# ENGLAND'S ONE TES

GW00771395

# ENGLAND'S
# ONE TEST WONDERS

RODERICK EASDALE

PARAPRESS LTD
GUILDFORD

© Roderick Easdale 1999
ISBN: 1-898594-63-5

First published in the UK by
PARAPRESS LTD
5 Bentham Hill House
Stockland Green Road
Tunbridge Wells
Kent TN3 0TJ

A catalogue record for this book is available
from the British Library

All rights reserved. No part of this publication may be reproduced,
stored in a retrieval system or transmitted in any form or by any
means, electronic, mechanical, photocopying, recording or otherwise,
without prior permission in writing from Parapress Ltd, Publishers.

Typeset by Vitaset, Paddock Wood
Printed in Great Britain by
Biddles Ltd, Guildford and King's Lynn

# *Contents*

For my mother and father

# 1 One Test Wonderdom

The most common number of caps held by an English test player is one. A seventh of England's test cricketers have played only one test. Why?

One test wonders have always fascinated me. Are they successes or failures? Picked to play for their country, the dream of so many, they failed to hold onto their place, and never got it back. Who are these cricketers who teetered on the narrow edge between success and failure?

The fascination is with the cricketers concerned, who they were and what they did. But arising out of this comes the question of whether it is possible to see any semblance of a pattern between the different stories. Or are the various experiences just so different and unconnected as to make this impossible?

Little attention has been paid to many of these people in cricket's existing literature. It sometimes appears as though almost as many books have been written about Don Bradman and W.G. Grace as there have been mere sentences about some other test cricketers, in particular many of England's one test wonders. Much of the coverage, when it comes, is frustratingly brief.

Arnold Warren is mentioned for playing for England only once, when he took five wickets in the first innings. And that's it: as though it were the most natural thing in the world to take five wickets in an innings and then be dropped. Surely there has to be more to his tale than this. When you delve into the circumstances surrounding Warren's test involvement there is indeed a story behind his dismissal. Similarly, Jim Parks senior gets mentioned as the only man to do the double of 3,000 runs and 100 wickets in a season. This is a phenomenal achievement, unequalled by any of the greats of world cricket, yet here achieved by a journeyman pro, a point often accepted apparently without question. But what suddenly caused Parks to exceed by far anything he – or indeed anyone else has ever done? 'Tate's Test' has been widely covered, but even here there seems an easy acceptance of the rather harsh judgement that history has handed down to Fred Tate. Although many accounts refer to the feud between MacLaren and Lord Hawke, there seems a reluctance to examine exactly what caused and fermented it.

This book seeks to fill this gap in cricket's literature. It seeks to place the cricketers, explain their achievements and, wherever possible, to outline the circumstances of their test selection, and subsequent deselection. In this there are sometimes obvious difficulties.

It is hard from the outside to know exactly what went on behind closed doors in selection meetings. Minutes are not produced, tour reports are kept confidential. Selectors do occasionally talk about their reasons and their selections, sometimes openly, sometimes by allowing information to seep through into the public domain. But even here there is often cause not to take the proffered information at face value. Keith Fletcher's explanation of David Gower's omission from the 1992–93 tour to India, that Gower was too old, was greeted with general disbelief in view of the fact that the captain was four years older than Gower and the recalled Mike Gatting only two months younger. Many saw the real reason being more connected with the conflicting attitudes between Gower and the captain to preparation and practice.

Sometimes, too, it is hard to establish exactly who made the various decisions. Even when the make-up of the selection committee is known, it is not always possible to divine exactly who was involved in making certain decisions. C.B. Fry, for one, seems to have had a more prominent role in England's selection history than his official positions would suggest. Sometimes the final decision as to whether to play, or risk, a certain cricketer rests with someone outside the official selection panel who is more closely acquainted with the player concerned, such as his county captain or coach. It is often they who provide the information on which the selectors make their decision, especially when it comes to physical fitness or mental attitude.

Many people can have an input to the selection process. Selectors are rarely full-time, for they normally have jobs and duties beyond their selectorial office and some of them have virtually full-time careers outside of cricket. Selectors have traditionally only been paid expenses for their duties. The selection committee picks sides for home tests but for overseas tours they pick only the parties – the final test elevens for overseas matches are selected from the members of the touring party by those on the spot. As such, the selection body for these matches has often been a much looser arrangement where the decision-makers have normally been members of the tour management and senior players. Touring English captains have traditionally tended to have more say in selection than captains in home tests

Even when selectors have jobs within cricket they are normally tied to a particular county, often as players, and are physically restricted in their cricket-watching to matches they are involved with. As selectors are often constrained in the amount, or variety, of cricket they can watch, on occasion they act more as accumulators and sorters of views than as witnesses of playing performances. Umpires and journalists are among those who have been used as sources of information and opinion. Umpires are in a particularly good position as they have the best view not only of the actual play but also, from working in amongst the players, of a player's character. Ultimately, however, the selection committee bears the responsibility for the selections.

With these difficulties in mind, the chapters on the various cricketers can neither claim nor seek to provide the definite reason or reasons for every individual's selection and subsequent exclusion. It is sometimes hard enough to explain adequately one's own decisions on occasion, let alone trying to explain those of others. However, by picking a careful way through the various facts and information available, it is often possible to gather together many, possibly all, of the pieces in the jigsaw puzzle. Sometimes these pieces can be put together in different ways to form different pictures.

The structure of this book recognizes this and in these cases is content to present the many pieces of the jigsaw which try to answer the question: if the one test wonders were good enough to be selected at all why were they not selected again?

The obvious, superficial response is that they simply were not very good. But if they were not good enough, why were they selected in the first place? Furthermore, if they were not considered good enough, how then can we explain away the fact that many one test wonders played well – sometimes very well – in their one match?

The spinner and one test wonder 'Father' Marriott took 5-37 and 6-59 against the West Indies in 1933, bowling England to an innings victory in the process. By any standard, this is a successful performance. But when you compare Marriott's achievement in taking ten wickets in a match, and five wickets in both innings of a test, with that of more generously capped test players, his achievement appears even greater. Bob Willis played 90 times for England as a strike bowler yet never took ten wickets in a match; neither did the Australian strike bowlers Ray Lindwall, in 61 tests, and Jeff Thomson in 51. The West Indians Joel Garner and Gary Sobers played 58 and 93 tests respectively without taking ten wickets in a match.

After Derek Underwood, the four most capped English spinners are Emburey, Illingworth, Titmus and Edmonds, who have 229 caps between them but no ten-wicket hauls. Mike Hendrick played for England 30 times as a specialist bowler without taking five wickets in an innings; neither did Barry Knight in any of the 29 tests he played as a bowling all-rounder.

No English one test wonder has made a century, although Oldfield was only twenty runs short. However, a West Indian, Andy Ganteaume, and a New Zealander, Rodney Redmond, did achieve centuries in their sole test. The circumstances of Redmond's test career are recounted in the chapter on Mitchell-Innes but the more famous is probably Ganteaume. In 1947–48 England sent a below-strength side to the West Indies. Compton, Edrich and Bedser did not tour and Hutton only joined the party for the final test. Before the test series the West Indies had decided to share the captaincy. George Headley would captain in the first and last of the four tests, the Trinidadian Jeffrey Stollmeyer in the second, at Trinidad, and John Goddard in the third. The first test, in which Headley strained his back, was drawn. Stollmeyer was injured for the second test; aware of the bigger picture, the selectors appointed the

Trinidadian Gomez as captain and brought in his fellow countryman Ganteaume as opener. It was often West Indian practice to favour local players, not only out of deference to local sensitivities, but from economic necessity as the impoverished West Indian Board often found it a strain to pay for transporting players often large distances from the other Caribbean islands. Another player from the Trinidad and Tobago side, Carew, had been recalled to the side for his second test match, thirteen years after his previous game.

England batted first and made 362. Carew and Ganteaume opened the innings for the West Indies. Carew, in a brown felt hat, batting in a carefree manner, went to his century just before close on the second day, which West Indies took at 160-0. Ganteaume, a clerk in the Trinidad Civil Service, was more circumspect. Disgruntled at not being named in the original party, he was determined to do well: "I decided that, unless something very unplayable came along, I would stay there and do my damnedest to get a hundred, just to show them."

When Carew was dismissed for 107 the next morning, he and Ganteaume had put on 173, a record for the West Indies' first wicket. Weekes came in and dominated a second wicket stand of 53 with 36, before he was bowled, to bring debutant Frank Worrell to the crease. Ganteaume's resolution allowed him to play out a maiden on 99. Then followed a drinks break and in the next over he took a single to bring up his century, after four and a half hour's batting.

Gomez sent a message out to the batsmen to up the tempo. Ganteaume recalled: "Frank read the note first and showed it to me without any comment. I said 'Well maybe we should try to press on,' but he said 'No, let's tan them some more.' I thought if the captain said try and press on, I should." Ganteaume was soon dismissed, lifting a shot to cover. "I suppose I was a little indiscreet, and I've always regretted it … if I'd got a big hundred I think they would have been more than a little embarrassed to leave me out of the next match."

In their second innings West Indies needed 141 to win in 57 minutes and Ganteaume did not bat as the West Indies rejigged their order in an unsuccessful chase. Carew was selected in the team for the next match, but Ganteaume was not, because new captain Goddard opened. Ganteaume was asked if he were available for the tour of India later that calendar year. He said yes, but was not picked. Carew was chosen instead on the basis that he was coming to the end of his career and Ganteaume had many years of playing ahead of him.

Despite performing well in trial matches, Ganteaume did not come near to test selection and eventually dropped out of cricket. Learie Constantine persuaded him to play in his Sunday sides and he made a first-class comeback, and was selected for a test trial when Alan Rae pulled out. He was picked to go to England in 1957 but, despite the West Indies using five different opening partnerships, he failed to play in any of the tests. Not comfortable in English conditions, in nineteen matches he made only 800 runs at 27, with a highest score of 92 made between the fourth and fifth tests.

Reflecting on his test career or lack of it, Ganteaume said "If you were to say that I am bitter ... you'd be correct." He eventually became a manager of West Indies touring sides, until in 1985 he learnt that the job of manager of that particular tour had been offered to someone else and he resigned.

Conversely, some players were extremely unsuccessful on their test debut yet went on to have long and triumphant careers. Ken Barrington, whose average of 58.67 is the third highest for England, started his test career with a duck. England's highest run scorer and most capped player, Graham Gooch, made a pair on his test debut. Len Hutton, who has made England's highest score made 0 and 1 on his. He had also made a duck in his first innings for Yorkshire 2nd XI and for the full Yorkshire side. Many of England's best batsmen have begun their first-class careers with ducks, W.G. Grace, Wally Hammond, C.B. Fry, Frank Woolley, Ted Dexter and Patsy Hendren among them.

What would some one test wonders have achieved had they been given more chances? Australia gave a test debut to a young batsman in the first test of the 1928–29 season. He made 18 and 1 and was dropped for the next match. One of his team-mates from the test side remarked that he clearly wasn't up to test standard. Injury brought the debutant back into the side of the third test, in which he became the youngest man to score a test century. This was Donald Bradman, who went on to score almost a quarter of Australia's runs in the 52 tests in which he played. Such was his domination of cricket that his ducks made headlines. It is from one of them that Walt Disney, a keen cricket fan, is said to have named Donald Duck.

Obviously someone of Bradman's talents would have forced himself back into the test side sooner or later. But what of those with lesser talents – which might well encompass every other batsman the world has known – could they not also have put in performances, if at a more modest level, which would have justified their selection?

In contrast, some test players are highly successful on debut yet fail to replicate this success. Seven Englishmen have made their sole century on their debut, most notably R.E. Foster. Foster made 287 not out in 1903–04 at Sydney, which remained the highest test score until 1929–30. This remains the highest score by a player on debut, by an Englishman in Australia and the record for any test at Sydney. In the remainder of his thirteen test innings he reached 50 only once, scoring 51 in his final test. He averaged 24 over the remainder of his innings.

Does a one test wonder reflect a lack of coherence or rigour in selection policy? Perhaps the best way to explore this would be through an examination of whether the decision to select and then de-select had been entirely rational. But this would be deeply difficult. The concept of 'rational action' requires certain pre-conditions. One is that the original beliefs which dictate the actions are rational. For example, if red-headed batsmen were considered the best – not that ludicrous an example when one considers that one test captain stated the colour of a batsman's eyes influenced how well he could play in the West Indies – then a rational action would be to select a side packed with red-headed batsmen. The action is rational even if the theory might not be.

Another requirement for rational action is that there must be no incompatible or conflicting aims. Selections often involve compromises. Take the assertion that you should always pick your best batsmen, bowlers and wicket-keepers. This already poses certain problems. What if your best batsmen are all openers? Do you still play them all, with most of them playing out of position? What if your best bowlers are all seamers? Do you still pick your best bowlers, even though this gives an unbalanced attack? What if your bowlers and wicket-keeper are all very poor batsmen? Do you still pick them even though your last few wickets might contribute very few runs?

When you combine still more factors, then the possibility for compromise is increased. A balanced cricket team is often considered to comprise six batsmen, five bowlers and a wicket-keeper. This equals twelve players, so there is a need for at least one all-rounder. But what if there isn't an all-rounder in the eleven best players? This is a problem England have frequently encountered in recent years. Do you go a batsman or bowler light, find a wicket-keeper/batsman, or bring in an all-rounder to achieve the balanced team, even if it no longer comprises the best players? The West Indies in their most successful years sacrificed specialist wicket-keeping for their perceived need for the team's balance between bowlers and batsmen. They are also an example of selection where the best bowlers were picked regardless of the lack of variety in bowling this gave them.

If the opponents are weak players of leg spin bowling, do you perhaps pick a leg spinner who is a lesser bowler than the best off spin bowler, but who might pose more problems for particular batsmen in the opposition side? On a turning pitch do you play this leg spinner against other opponents at the expense of a better pace bowler who is not expected to be favoured by pitch conditions? As the courses change so might the horses.

Eleven players bring certain talents to a team, forming a team with certain properties, and it is this unit which takes on another unit, albeit often in a series of one-on-one interactions. Thus when one player changes so might others, to maintain the properties of this unit.

A side's opening batsman might be injured and be replaced by an opening batsman from outside the side. If the original opening bat was the side's off spin bowler, and his replacement did not bowl off spin, then a further change might be made to bring in another off spinner. This would involve replacing another member of the side. Thus the number six batsman, say, might lose his place through the opener getting injured. Conversely if the replacement opener was a handy medium paced bowler, perhaps then one of the seam bowlers would lose his place instead as a result of the change of opening batsmen.

Selection often involves compromises and factors beyond the designs and, influence, of selectors. It has always been so. In January 1877, after playing a few games in Australia, the English tourists set off to New Zealand for two months' cricket, before returning to Australia to play what were later to become the first two test matches in cricketing history. Len Hutton is often referred to as England's first professional captain but the professional James Lillywhite was actually England's first-ever test captain and in their early tests England were led as often by a professional as an amateur. While in New Zealand, the English wicket-keeper, Pooley, bet a local man, one Ralph Donkin, that, for odds of 20-1, he could nominate in advance the scores of each Christchurch batsman. Donkin took up the bet for a stake of a shilling per batsman, Pooley guessed a duck for each, and enough of the eighteen batsman made a duck – even one would have put him up on the deal – for him to make a tidy profit. Donkin claimed it was a trick and refused to pay. A scuffle ensued. The side went on to Otago, but after the game there, Pooley and the side's baggage-man were arrested. They were fined £5 for assault and remanded on bail on a charge of 'injuring property above a value of £5'. Six weeks later both appeared before the supreme court at Christchurch and were acquitted. The locals, believing the Englishmen to have been badly treated, subscribed fifty pounds for them and also presented Pooley with a gold watch.

Meanwhile, England played Australia without Pooley. The under-study 'keeper, Henry Jupp, had eye trouble and so, after experiments with Selby and Emmett, the latter a bowler, Selby 'kept in both tests. However, Australia's Ted Evans, considered the country's best all-rounder, had declined the invitation, as did Frank Allen – 'The Bowler of the Century' – who had agreed to meet friends at a fair. Furthermore, Spofforth refused to play unless his regular wicket-keeper, Murdoch, 'kept for the side.

Sometimes, though, selectors are clearly culpable of error. One such instance was the selection of Ken Burn as the second wicket-keeper in the Australian party to tour England in 1890. When he joined his team-mates on the ship at Adelaide he told them he had never kept wicket in his life. Boyle and Blackham, who had selected the side, the latter a wicket-keeper himself, had mistaken him for another Tasmanian, John Burn, who had kept wicket against Victoria in 1869. (Other sports have their strange selections too. In 1906 the first South African rugby touring team took on England at Crystal Place. In the English side was Arnold

Alocock, an average forward and a surprising selection. His selection
was as a result of a misprint for Slocock. Launcelot Slocock was a well
known player good enough to score three tries in his eight internationals.)

The first test match is generally considered to have started on 15
March 1877, when the fourth touring team of English cricketers to visit
Australia played two matches against a combined Victoria and New
South Wales eleven. Previous touring teams had taken on opposition
against odds, normally against teams of 22. The first English tour to
Australia had been in 1862 under H.H. Stephenson. Spiers and Pond,
proprietors of the Café de Paris in Melbourne, brought out a team to
promote their catering business. The cricketers were their second choice
after Charles Dickens failed to reply to their invitation to undertake a
lecture tour. They sent a Mr W.B. Mallam to England to recruit players.
He went to the North versus South match at Birmingham, and invited
the best players in the two teams to tour Australia at £150 a man plus
first-class expenses. George Parr and his Northern team-mates declined,
so Mallam arranged a tour with H.H. Stephenson, the Surrey captain,
who was captaining the South. Stephenson's side played thirteen games
on the tour. Eleven were against teams of 22 players and one was against
a team of eighteen, which they beat. This was the first game and was
scheduled to be against a side of 22, but the tourists complained they
were still weary after the sea voyage and agreed to take on only eighteen.
The other game was a match billed as Surrey against the World. The six
Surrey players in Stephenson's party were joined by the best local talent,
and they took on the remainder of the tourists and some locals in an
eleven-a-side match which ended as a draw. Stephenson's side won five
of the matches against 22, lost two and drew the rest.

George Parr captained the second touring party in 1873–74, which
included England's best professionals and the amateur E.M. Grace;
midway through the tour the party went to New Zealand where they
played four games. The third English touring party came out under the
captaincy of W.G. Grace, after he had accepted an invitation from a
syndicate of Melbourne Cricket Club members to bring out a side.

In 1876–77 James Lillywhite brought out a side which he and Alfred
Shaw had recruited from the professional ranks of Sussex, Yorkshire,
Surrey and Nottinghamshire. In January, having played a number of
games, they left for a two-month visit to New Zealand. This was
scheduled to be the end of the tour, but in their final game in Australia
they had drawn with an eleven of New South Wales. This was the first
time that an English touring team had taken on an opposing eleven. The
success of the local side encouraged the cricket authorities in Melbourne
and Sydney to offer Lillywhite two more games after their visit to New
Zealand. These matches later became classified as the first two test
matches. Even so, the England team was not representative of the best
cricketing talent in the country – it had been estimated that only four of

that first test team would have figured in a best England XI – and only five of the team were to play in another test series.

This was to be much the pattern of early tourists and tests. They were privately arranged tours for the financial gain of the organizers. It was not until 1903–04, and the sixteenth English tour, that the MCC sent an 'official' touring team to Australia, and not before 1905–06 that such a side went to South Africa.

Teams that went to South Africa in particular were a long way short of being the best cricketing talent from England. B.A.F. Grieve and the Hon. C.J. Coventry both began their first-class careers in England's first ever test with South Africa, and ended their first-class careers with the second test. In the opening test with South Africa, C.A. Smith became the only one test wonder to captain England. J.E.P. McMaster took his place for the second test, batted number nine, made nought and did not bowl. This was his sole first-class match. This was in 1888–89. Another English team toured South Africa in 1891–92, playing one test; this side included two Australian test cricketers, one a previous captain. This was particularly notable as 'England' were also touring Australia at the time, and two days after the test with South Africa ended, another English test team, under W.G. Grace, played the second test of a series with Australia. Eight of the eleven who played against South Africa did not play test cricket again. England also played coincidental rubbers against West Indies and New Zealand in 1929–30, and both are deemed test series.

126 men made their test debuts for England in the nineteenth century. Of these, 65 played in only one series, 42 of them playing all the games of their series. Nineteen of them did so in a one test series, thereby becoming one test wonders. As a further dozen also played in only one test of a longer series, a quarter of all nineteenth-century test cricketers are one test wonders.

In examining one test wonders I decided to exclude nineteenth-century test players. The teams often could not be considered to equate with a concept of a national first eleven and selection was haphazard. Prior to 1899 the sides were chosen by the ground authority where the match was to take place. The last occasion test sides were so determined was in 1896 when the Indian prince Ranji was not picked for the first test at Lord's because Lord Harris was not convinced of his 'English-ness'. He made his debut in the next test at Old Trafford and became the first man to score a century before lunch in a test. A.E. Stoddart declined an invitation from the Surrey committee to play in the third and final test of the rubber at the Oval so as to play in a match at Lord's for Middlesex. In 1899 the MCC, which had previously shared the selection duties with the committees of Lancashire and Surrey county cricket clubs, depending upon where the matches took place, took over responsibility for selection for all home tests irrespective of venue. As such the committee that the MCC formed to deal with selection for that summer's tests might be considered to be the first England selection committee, as we have come to know it.

Even excluding the nineteenth-century one test wonders leaves too many players to examine in depth within the scope of this book. Therefore I have limited the period to that prior to 1939. Taking all test matches up to the present leaves the problem of who is and isn't a one test wonder with current first-class cricketers. Of the 25 post-war one test wonders, about a third are still playing first-class cricket. Will all of them remain so? Will they, even by the time you read this? It is not always easy to prophesy who will remain a one test wonder. The Derbyshire fast bowler Les Jackson was picked for his test debut for the third test in 1949, but failed to make the team for the next test. Twelve years later he was recalled to the side to open the bowling, aged 40. Jim Parks junior, played one test against Pakistan in 1954, and did not play again for almost six years; when the side in South Africa was hit by injuries he was on hand, coaching in South Africa, and was drafted into the side. He made a century and remained in the side. George Gunn went seventeen years and 316 days between his eleventh and twelfth caps.

After each chapter, as well as giving the subject's first-class career details, I have given their record in Gentlemen versus Players fixtures. To be picked for one of those sides was an honour second only to being picked for England. In many seasons there were no tests – England played only three home series between 1919 and 1927 inclusive – so to be picked for these matches in those seasons was the highest recognition that cricketers could receive. I do not claim these figures are a reliable guide to the cricketers' ability to compete at the highest level, but in some cases they might give some indication.

# 2    F.W. Tate (Sussex)

Born: 24 July 1867, Brighton, Sussex. Died: 24 February 1943
4th Test, 1902 v. Australia
Batting:   1st Inns: (No.11)   5 no    2nd Inns: (No.11)    4
Bowling:  1st Inns: 11-1-44-0        2nd Inns: 5-3-7-2

The selection of Fred Tate had its roots in events at the end of the previous century. In August 1899 Major Wardill, Secretary of the Melbourne Cricket Club, invited the Marylebone Cricket Club to send a team in the season 1901–02. The Lord's-based MCC agreed. According to reports, Lord Hawke, who had been chairman of the first English test selection panel in 1899, was going to manage and captain the tour, with

Archie MacLaren captaining the test side. But when the time came, the MCC were unable to gather a team, as some of the leading amateurs were unavailable. According to MacLaren, Hawke had invited him to be captain of the party soon after Melbourne's invitation had been received. MacLaren delayed a decision because of his father's illness. Later, hearing there were difficulties with the tour, MacLaren went to Lord's where W.G. Grace and A.E. Stoddart told him that many of the amateurs were not available to tour. Believing the tour no longer viable, MacLaren informed Lord's that he, too, was unavailable. As a result Lord's informed Melbourne that a tour would not be possible.

But the Australian public were expecting a touring team, and so MacLaren was contacted by the Australians to see if he could bring a side out to Australia. MacLaren agreed to try. Lord Hawke, as Yorkshire captain, refused to let the Yorkshire professionals Hirst or Rhodes tour with MacLaren. He suspected the decision was made out of pique. Hawke claimed at the time that he wanted his bowlers to rest. In an article in *Cricket* he stated that the pair were not offered enough money for the tour: only £300. In the 1932 *Wisden*, Lord Hawke wrote, "I based my refusal, in which the Committee supported me unanimously, upon the solid grounds, as I and they thought, that it was not cricket that all the profits of these tours, to obtain which the English representative professionals did their full share, should go to individuals and to the benefit of Australian cricket only." The incident created great discord between MacLaren and Hawke. In a speech at Victoria early on in the tour MacLaren expressed a wish for "a few more sportsmen on the Yorkshire county committee".

In the absence of Hirst and Rhodes, MacLaren had plucked Sidney Barnes from the leagues. Having taken 5-65 in the first innings of the first test, won by England by an innings and 124 runs, Barnes broke down in the third test through being overbowled. England lost the series 4-1.

MacLaren's change of mind about his availability to tour was probably motivated by financial considerations. He was not a wealthy amateur and he sought to make a living from various sources. One of the main sources was cricket through coaching, lecturing, the Assistant Secretaryship of Lancashire, marketing pneumatic pads and bats made from Spanish willow and the hiring of cricket films. Other sources of his income included banking, cotton, school-teaching and even working as an extra in Hollywood films. As captain of an MCC team, MacLaren would have received only expenses, but as leader of a private party he would have received much greater reward.

Lord Hawke appears, from his various comments and actions, to have a degree of ambivalence about national cricket. He declared that test matches were duller than other forms of cricket and stated of his position as Chairman of the Selectors that, "The one pleasure I had in it was to act as host to other good fellows. Nowadays selectors get their expenses so the same opportunity would not arise."

For the series against Australia in 1902 Lord Hawke was again appointed Chairman of Selectors. That year he became President of Yorkshire, a position he retained for the thirty years until his death. He had been appointed Yorkshire's captain in 1883, two years after his debut, thus becoming Yorkshire's first amateur captain, following the appointment of four professional captains. He remained Yorkshire's captain for twenty-seven years.

His fellow appointed selectors were Gregor MacGregor and H.W. Bainbridge. F.S. Jackson and A.G. Steel were co-opted onto the selection panel. C.B. Fry, somehow, seems also to have got involved in the selection of the team. This meant that three of the English team were part of the selection process, yet the captain was not. When he became acquainted with the twelve for the fourth test, MacLaren is reputed to have exploded: "My God, look what they've given me! Do they think they are playing the blind asylum?" MacLaren's sole input to the selection process was to decide who, from the twelve names he was given, was to be the twelfth man. It was a power he was to use to effect.

The first test of the series was drawn after rain had delayed the start of play on the third day until 5.15pm. With a batting order of players who had all managed first-class centuries in their careers, England declared at 376-9. Australia were then bowled out in 80 minutes for 36, Hirst taking 3-15 and Rhodes 7-17. Following on, Australia finished at 46-2. In the match after the test, Yorkshire, through Hirst and Jackson, bowled Australia out for 23. Rain delayed the start of the second test until 2.45pm and allowed only an hour and three-quarters' play and washed out the other two days. Australia won the third test, at Bramall Lane, by 143 runs.

According to C.B. Fry, the selectors met to choose the team for the fourth test during a rare spell of fine weather in a wet summer. Ranji, who had missed the last test through injury, was brought back for Fry. Fry had scores of 0, 0, 1 and 4 in the series. Jessop was dropped in favour of Palairet. The dropping of Jessop was a strange decision. He had top scored for England in the last test, was an all-rounder – who had already taken 8-58 in the season at Lord's for Gloucestershire – and a good fielder, in a side in which this commodity was becoming scarce. Abel and Lockwood could not throw. The latter had been brought back in place of Barnes, who was still troubled by the knee injury of the previous winter. Barnes had not been in the selectors' party for the previous test either, but MacLaren had sent him a telegram and picked him anyway. Barnes was at home in Manchester when he received the telegram at nine o'clock on the morning of the match inviting him to play at Sheffield. He got to the ground late, and the Yorkshireman Schofield Haigh, who was part of the party, had taken his place in the field as twelfth man.

Barnes entered with the new batsman at the fall of the first wicket. The Yorkshire crowd had naturally presumed that Haigh was in the eleven, and they booed Haigh's removal, at least one of the spectators taunting Hawke: "There's one of the selectors, and he's a Yorkshireman." He wasn't, in fact – Hawke had been born in Lincolnshire. Barnes took 6-49 in the innings.

These changes created a complete eleven, and this was the team that was first announced to the press. But it was decided, in view of the inclement summer, to add a wet-wicket bowler. Schofield Haigh, who was having a fine summer, was suggested. He was to end the season at the head of the national averages with 158 wickets at 12.55. Already in the side were Jackson, Rhodes and Hirst, and Lord Hawke objected to seeing his Yorkshire attack further weakened by contributing another to the England team, especially one who would only play depending on the weather. He insisted that the wet-wicket specialist was Fred Tate, who was also having a good summer. C.B. Fry said that he warned the committee that Tate could not throw. Tate was a specialist slip fielder for his county but the team already possessed three specialist slips in Braund, Ranji and MacLaren.

1902 was a wet year and Tate was thriving in the conditions. At the end of the first week in June, he had taken 9-73 against Leicestershire in the first innings and 4-44 in the second. In the middle of that month, at Lord's, Sussex had a day's batting under favourable conditions and made 354-8. There was no play on the second day and at the start of Saturday's play Ranji declared. Tate bowled unchanged throughout the day and took 7-28 and 8-40 as Middlesex were dismissed on 51 and 79. Later he was picked for the Players at Lord's at the beginning of July, taking 3-67 in the first innings.

It rained during the Tuesday and Wednesday prior to the test match. A wet wicket was considered a distinct possibility, and Haigh could have been added to the party in this period. But come the beginning of the fourth test the wicket was wet. Tate was the wet-wicket bowler, and MacLaren picked him. The logic here is impeccable. This, though, entailed leaving out Hirst: a decision MacLaren would have enjoyed, and may even have motivated the decision to play Tate. Lord Hawke had overruled his fellow selectors to prevent the possibility of one of his treasured county attack becoming England's twelfth man. Instead he now found one of his bowlers acting as England's twelfth man. Hirst had gone wicketless through twenty-five overs in the previous test, and was reported as having lost his swerve after his early season successes. He was averaging 30 with the bat at this stage of the season. Of Tate one of the national newspapers had declared, "succeed or not, he was, on general form, the man for the wicket we may yet have." It was his thirty-fifth birthday.

The match began in front of 20,000 spectators. The pitch was soft and damp. It was overcast and there was no wind, so the pitch would dry quickly. Once the pitch began to dry it would favour the bowlers. With the footholds too soft for Lockwood, he was kept out of the attack. Australia, keen to make use of the pitch before it worsened, began aggressively and scored 42 runs in the first 25 minutes, and soon after this Tate came on to bowl. His first four overs cost 13 runs. Trumper hoisted his 50 within 52 minutes of the start, and with his fellow opener, Duff, he put together a century partnership in 57 minutes – this remains the fastest century opening partnership in test history. This was despite defensive field placings from MacLaren who was keen to keep the batsmen quiet until the wicket turned in England's favour.

The partnership had reached 129 when Lockwood was able to come on and seven runs later, when the partnership was 78 minutes old, he had Duff, who had just been missed at slip by Braund, dismissed to a catch at the wicket. Trumper moved to a century before lunch with his fourteenth boundary and Australia lunched at 173-1, with Trumper on 103.

Trumper was dismissed to the fifth ball after lunch, caught low and right-handed by the wicket-keeper from Rhodes' bowling. Noble fell to the same bowler to be caught and bowled which he disputed, claiming a bump ball, and when Gregory fell cutting, the Yorkshireman had taken 3-6 in four overs.

Darling and Hill, two South Australians, came together and put on 73 in three-quarters of an hour. Darling twice hit Rhodes out of the ground for the first sixes scored in tests in England. Darling had previously hit the first six in Australia to bring him to his century in Adelaide in 1898. He also hit three balls out of the playing arena on the full for four. Sixes at that stage required to be hit out of the ground. Australia were a commanding 256-4 when Hill fell. Lockwood, by now bowling at his quickest, then took 5-8 in an eight-over spell to rein the visitors back to 299.

England had leaked a number of runs in the Australian innings through their limited fielding. Jessop wrote that "no England team can ever have been picked with less regard for its fielding capabilities than this one [...] since there were in all three fieldsmen who had not thrown a cricket ball fifty yards for quite a number of years."

England were left with an hour and a quarter's batting at the end of the first day and after 35 minutes were 30-4. Abel was caught at first slip from a top edge in Saunders' fourth over, Palairet was caught at backward point, MacLaren was bowled through the gate playing forward, and Ranji trapped lbw playing back. Tyldesley, reckoned by many as the best bad-wicket player in England, was joined by Jackson and these two added 14 in a quarter of an hour before Tyldesley was caught at third man from a cut over gully. Braund came in at five past six and in the remaining 25 minutes 26 runs were added, Braund ending on 13 and Jackson 16.

In the first hour of the second day's play the sixth wicket added a further 54 runs; five minutes later Jackson went to his 50. Five minutes shy of lunch, Braund took sixteen runs from an Armstrong over before he pulled an outswinger from Noble onto his stumps. He and Jackson had added 141 in two and three-quarter hours. England lunched at 186-6.

Soon after lunch wicket-keeper Lilley was bowled and Lockwood joined Jackson. On 92, the latter cut a ball to short third man, who misfielded. The batsmen became stranded in mid wicket and Lockwood sacrificed his wicket to applause from the spectators. At five past three Jackson went to the third of his five test centuries – the product of 225 minutes' batting – before he was last out, caught at deep wicket, having just been dropped.

Australia went in to bat again at five past four to face the bowling of Lockwood and Braund. Lockwood soon had Australia in trouble, bowling very quick deliveries – which broke the batsman into a field of three slips, a gully, short forward leg and short backward leg. At 9-2, with Trumper out to a catch at second slip at the second attempt, and Duff having played on, Darling promoted himself in the order. One run later Hill was bowled off stump.

With the score at 15-3 Braund began an over to Gregory. From the fifth ball the batsman took a single. This meant rearranging the field for the left-handed Darling. Seventeen years later the consequences of this single were still being debated, and the England captain, in response to comments in *The Times*, felt obliged to write a letter explaining his deployment of the field for this one delivery.

The result of the various manoeuvres was that Tate ended up fielding in the deep, backward of square. It is normally stated that Braund wanted his Somerset team-mate, Palairet, who usually fielded at deep square leg for his bowling, to move across the field to this position for the left-hander, but MacLaren signalled, in order to save time, that Tate should move from his slip position instead. This seems to be contradicted by MacLaren's letter, where he states that Braund never had a slip.

Darling, who was seeking to hit his side out of trouble, struck out at Braund's final ball of the over, a leg break. The ball went up in the air towards Tate, curving to the left through a combination of the spin imparted by the bowler and that added by the batsman. A specialist slip, Tate was not used to coping with such movement. Tate moved to his right, but the ball moved even further in this direction. With a despairing lunge, Tate was able to get his hands to the ball but could not hold it. The crowd, hushed, now sighed and, according to most accounts, Tate was moved back to slip.

In Braund's next over Darling hit him out of the ground into the station. Tate had no opportunity to atone for his mistake until he was brought on to bowl. He promptly had Gregory lbw to an off cutter to make the score 64-4. Tate was then taken off. At 74, Darling mistimed a hit and was caught at long on, and Lockwood came back, rested, and took two more wickets. Australia closed at 85-8.

It rained for five hours during the night, putting the bias back in favour of the bowlers when play got underway at noon. MacLaren opened with Rhodes and his wet-wicket specialist, and they took a wicket apiece – Trumble showing dissent when adjudged lbw to Tate – to dismiss Australia for the addition of only one run.

MacLaren promoted himself, to force the pace, in place of the more restrained Abel. In the 50 minutes' batting before lunch he and Palairet put on 36. This was a crucial period of the match, and another instance when they might have missed Jessop. Not only would he have saved some of the runs donated in the field, a natural big hitter, he would have proved useful in forcing the pace. But MacLaren was confident at lunch. Reportedly, on a visit to the Australian dressing-room he called out to the Australian captain, Joe Darling, "We've got you this time." Darling replied, "You can never tell, Archie, until we've been really beaten."

Eight runs were added in two overs after lunch and then Palairet was bowled by Saunders. Two dozen runs later, Tyldesley fell to a slip catch by Armstrong, bringing Ranji to the crease. By this time storm clouds were gathering and MacLaren decided to try to increase the scoring rate. He off drove Trumble for four, bringing his score to 35. This meant that at this stage no man had scored more test runs against Australia than he. The next ball from Trumble, round the wicket, was slower and more flighted, and MacLaren hit it to deep mid on where Duff took a catch just inside the boundary.

Four runs later, play was suspended for a quarter of an hour because of rain. Ranji struggled when play resumed, and with England seeking runs quickly, he was unable to provide any at any pace. Clem Hill said that he never saw Ranji bat so timorously. (The following season, after Sussex had scored 41 for the first wicket in the game with Lancashire, Ranji came in and failed to get off the mark for thirty-five minutes. The crowd began to barrack and MacLaren brought himself on to bowl to enable Ranji, godfather to his son, to move off the mark. He went on to make 144 not out.)

This time, with the score at 92, Ranji was excused from his labourings when he fell lbw to the third appeal in the over. Abel, with instructions to score quickly, which was not his usual game, was bowled hitting out and England were 97-5.

This brought together the partnership which had put on 141 in the first innings. A snick for three by Braund brought up the century before Jackson drove at a full toss from Saunders and was caught by Gregory diving high to his right. Trumble bowled Braund a delivery which went between bat and pad but missed the stumps. But the batsman then fell to a brilliant stumping and Lockwood fell third ball to reduce England to 107-8 and the crowd to silence. Rain twice drove the players from the field. Rhodes, who had come in at the fall of Lockwood's wicket to partner Lilley, off drove a four from Saunders to the mid on boundary. Lilley who had scored a two and a single, during which he nearly ran himself out, then hit out at a ball from Trumble, sending it skimming towards mid wicket where Clem Hill was fielding. He later recalled, "I raced after the ball with not the slightest idea of bringing off a catch, but with the full determination of saving a fourer. Almost on the boundary, after having run the best part of twenty five yards, I threw everything to chance and made a dive at the leather. No one was more astonished than myself to find that the ball had stuck to my hand. As a matter of fact for a fraction of a second I could hardly believe that I had brought off the catch, but the next instant I was the proudest man on the ground [...] Poor Dick Lilley, passing me on the way to the pavilion, said, 'Oh Clem, what a bally fluke!' For appearance sake I had to reply, 'Never on your life!' but the English wicket-keeper knew the truth and spoke it."

A parson amongst the spectators later called this a 'sinful' catch. C.B. Fry later wrote of the catch that "Clem ran along the pavilion rails and though going fast he took the ball easily with both hands chest high."

Tate came out to bat, and as he did it began to rain. The umpires conferred, with Tate becalmed and nervous in the middle. After a deliberation the umpires brought the players off. In the dressing-room MacLaren was blaming himself for getting out. But at that stage England had been on top and it would have been negative captaincy for a side behind in the series not to seek victory in the face of inclement weather. What is more debatable is whether the later batsmen should have been more protective of their wickets. Abel, for instance, perished playing a game alien to his instincts.

At a quarter to five play resumed after a forty-minute hiatus. Rhodes sought, but failed to gain, a single from the last ball of Trumble's over, leaving Tate to face Saunders. The first ball was quick and aimed at leg stump. Tate dabbed his bat down on it, deflecting the ball to long leg, where the ponderous Armstrong gave chase. He made an unavailing attempt to scoop the ball back with his foot but the ball went to the boundary amidst wild cheering. Tate was within a stroke of becoming a hero. He kept out two more deliveries before Saunders came in to deliver the fourth ball of the over. The ball swung late and his leg stump was knocked out of the ground. The crowd were stunned into silence and the Australian players at first did not react, then they began to grasp each others hands in congratulations. Clem Hill recollected, "We were like a lot of schoolboys after that match. Never in all the games I have played has the tension been so great, nor have I witnessed such scenes of ecstasy in an Australian dressing-room."

Tate was booed by some in the crowd as he left the field. It always seems so unjust to blame the last batsman in these circumstances. The reason they are at number eleven is that everyone else in the team is considered a better bat, and it is from these people, especially the early batsmen, that the runs are expected to come. Tate in this game had scored more, and been out less, than Ranji. His batting achievements equalled that of number ten Rhodes and exceeded those of number nine Lockwood. But Tate also had the dropped catch to contend with, as well as his controversial selection, for which he certainly cannot be blamed. But this combination of circumstances meant that the test is always 'Tate's Test'. C.B. Fry argued, thirty years on, that it would be more logical to call it 'Lord Hawke's Match'.

The selectors were blamed. One source of this view saying that "ministers of religion publicly prayed that heaven would open the eyes of these misguided men [...] when England lost by three runs we felt this was the clearest instance of Divine retribution since the destruction of the cities of the Plain."

Tate was very upset by his dismissal and the crowd's reaction. He sat in the dressing-room in tears. Len Braund went with him to Manchester station and travelled south with him. Later he told John Arlott about the journey: "Suddenly, as the train was passing determinedly through central England, Fred Tate looked up and said 'I've got a little kid at home there who'll make it up for me.'"

Braund remembered this wild statement as a sign of the great miserable turmoil of his friend. His son was seven years old, and had showed no aptitude for cricket.

In the summer of 1919, following comments in *The Times,* MacLaren wrote a letter stating his version of events:

> I forward facts which can be corroborated by such as Braund, the bowler, or Lilley, the wicket-keeper, who heard the conversations which took place.
>
> When Darling faced Braund after a single by Gregory, the point and mid off to him were then the only two men on the on side. With Darling facing Braund these naturally should fall back on the leg boundary for the left-handed batsman as no less than five of the seven fieldsmen on the leg side to Gregory had to cross over to the leg side for Darling after a single had been scored. L.C.H. Palairet was moved the whole length of the ground, from the leg boundary when Darling faced Braund. The Maharaja Ranjitsinjhi was dead lame, and consequently was useless as an outfielder, since he would have made little or no ground to a catch, and for that reason I refused his offer to fall back. As Darling was hitting out at every ball I felt that, with the great amount of what became off break to the left-handed batsmen that Braund was getting on the ball, the spin would most likely cause Darling's hit to carry behind rather than in front of the square leg boundary, and I accordingly placed Lionel Palairet in that position with Tate in front. Braund then asked me if he might not have L.C.H. Palairet in front where Tate was fielding, and

although I pointed out that the finer long leg was more likely to get the catch, he still preferred to have Lionel Palairet in front where Tate was fielding, and as I never went against any bowler of judgement, Tate was allowed to take the fine-leg position and Palairet came in front to occupy the position in which he usually fielded for Somerset. Tate got the catch and had the misfortune to drop it. No one was more sorry for Tate than myself. Although I had the greatest respect for Tate as a bowler, it was in my opinion far too late in his career to ask him to play for his first time at so critical a period in the test games, when we were one down with only two games to play. Your correspondent says he cannot vouch for it, but the story goes that both the Hon. F.S. Jackson and Ranjitsinjhi offered to take the long field. The Hon. F.S. Jackson, a fine infield, on the contrary asked to be allowed to take that position.

Your correspondent says that short slip and mid on were the only two places for Tate. Braund never had a slip and Ranjitsinjhi, lame, occupied mid on. We had no less than four men on the deep leg boundary for Braund, and if all four moved right across the ground for six singles in one over, when a left-handed batsman was in, each fieldsman would have covered some 1,200 yards in the over. It is always necessary to save not only your fieldsmen as much as possible, but also time. Tate had the very bad luck to do what all of us have done, times without number: drop a catch which, owing to the greatness of the occasion, advertised its costliness.

Yours faithfully,
A.C. MacLaren, captain

The traditional view of Fred Tate is that he was not good enough for test cricket, and this showed in the events of the test. This is a harsh analysis of Tate's performance. He was offered two catching chances, one of which, at slip, he took and the other he spilled. In the context of the game, Saunders' miss of Jackson, then on 41, was more significant as the batsman added 88 runs after this reprieve. The Jackson/Braund partnership, which dominated England's first innings, putting on over half of England's runs, had then only reached 70, and was to put on another 71. Had Saunders accepted this sharp caught and bowled chance Australia would have cruised to victory. As it was, England, despite consistently receiving the worst conditions, almost won.

Tate's bowling was respectable, yet he had the misfortune to be dismissed with England in sight of victory. But he did not give Australia this victory as is sometimes implied. In such a close match there are so many significant moments and passages of play. The match is better remembered for the many brilliant performances. Trumper made the first century before lunch of the first day of a test, something which has still only been achieved by two others. Jackson made his highest score in test cricket and Lockwood returned his best test match analysis of 11-76 in this, his penultimate test.

Nor could Tate be considered ridiculously old for a debut based upon others' experiences. At exactly 35 years old, he is fourteen years and 119 days younger than the oldest man to make a debut for England, James Southerton. Four Englishmen, including three subjects of this book, have made test debuts aged over forty. In the first test of the 1928–29 Ashes series Ironmonger became Australia's oldest debutant, and in the next test Blackie who, at 46 years and 253 days, was just over a fortnight older than Ironmonger, became Australia's oldest test debutant. Pakistan's Miram Bux was 47 years and 284 days old on debut in 1954–55. Three Englishmen have played test cricket in their fifties.

What perhaps is true is that playing the game for so long in the comparative backwater of Sussex county cricket, in a side which rarely promised or delivered success, Tate was exceedingly nervous of playing in such a major match. But he had played for the Players against the Gentlemen, a match exceeded only by tests in their importance.

Fred Tate had made his debut in 1887, playing one match, against Yorkshire at Bradford, as many of Sussex's amateurs were unavailable. He scored 1 and 26 – equal top score in the second innings – and went wicketless through a dozen overs, which cost 26 runs. He played through-out the next season and came second in Sussex's bowling averages with 26 wickets in twelve matches. That year he took his first 'five for'. On a sodden pitch Sussex had made 51 and 96, and when Tate came on in Kent's second innings they were at 41-4, needing only three for victory. Tate then clean bowled five batsmen in 11 balls, and the final man came in with two still wanted. Two scrambled singles brought victory. Tate had returned 5-1 from four four-ball overs. He had less success the following season; so did his county, winning only one of a dozen games. He did not play at all in 1890.

The 1892 *Wisden* reported that "a considerable measure of the success which fell to Sussex in 1891 was due to the brilliant batting of Bean and the bowling of Tate, who on slow wickets showed himself quite a first-rate bowler." Tate took 80 wickets including returns of 6-23 versus Kent at Brighton, and 7-33 versus Oxford University, when, in his second spell, he took 7-6 in 8.3 overs. In these two analyses, ten of the thirteen wickets were bowled. A.E. Stoddart recalled, "Tate clean bowled more first-class batsmen on perfect wickets than any other medium-pace bowler, and it is certain that on a sticky or crumbled pitch, Tate can bowl out any side for a small score."

Of 1892, *Wisden* reported that "though he bowled well now and then and got through a lot of work, it cannot be said that he increased his reputation." In 1893 he took 31 wickets and in 1894 only 16, playing in only one championship game, the first of the season.

In 1895 he took 85 wickets and *Wisden* wrote, "Considering that he had to bowl very frequently on the Brighton ground – admittedly one of the easiest in England for run-getting – his record is decidedly better than it looks on paper." Against Kent he took eleven wickets in the match, enabling Sussex to win by 45 after being 178 adrift on first innings. Kent were bowled out for 122 in their second innings, Tate bowling 32 overs unchanged. Tate was now established as the stock bowler of the side, and in the following year he took a hundred wickets in a season for the first time, always bowling more than his share with great endurance and cheerfulness.

The next year he took fractionally fewer wickets and in September he played for the first time for a side other than Sussex, in a festival game at Hastings. In 1899 he captured 121 wickets and scored 510 runs – his previous seasonal best had been 264 – and reached the first fifty of his career in his 288th innings, with 59 not out versus Somerset.

At around this time C.B. Fry in *A Book Of Cricket – A New Gallery of Famous Players* wrote of Tate that he was "one of the two or three best medium-pace bowlers in England [...] he has a beautifully elastic action, and a wonderful natural spin. He makes the ball whip off the ground with that extra bit of pace which indicates a born bowler. He commands a strong off break, can send down a lovely faster ball that goes straight on, and often succeeds with a deceptive yorker. Tate is a useful bat on fast wickets; his style has vastly improved of late. He is a neat catch at slip, and a clever extra cover. He cannot throw, but returns with an uncommonly good jerk."

In 1901 he took 141 wickets, a total he increased by one the next season, of which *Wisden* wrote, "Tate probably bowled in finer form than at any previous period of his long career. He lacks some of the pace he at one time possessed, but he has great command over the ball, and last summer, at the age of 34, was certainly one of the best medium-pace bowlers in the country." Tate took 14 wickets against Kent at Tonbridge.

Tate was granted a benefit that year, and in the match Sussex made 560-5 declared against Yorkshire; Yorkshire replied with 92 but then saved the game in their second innings. Tate gathered £1,051.18s, then a Sussex record. With this help he became landlord of the Burnell Arms at Haywards Heath, opposite the station. His batting form, which had dipped deeply in 1900, came back again, and he made the highest score of his career, making 84 out of 96 to save a game against Nottinghamshire.

After the fourth test of 1902 the Australians had a match against Essex, and then one against Sussex. Tate toiled through 41 profitless overs, conceding 136 runs as the Australians declared at 580-6. When Sussex batted, Tate made an undefeated 22. How he would have traded all 22 for just four more runs in the test. A month after the test he took 8-28 versus Hampshire at Southampton. In mid-September he turned out for the South of England at Bournemouth against the Australians. On a treacherous pitch he and Arnold of Worcestershire bowled unchanged throughout both innings of 123 and 91. In the first innings Tate took the wickets of his two tormentors from the test, Darling, (clean bowled), and Saunders, in figures of 27-5-67-2. The second innings brought figures of 13-2-48-6. Darling escaped him the second time around with Arnold dismissing him, but Saunders fell to him again.

His total of 180 wickets that season was surpassed only by Rhodes, with 213 and his 153 wickets for Sussex were a county record. He contributed an unbeaten 61 at Hastings against Surrey as Sussex made 705-8 declared, their highest score. With Ranji he put on 160 in 70 minutes for the ninth wicket. The match aggregate of 1,427 runs, was a record for three-day first-class cricket in England. Sussex came second in the championship, their highest position ever, and one which they were to repeat the following season and also in 1932–34 and 1981.

In 1902, *Wisden* reported that, "The main factor in the success of Sussex was the wonderfully good and consistent bowling of Tate. The summer favoured him but it is no exaggeration to say that he was a better bowler than at any previous period of his now somewhat long career. In match after match he made the most of the advantage afforded him by the state of the grounds, combining great accuracy of pitch with his always formidable off break. He had no bowlers of anything like his own class to support him and this being the case, his record of 153 wickets in 20 county matches at a cost of little over 14 runs each was even more remarkable than it looks on paper. There has been no such effective bowling for Sussex since Walter Humphreys had his great success with lobs in 1893."

After this year of achievement – achievement which brought sorrow – Tate's play faded away. Some said he was never the same person again after the test match. In 1903 *Wisden* described his bowling as 'comparatively harmless'. He took 62 wickets that year; in the following year he took 51, and in 1905 he took 13 at 46 runs apiece and finished at the bottom of the first-class averages. He did not play first-class cricket again. All but eight of his 310 first-class matches had been for Sussex.

In the winter of 1898–99 he had become one of the earliest English professionals to coach overseas when he went to Western Province. In 1907 he became coach at Oundle and in 1921, aged 54, he became coach to Derbyshire, before joining Trent College as coach.

When his coaching days were over he moved to Haywards Heath to the pub he had bought with his benefit money. He was always willing to talk about 'that tragic test'. He thought it would be an eternal stain on his memory and used to say that years after he was dead and buried the tale would go on of how Fred Tate lost a test match. But he quite enjoyed making the most of the story.

What of the little kid at home, who was going to make up for it? He did not show much early ability. He grew up around cricket as he later recalled: "Nothing else seemed to be talked about. My baby milk was diluted with cricket; I was weaned on it and it was served up with every meal."

Keen but unable, at prep school he resorted to bribing the captain with the aid of his shilling-a-week pocket money in order to get into the team. Despite this, he was picked only once – though the captain took the money. He was more of a success as a football goalkeeper and a master told him, "We know your father is a great cricketer, but you'll never be one. You stick to football."

Yet his father's faith never wavered. "One day you will play for England," he said with conviction. "I never allowed my failure to get into the school team to daunt me," recalled the son.

Having waited weeks for the chance to play for Haywards Heath in the summer of 1910 he was finally selected to play for their second eleven. There then followed days of careful preparation, and nights when he could not sleep for the excitement and anticipation. But King Edward VII died and the game was cancelled. He took it badly and locked himself in the stable. His grandmother called through the door to come out and have some food but he called out that the king had died just to spite him. He emptied some sacks of vegetables and pelted anyone who came near. One of his sisters said it was weeks before he got over his disappointment.

In April 1910 Fred Tate received a letter from Sussex asking if he would send his son to Hove for a fortnight's trial. For the first three days it rained. When the trial could get under way his son was sure that he was the worst of the fifteen candidates. Convinced he had not done himself justice, "It seemed a foregone conclusion that I was a failure. I would go home in tears in the evening at the thought I had done so badly." But he was offered an engagement for the season.

Ten years after the fateful test, Fred Tate's son made his debut for the Sussex 1st XI. Still he failed to impress: when war came he had been on the staff for five years, yet he had played only ten times, taking seven expensive wickets. He returned from the war tougher and stronger. His pace had increased, but there was little spite in his deliveries, and he was no better than first change. Then in a game in 1922 versus Hampshire, Arthur Gilligan had been changing the bowlers around: Tate, Roberts, Cox, himself, his brother Harold and Bowley. Immediately after lunch Tate was brought on versus Mead. Arlott wrote that "Tate swung all his body into bowling Mead a quicker ball and, almost inadvertently, bowled him a cutter. The ball pitched off stump and hit top of leg stump like a rifle bullet."

It was at that moment that, belatedly, Tate showed that he had something special as a bowler. In 1924 he fulfilled his father's prediction, when he played for England in the first test of that summer, taking 4-12 in the first innings and another four wickets in the second. Maurice Tate was to play thirty-eight more times for England, becoming one of her greatest bowlers.

In 1923, in a match report, Archie MacLaren wrote that "it is good to see bowlers who have been well-taught by their fathers, who were really great bowlers themselves as Fred Tate undoubtedly was."

In 1937 Fred Tate wrote, "I only once had the great honour of playing under Mr Archie MacLaren. That was for England in 1902, but I always adhere to the assertion that he was the finest captain I ever played under."

On 24 February 1943 Fred Tate died, aged 75. A few days later *The Times* made him the subject of a leader entitled 'Dropped Catches' in which Fred Tate's infamous miss was recounted, and it discussed why cricketers are exposed to such life-long reproaches while open goals and missed putts are soon forgotten and forgiven. It concluded it might be because, "There is something ineradicably boyish at the heart of a cricket crowd which never ceases to identify itself with the players [...] When a momentous catch is dropped these kindly people leave the ground with a sense of sin which time cannot expiate. It is a part of them that has erred."

First-Class:

| Matches | Inns | NO | Runs | HS | Aver |
|---|---|---|---|---|---|
| 320 | 458 | 150 | 2952 | 84 | 9.58 |

| Wkts | Average | SR | Best | 10wm | 5wi | ct |
|---|---|---|---|---|---|---|
| 1311 | 21.55 | 51 | 9-73 | 29 | 104 | 236 |

Players: 1 appearance

| Inns | NO | Runs | HS | Aver | O | M | R | W | Aver | BB |
|---|---|---|---|---|---|---|---|---|---|---|
| 1 | 0 | 0 | 0 | 0.00 | 28.3 | 9 | 95 | 3 | 31.67 | 3-67 |

# 3  A. Warren (Derbyshire)

Born: 2 April 1875 in Codnor Park, Derbyshire. Died: 3 September 1951
3rd Test, 1905 v. Australia
Batting:  1st Inns: (No.10)  7 no
Bowling:  1st Inns: 19.2-5-57-5        2nd Inns: 20-4-56-1

Many players get dropped because they fail. Arnold Warren appears to have been dropped through one of the consequences of his success.

Rarely do English selectors choose from Derbyshire when picking the national team and when they do they tend to pick opening bowlers. Of the couple of dozen players who have played for England whilst at Derbyshire, almost half have been opening bowlers; of the remainder, a third have been wicket-keepers.

In 1905, when over a hundred cricketers had represented England, Arnold Warren became the second Derbyshire cricketer to do so, and the first in a line of opening bowlers.

On his day Warren was one of the quickest bowlers in the country. W.T. Taylor, the long-time Derbyshire secretary, reckoned Warren to be the fastest Derbyshire bowler he had seen with the exception of Michael Holding. Warren generated his pace from a long, bounding approach and a fluent action, making the ball lift and break off the seam into the batsman. With Bill Bestwick he formed a fearsome opening partnership, Warren providing pace and hostility and Bestwick stamina and consistency.

Warren's father was a prosperous builder who apprenticed his five sons into the trade. Warren was born into a mining community and was a product of his environment at a time when Derbyshire cricketers were considered to be a 'somewhat rough lot'. In his later years he worked as a bricklayer at Ormonde colliery and his youthful cricket was played in a brickyard quarry not far from his home.

Like some other cricketers of his time, notably his opening partner Bill Bestwick, Warren was a heavy drinker. This partly explains his erratic performances, beyond the natural tendency of quick bowlers either to 'spark' or 'misfire'.

Sometimes Warren's drinking had beneficial effects upon his bowling, such as at Ashby-de-la-Zouch in 1912, which he considered his best bowling performance. Needing 181 to win, Leicestershire looked to be heading for a comfortable victory on a pitch unhelpful to the bowlers when lunch came. Warren spent the lunch interval in the refreshment tent, downing several whiskies, and after lunch he ripped through the Leicestershire batting to bowl them all out for 97 with figures of 7-52. This was in the era when amateurs had cooked lunches provided for them by the host club and professionals were left to their own resources.

On other occasions both Warren's and Bestwick's bowling was adversely affected by their lifestyle. Warren and Bestwick shared a similarity of circumstances in that both their wives died young, leaving them to bring up a young son on their own, and both had a brush with the law following a brawl. Bestwick had a run-in with a man named Brown one evening in 1907 after both had been drinking. Later that evening they had another fight, where it is said that Brown produced a knife and Bestwick suffered a facial wound. That night Brown was found dead through knife injuries and Bestwick was arrested for murder. A jury subsequently returned a verdict of justifiable homicide in self-defence. On another occasion, when under the influence, Bestwick barracked his own side from the crowd. At one stage on away trips one of the side always accompanied him in the evenings to ensure fitness to bowl in the morning. Bestwick's unreliable behaviour eventually led to him being suspended from the side in 1909 and later sacked.

Sport and drink have always been entwined. In 1897, Bobby Peel seems to have celebrated his highest first-class score, 210 not out, enthusiastically. The next day, so the story goes, he was caught short on the pitch and relieved himself, was sent from the pitch by his captain, Lord Hawke, and never played again. Three years after Warren's test appearance, the South African Charles Hefferon was leading the Olympic marathon by the huge margin of almost four minutes with six miles to go. With only two miles to go he was still in a comfortable lead when he accepted a glass of champagne from a spectator. Less than a mile from the finish, with victory looking a certainty, he was hit by stomach cramps and dizziness and was subsequently passed by two competitors, one of whom was later disqualified. The austere Douglas Jardine ushered an ill Eddie Paynter on his way to an epic 83 at Brisbane with a glass of champagne.

Warren made his first-class debut for Derbyshire in 1901, meeting with a notable lack of success: his seven wickets that season came at an average of 84. In 1902 he became a regular member of the side, playing in eleven championship matches, taking 38 wickets at 24.57 in the process.

In 1903 Warren was at the fore in both the first-class matches Derbyshire won that season, including a historic first win over their neighbour Nottinghamshire. Warren took 6-93 in the second innings as Nottinghamshire, set 316, lost by 114 runs.

In 1904, when England played no test matches, Warren became the first Derbyshire player ever to take a hundred wickets in a season, finishing with 124 wickets at 20.94. He and Bill Bestwick, who that year took 92 wickets at 26.34, dismissed the MCC at Lord's for 55, the wickets shared equally between them. He achieved his best figures of his career on a wet wicket at Welbeck in this season, when, of the 18 Nottinghamshire wickets which fell, he took 8-69 and 7-43.

In the middle of June 1905 Derbyshire defeated Yorkshire in two days, one of only three defeats for Yorkshire that season. Warren returned figures of 20-5-57-7 in Yorkshire's first innings of 123 and 20.3-5-69-5 in their 161-run second innings as Derbyshire won by nine wickets. The England and Yorkshire captain F.S. Jackson, although not playing in the game, was impressed by Warren's bowling. *Wisden*, reporting on this performance, said, "On the strength of it, in all probability, he was chosen as England's fast bowler at Leeds."

The close of the first day's play of the Leeds test came at the end of England's innings of 301, almost half of which were made by F.S. Jackson who, on home turf, became the first test centurion at Headingley. On the second morning, with Warren bowling rapidly, Australia were reduced to 36-3 after half an hour's play when Hayward fell to a catch off Warren, Warren having clean bowled Trumper for 8. He maintained his pace throughout the innings, getting the ball to rise awkwardly to take 5-57 to bowl Australia out for 195. England declared their second innings on 295-5, but were unable to dismiss Australia a second time, the tourists hanging on at 224-7. Warren, although dismissing Trumper for nought before Australia had scored, bowled without the fire of the first innings and Trumper was to be his sole victim in twenty overs, although Hill was badly missed in the slips in his second over.

The difference in the quality of the bowling from one day to the next could be explained by the evening in between. That evening Warren had embarked upon a vigorous, alcoholic celebration of his first innings' performance, in which he was joined by friends and relatives. This appears to have had an adverse effect on his performance the next day. F.S. Jackson heard of Warren's exploits during that evening and was unimpressed, and this influenced the selection of the next team in which the Lancastrian fast bowler Walter Brearley was selected to play on his home ground. Warren appears to have been a victim of his own success. Had he been less successful in the test he might have played more tests; had his five wickets come in the second innings he almost certainly would have done.

Brearley took 4-72 in the first innings of the next test, and after Australia had closed the second day on 113-1, he took four wickets on the last day to skittle Australia out for 169 to bring England victory by an innings, thereby retaining the Ashes. After this performance he retained his place for the final test where he took five wickets in the first innings.

In between the third and fourth tests Derbyshire played a remarkable game against Essex at Chesterfield. When Bestwick took an early wicket to move Essex to 12-1, Perrin came to the wicket. On a scorching day, hindered by a knee injury, Warren conceded 58 runs from his first 13 overs, not taking a single wicket. But in his fourteenth over he caught and bowled Gillingham for 43 to end a fourth wicket partnership of 121 in 70 minutes to make it 300-4. In his sixteenth over Perrin, on 152, was missed by Bestwick at mid on. With the fifth ball of the over Warren bowled Sewell and next bowled Reeves to make the score 314-6. Perrin re-established the bat's dominance by taking two boundaries from each of Warren's next five overs. By close of play Essex were on 524-8 with Perrin not out 295, including 58 boundaries – only eight fours short of MacLaren's record 65 in his 424. Declarations were not then allowed until lunch on the second day. Next morning Essex took their score to 597, with Perrin not out 343, the product of five and three-quarter hours' batting, including a record 68 fours.

Derek Lodge in *Figures On The Green* writes that "for many years it was fashionable to say that P.A. Perrin was the best batsman never to play for England." Perrin made almost 30,000 runs at an average of 36, with 66 centuries. Another batsman also often described as the best not to have played for England is John Langridge, who made 76 first-class centuries, eight of them doubles and reached two thousand runs in a season eleven times. He scored over 34,000 runs at an average of 37.45. John Langridge was selected for the 1939–40 tour to India, which was subsequently abandoned. Only Alan Jones, with 36,049 runs at 32.89, including 56 centuries, scored more runs yet never played test cricket. Third equal in the list of prolific non-test batsmen are Les Berry of Leicestershire and Ken Suttle of Sussex, with 30,225 runs. Suttle toured the West Indies in 1953–54, taking a catch as substitute in the fourth test. Berry never made an overseas tour. Only one Englishman has gone on two tours without ever playing test cricket. George Brann of Sussex. He toured Australia in 1887–88 and South Africa in 1891–92 without playing in the sole test match on each tour.

In reply to Essex's 597, Derbyshire made 548, Olliveire making 229, their innings closing at 12.40 pm on the final day. Carpenter was caught by Warren off Bestwick in the slips and Warren shattered Fane's stumps. Perrin took two leg side boundaries off Warren and then drove the third delivery of his fourth over back with almighty power, but Warren clung onto a difficult return catch, and at lunch Essex had subsided to 27-6. After lunch they were eventually all out for 97, Warren taking 4-42, leaving Derbyshire to make 147 for victory in 125 minutes. Despite the fall of an early wicket Derbyshire scored 149-1, with forty minutes left, Olliveire scoring an unbeaten 92.

Later that summer Warren was selected for the Players for the match at the Oval where he took 5-105 in the first innings from forty overs and 3-52 in the second innings.

That season he took 94 wickets at 24.54, and in 1906 and 1908 he took a seasonal hundred wickets; in 1909 he missed it by the smallest possible margin, his wickets costing 22.25.

As his career batting of 13.73 suggests, his batting was that of a competent tail-ender. In June 1910 Derbyshire played against Warwickshire at Blackwell, one of only seven fixtures ever played at that venue. The colliery manager was on the county committee and persuaded his colleagues to host matches there. Warwickshire, 429-5 at the end of the first day, declared at 504-7. Derbyshire replied with 262 and, on the final day, following on, collapsed to 131-8. John Chapman, the captain, came in to join Warren, who had come in at the fall of the sixth wicket. At that point in the season Chapman was averaging 15, which was three more than Warren. The innings defeat was not expected to be long in coming. Warren, using his height to good advantage, started to strike the ball hard and Chapman put an indifferent start behind him as 73 were added in the 40 minutes up to lunch, by which point Derbyshire needed only 38 to avoid an innings defeat. After lunch Warren was the first to his fifty and at 264 the partnership reached 133 – a new county record for the ninth wicket. Chapman was by now beginning to take on the mantle of the senior batsman as Warren was suffering from a knee injury, which limited his stroke play and his running between the wickets. Despite this handicap, the stand passed the English ninth-wicket record stand of 193 by W.G. Grace and S.A.P. Kitcat for Gloucestershire against

Sussex at Bristol in 1896, and the world record of 232 by C. Hill and E. Walkley for South Australia v. New South Wales in 1900–01. With the stand worth 283 and in its 175th minute, Warren fell to a superb slip catch for 123, having hit fourteen boundaries. His century had come in two hours and thirty-five minutes. The stand remains a world record. The closest attempts on it were by J.B. Commins and N. Boje when they made 268 for South Africa against Mashonaland in 1994–95 and, in 1921, when J.W.H.T. Douglas and S.N. Hare had put on 252 against Derbyshire for Essex.

This was the season after Warren's retirement, which had come at the amazingly late age for a fast bowler of 45. Not having played for Derbyshire since 1913, he returned to the team for a couple of matches in Derbyshire's appalling 1920 season when they lost seventeen of their eighteen first-class games; the other match was abandoned without a ball being bowled. That season Warren came second in the averages behind Bestwick, who had returned to the side in 1919, aged 44. Bestwick enjoyed an Indian summer, playing for the Players at Lord's that season, and took 147 wickets in 1921.

In sixteen seasons for Derbyshire Warren played 250 matches, taking all bar twenty-one of his first-class wickets for them. In 1923 he became a first-class umpire. Bill Bestwick also became an umpire, and umpired in Denis Compton's debut match for Middlesex. Compton came in at number eleven, to join his captain Gubby Allen, with Middlesex 24 behind. Together they took Middlesex into the lead when Compton was given out lbw. Allen complained to Bestwick that it was never out. "I know," confessed the umpire, "but I was dying for a pee."

Warren had also been a good football player, and had played wing half for Derby County in the 1906 FA Cup Final, which resulted in a 6-0 victory for Bury – it remains the heaviest cup final defeat in FA history. Warren died aged 76, but he lived to see Derby County come back and win the FA Cup in 1946.

First-Class:

| Matches | Inns | NO | Runs | HS | Aver | 100 |
|---|---|---|---|---|---|---|
| 235 | 445 | 44 | 5507 | 123 | 13.73 | 1 |

| Wkts | Average | SR | Best | 10wm | 5wi | ct |
|---|---|---|---|---|---|---|
| 939 | 24.55 | 46 | 8-69 | 15 | 72 | 195 |

Players: 1 appearance

| Inns | NO | Runs | HS | Aver | O | M | R | W | Aver | BB | 5wi |
|---|---|---|---|---|---|---|---|---|---|---|---|
| 2 | 0 | 23 | 14 | 12.50 | 58 | 9 | 157 | 8 | 19.63 | 5-105 | 1 |

# 4  J.H. King (Leicestershire)

Born: 16 April 1871, Lutterworth, Leicestershire. Died: 18 November 1946
2nd Test, 1909 v. Australia
Batting:  1st Inns: (No.5)  60  2nd Inns: (No.5)  5
Bowling: 1st Inns: 27-5-99-1

In 1909 King became involved in one of the biggest selection contro-
versies in English test history. *Wisden* wrote of it that "never in the history
of test matches in England has there been such blundering in the selection
of an England XI. When the names of the players were announced every
one was astonished to learn that Jessop and Walter Brearley had been
left out, and almost as much surprise was felt at the Leicestershire pros,
King and Jayes being chosen ... On no other occasion has there been
such a storm of protest, nearly every newspaper in England condemning
the action taken."

In his Notes, the Editor of *Wisden* wrote, "Complaint has been made
that the selection committee came in for unfair attack, but I do not think
the complaint can be justified. To this day the extraordinary blundering
in connection with the team for the Test Match at Lord's – the game that
was the beginning of England's troubles – remains unexplained [...] How
these three gentlemen came to make such a muddle of the business no
one has ever been able to understand."

The selectors in 1909 were Lord Hawke, who acted as chairman, C.B.
Fry and 'Shrimp' Leveson-Gower. F.S. Jackson was invited to captain
the side but, due to other commitments, declined. He had hardly played
first-class cricket since 1905. Archie MacLaren became captain instead.

The English cricket-supporting public was confident that their team
could carry off the series. Not for the last time it seems that the English
had underestimated the merits of the Australian tourists. Prior to the
first test the Australians had played six matches, losing to Surrey by five
runs and MCC by three wickets and beating Nottinghamshire and
Northamptonshire.

After selecting fifteen names for the first test, Lord Hawke's back
trouble necessitated a visit to Aix-les-Bains. Because of wet footholds it
was decided to leave out the fast bowler Brearley, and the attack was
opened by two left-arm spinners, Hirst and Blythe. Bowling unchanged
through the first innings, they took 4-28 and 6-44 from 23 overs each to
bowl Australia out for 74. England made 121 and Blythe and Hirst once
again dominated the second innings' bowling, both taking 5-58. The
bustling medium pacer G.J. Thompson bowled four overs on debut, and
the slow left-armer, Rhodes, bowled a solitary over. England won by ten
wickets.

In Lord Hawke's absence, the selection of side for the second test was left to Fry and Leveson-Gover, and MacLaren as captain. Fry does not appear to have had a strong role in selection as he was involved in a court case at the time, which also meant him missing the test as a player. When the fourteen names were announced, omitting Jessop – described by *Wisden* as "the one indispensable player" – and Brearley there was a great public outcry.

*Cricket* wrote: "Since Friday evening, when the names of the players from whom the England side would be chosen for this week's test match at Lord's became known, the Selection Committee has been very freely criticized. The absence from the list of the names of Jessop and Brearley has given rise to much speculation and many rumours. There is no need to dwell upon the matter at any length; suffice it to say that if, as many people imagine, the pair named had not been invited because they were not considered worth their places, the Selection Committee would at once have forfeited the confidence of the public.

"No one would quarrel with the selection of George Gunn and Haigh," it continued, "but many unkind things have been said concerning the invitation extended to King and Jayes. There certainly seems to have been little to justify the choice of the last-named, but King has been well above the average of all-round players for several seasons past. The selection of King struck me as a very happy one. It is always advisable to have a sound left-handed batsman in a side, and when there is available one who has been showing good form, and one, moreover, who is a very useful bowler, what is more natural than he should be picked.

"Of King it may truly be said that if he had been associated with a more prominent county his real worth would have been appreciated more as it deserved to be."

MacLaren, in a letter to Jessop, said he had wanted Jessop and Brearley. Leveson-Gower, in his autobiography, wrote of the decision to omit Brearley that "I thought at the time, and still think, that it was a mistake, though the captain disagreed with me. Brearley however was of my opinion." MacLaren had asked Brearley, who was at Lord's as a spectator, to play at 11.15 on the morning of the match. But according to a letter MacLaren wrote to Jessop, "Brearley could have played but would not when I saw him before the game – his bag being at Tonbridge – but he would not wire for it." Brearley instead stationed himself under Leveson-Gower's clock-tower box and sang about his omission: "I often get six wickets in an innings, and generally the leading batsmen. I don't always trust the fieldsmen so I clean bowl them." Brearley's singing attracted quite a crowd until a policeman moved him on, allegedly telling him that Christmas was a long time off and he would have plenty of time before then to perfect his carols or whatever it was.

It was not to be the only time dissenters voiced their views to Leveson-Gower about his selections. Later, when he was chairman, he received a

letter telling him that if a certain player was not in the next test team he
would be shot on his next visit to the Oval. When the player was not
selected he received a parcel containing a packet of black-edged 'in
memoriam' cards and a letter:

> Dear Sir,
> As you have failed to take my advice and play — you will still be shot,
> and I am sending some In Memoriam cards for you to post to your friends
> (if you still have any) so they may have the pleasure of seeing the end of
> you as an Ignorant Selector. I have several more cards as there is certain
> to be a great demand for them to welcome your departure.

Blythe had to be omitted from the team on doctor's orders, because
he was not up to the nervous strain of a test match, though he could
cope with the lesser demands of county games. At this time Blythe was
the form bowler in England. In the absence of Blythe and Brearley the
selectors seemed to be hoping for a repeat of the success of the first test
when two slow, medium, left-arm bowlers bowled England to victory.
*The Times* described the bowling attack England went into the match
with – Hirst, King and Relf, who had been in the party for the previous
test but not played, and Haigh – as 'rash'. Selection was further
hampered by Fry's last-minute withdrawal, which brought Hayward into
the side although his leg was not fully fit. He missed a running catch and
was run out in the second innings. King's Leicestershire colleague Jayes
was left out, and was never to play test cricket, leaving King, alone, to
become the first Leicestershire player picked for a home test.

Coming in at number four as England batted first, King, "never in
difficulties", made a chanceless 60 out of 131 in 155 minutes, an innings
containing "some delightful off drives and leg hits", and six boundaries
as England made 269. Just before close King opened the bowling with
Hirst, Australia moving to 17 without loss by the close of play. On the
second day, during the course of a King over, MacLaren, in the slips,
put down a chance from Ransford, on 13, and Hayward spilled a catch
at point from a scoreless Trumper. Ransford's miss was extremely costly,
for he went to make an unbeaten 143 out of Australia's 350. Trumper
made 28. *Cricket* reported that "King at one point bowled extremely
well, but he never got over the disappointment of seeing Ransford and
Trumper missed off him in one over." After being dropped, Ransford
took eighteen runs from two King overs.

In the second innings England, having conceded a first innings lead
of 81 through poor fielding, collapsed to Warwick Armstrong's leg spin,
King being bowled by him for 4. At one stage they were 41-6 before
rallying to make 121. Australia knocked off the runs for victory from
the bowling of Hirst and Relf for the loss of one wicket.

*Cricket* wrote of the second test: "Few Englishmen will recall it with any satisfaction, for it has provided one of the blackest pages in the chronicle of this country's cricket [...] England, as was expected, severely felt the absence of a really fast bowler, but that does not excuse the very weak batting display they gave on a plumb wicket in their second innings."

Lord Hawke returned from France and set about repairing the situation. MacLaren offered his resignation to Lord Hawke but Hawke refused to accept it. It is not clear that it was MacLaren's fault that selection had gone awry, and, of his performance in the field, F.S. Ashley-Cooper wrote, "MacLaren handled the bowling at his command with considerable skill."

Brearley, Jessop, Barnes and Rhodes were restored to the party for the fourth test and Sharp, rated highly by MacLaren, was included. Jayes and King were omitted. This seems harsh on King, for he had top scored in England's first innings, and had bowled much better than his figures suggest. However Hawke had not seen the bowling performance. King seems to have done enough as a batsman certainly to be retained in the party from which the final eleven was to be picked. His original selection may have been freely criticized – although *Cricket* approved of it – but his performance in the test had justified the selectors' faith. Or would have had they demonstrated any; that they didn't was shown by how quickly they disposed of him. England's batting again failed in the third test as they were bowled out for 87, albeit a man short as Jessop was unable to bat in the match. With Hobbs and Jessop injured, three more batsmen were called up for the fourth test, bringing recalls for Spooner, Hutchings and Warner. The last named, a selector in 1905, had not played test cricket for four years and was replaced by debutant Frank Woolley for the final test.

It is difficult to determine whether King was victim or beneficiary of the summer's selection confusions. The argument for the former view would be the way in which he was ditched; for the latter one could point out that, had not the selections for the second test been so idiosyncratic in the first place he would not even have had an England cap. However, his record, both before and after his test appearance, suggests it was an honour well deserved.

King played first-class cricket for thirty years, and throughout this time he was one of the best left-handed batsmen around. An attractive bat, particularly effective against fast bowling, he was a fine cutter and driver. A left-handed bowler, he varied between slow and medium-paced deliveries bowled from around the wicket with little follow-through. He bowled with a puzzling flight to a good length. Fourteen times he made a thousand runs in the season, and twice he took a hundred wickets; in 1912 he did both. A good field in the early part of his career, in his later years he was hampered by rheumatism.

It seemed that King was to get selectorial recognition either grudgingly or fortuitously, depending upon one's viewpoint. In 1904 he became the only player to score centuries in both innings of a Gentlemen and Players match making 104 and 109 not out on a wicket described as 'fiery'. He had only played because at the last moment Tyldesley withdrew with an injury and the twelfth man had missed his train and had not arrived at the ground when the game was due to start. King, on hand as a member of the ground staff, was co-opted to the team. In 1906 at the Oval in this series he scored 89 not out and 88, but was not selected again until 1909.

It had originally been intended that King, the son of a local builder, would join his father's business but he joined the Leicestershire ground staff instead, and for many years was on the ground staff at Lord's. He first played for Leicestershire in 1895, but did not play regularly for them until 1899.

Against Sussex at Hove in 1903 he performed the hat trick, which he also did against Somerset at Taunton in 1920. At the Oval in 1906 he had hit the ball twice in defence, but then ran to be given out – the most recent man to have been so dismissed in England. Despite gaining his test recognition when 38 years old, most of his best performances came after this. In 1911 he took 8-17 against Yorkshire, including a 20-ball spell of 7-0. In 1912 he performed the 'double', scoring 1,074 runs at 22.85 and taking 130 wickets at 17.63. In 1913, in a match with Northamptonshire, he scored 111 and 100 not out to record his second accomplishment of centuries in both innings of a match. A year later he scored his first double-century, an undefeated 227 against Worcestershire at Coalville. In 1923, when 52 years old, he scored 205 against Hampshire at Leicestershire. He retired from first-class cricket in 1925. By now a rheumatic 55 year-old, he recorded the first century that season. He became an umpire after retiring from the game.

First-Class:

| Matches | Inns | NO | Runs | HS | Aver | 100 |
|---|---|---|---|---|---|---|
| 552 | 988 | 69 | 25122 | 227no | 27.33 | 34 |

| Wkts | Average | SR | Best | 10wm | 5wi | ct |
|---|---|---|---|---|---|---|
| 1,204 | 25.17 | 58 | 8-17 | 11 | 69 | 340 |

Players: 5 appearances

| Inns | NO | Runs | HS | Aver | O | M | R | W | Aver | BB |
|---|---|---|---|---|---|---|---|---|---|---|
| 9 | 3 | 468 | 109* | 78.00 | 27 | 4 | 80 | 3 | 26.67 | 2-37 |

# 5   D.W. Carr (Kent)

Born: 17 March 1872, Cranbrook, Kent. Died: 23 March 1950
5th Test, 1909 v. Australia
Batting:   1st Inns: (No.11)   0
Bowling: 1st Inns: 34-2-146-5     2nd Inns: 35-1-136-2

Douglas Carr had been in the eleven at Sutton Valence school for four years before going up to Oxford University. There he played in the Freshman's match in 1891 where he scored 4, batting at number four, and took 3-27, including the wicket of university captain M.R. Jardine. He was then picked for the 16 Freshmen against 'The Twelve'. Figures of 0-17 and a knee injury, picked up in a game of football, meant he played little further cricket at university.

When he was a master at Stanmore School, his knee now well recovered, he played as a steady medium-pace bowler and occasional middle-order batsman in Kent club cricket. In 1897 he did well enough to be selected for Kent 2nd XI against Sussex 2nd XI at Brighton. It was for his bowling that he was chosen, but it was as a batsman that he proved more successful, scoring 39 and conceding 145 runs in taking two wickets. Around this time he scored 165 for Free Foresters against the Royal Engineers at Chartham, his highest score in any class of cricket.

Originally in club cricket he bowled medium pace with ordinary off break. He had always possessed a leg break and for many years proved effective as a leg break bowler with a useful fast ball. Playing as a medium pacer for Blue Mantles against Newbury in 1896 he finished off the first innings with a hat trick and, when Newbury followed on, took wickets with the first two balls of the second innings. In another match he had five runs added to his analysis thanks to cover point fielding the ball with his cap.

Having played several times with Bosanquet, and envied his success, he spent the winter of 1905–06 in trying to acquire the googly, eventually succeeding in making the ball come back with the leg break action, only to find that he had lost his old leg break entirely. There followed a year during which he was practically unable to make the ball turn in either direction. But, getting at length some control of both breaks, he began to perfect the method through 1907.

In 1905–06 the South African googly bowlers became a force in world cricket as South Africa not only beat England for the first time in a test match – England had won all the previous eight tests – but won four of the five tests in the series. Carr learnt further from watching these South African bowlers – Schwartz, Vogler, White and Faulkner – when they toured England in 1907.

Carr bowled faster than many of his type, relying on length and concealment of the googly rather than flight. C.B. Fry described his style as being much like the South Africans' in method. He was surprisingly accurate for a leg spinner and was able to take punishment without losing confidence or length.

The googly was then rarely encountered in county cricket let alone club cricket and Carr had considerable success with his new method of bowling in Kent club cricket in 1908. But the county side were very powerful and had a bowling attack so strong that Fielder, Blythe and Woolley, who between them took 5,807 first-class wickets at 19 during their careers, rarely needed extra help, and when they did it was readily available from Fairservice and Humphreys. They did not wish to drop an established player for a 37 year-old whose batting and fielding, for a first-class cricketer, were very ordinary, and who had to find time from his teaching duties to play. The committee compromised by giving him a game against Oxford University at the end of May. He took 7-95 in the match, including a first innings five-wicket haul.

The Australians were touring that year and the selectors decided that the Gentlemen versus Players matches would not involve those who would otherwise have been playing in a championship game as the counties had already complained of missing players due to the tests. Carr was therefore chosen for the Gentlemen, for the match beginning on 8 July, in which he took 3-58 and 5-80 including the wickets of the first four batsmen in the second innings. In the return match two days later he took 6-71 in the first innings. These figures were the more remarkable for being obtained on slow pitches unsuited to leg break and googly bowling. These performances made quite a stir, as *Cricket* reported on 22 July: "D.W. Carr's bowling is one of the chief topics of conversation in cricketing circles."

Carr was chosen in the twelve for the fourth test despite not yet having played a county championship match. *Cricket* reported that "he was chosen, with the unanimous approval of the critics." On the morning of the match he was left out as the pitch was considered too soft for his style of bowling. Time proved this to be a dubious belief as he was very successful on the predominantly soft wickets in August 1912.

He joined the Kent county championship side and took 6-85 against Essex, 8-106 against Middlesex and 6-99 in the match with Hampshire and he was picked for the final test. *Cricket* urged his selection on 'moral grounds', arguing that "googlie bowling, even when not deadly, is apt to be demoralising by inducing hesitation and two minds. Hence a googlie bowler can help other bowlers to wickets and is always worth playing, if at all good."

England went into the test without a fast bowler. Carr opened the bowling. He bowled Gregory at 9, had Noble lbw at 27 and Armstrong lbw at 55, at which point he had figures of 3-18. He was the only England bowler – the others were Sydney Barnes, John Sharp, Wilfred Rhodes and, a fellow debutant, Woolley – to trouble the batsmen. As a result, the captain, Archie MacLaren, kept him on for more than one and a half hours: the longest spell he had bowled in first-class cricket. He lost his nip for being bowled so long, and ended up taking 5-146 as Australia made 325; the figures for the other bowlers were, respectively, 2-57, 3-67, 0-34 and 0-6. Rhodes had only come on to bowl when the total reached 166.

It was part of the style of MacLaren's captaincy to bowl his strike bowlers for long spells, arguing that a tiring strike bowler was better than a fresh change bowler. Monty Noble, Australia's captain in this series, remarked of MacLaren, "If there was a weakness in his method of general attack it was a tendency to give his stock bowler too long a spell at the crease." Another example of MacLaren employing this tactic was in his use of Barnes on the 1901–02 tour of Australia which had resulted in Barnes breaking down from overbowling. In Australia's second innings of 339-5 Carr took the wickets of Armstrong and Trumper for 136. MacLaren's overbowling of Carr was considered by many a gross misjudgement, and he never captained England again.

The selectors' decision to omit the fast bowler Buckenham on the morning of the match on a good pitch with the weather favourable, was roundly criticized. *Cricket* wrote, "The reason why the selectors decided to leave a fast bowler out of the side in the final test is known only to themselves. To everyone else their action was quite incomprehensible, especially as the conditions called for a fast bowler. Noble had included Cotter in all the tests, and his success at the Oval, where he was most judiciously nursed, affords ample proof that our selectors made a most egregious error in leaving Buckenham out." *Wisden* was most un*Wisden*-like in its language, describing it as "a fatal blunder [...] a blunder for which it was generally understood MacLaren was responsible [...] Experts occasionally do strange things and this was one of the strangest [...] touches the confines of lunacy."

In five more county championship matches that season Carr took 31 wickets, including 12-116 against Somerset, as well as taking 8-105 for Lord Londesborough's XI against the Australians

Each summer up until World War I he became available for Kent after the school term, playing in about ten matches each season. For Kent in the county championship he took 31 wickets at 14.21 in 1909; 60 at 12.16 in 1910; 55 at 16.46 in 1911; 49 at 9.59 in 1912; and 47 at 18.55 in 1913. Kent won the county championship in 1909, 1910 and 1913.

In a brief first-class cricket career lasting from May 1909 to August 1914 he captured 334 wickets at the impressive rate of 5.76 per match. He was never awarded his county cap, (neither, incidentally was another of England's leg spinners, Eddie Leadbeater, despite two test appearances and 81 matches for Yorkshire and 27 for Warwickshire).

Douglas Carr was amiable and not easily ruffled on or off the field. He enjoyed the story of a day in 1926 when Arthur Carr was picked as captain of England. On hearing the news Lord Harris, the dominant force in Kent cricket, replied, "Carr – ah Carr – bit old, but Kent – we can't go wrong there." Douglas Carr was then 56 years of age.

First-Class:

| Matches | Inns | NO | Runs | HS | Aver |
|---|---|---|---|---|---|
| 58 | 68 | 18 | 447 | 47 | 8.94 |

| Wkts | Average | SR | Best | 10wm | 5wi | ct |
|---|---|---|---|---|---|---|
| 334 | 16.72 | 32 | 8-36 | 8 | 31 | 19 |

Gents: 4 appearances

| Inns | NO | Runs | HS | Aver | O | M | R | W | Aver | BB | 5wi |
|---|---|---|---|---|---|---|---|---|---|---|---|
| 7 | 4 | 15 | 7 | 5.00 | 129 | 18 | 458 | 20 | 22.90 | 6-71 | 2 |

# 6   N.C. Tufnell (Sussex)

Born: 13 June 1887, Simla, India. Died: 3 August 1951
5th Test, 1909–10 v. South Africa
Batting:   1st Inns: (No.9)   14
Fielding:  1st Inns: –                         2nd Inns: 1 st

Neville Tufnell was in the Eton XI from 1905–07, playing as a wicket-keeper/batsman. In his final season he was promoted to opening the innings. Despite failing in the major match of the season, against Harrow at Lord's, when he made 2 and 0, he came second in the batting averages, with 343 runs at 28.58, with a highest score of 65. In the match with Winchester, Eton's second most important fixture, he made 43 and 26.

He toured with E.G. Wynyard's team to New Zealand in 1906–07. He started the tour with a pair against Auckland, but in the fourth match, coming in at number eleven, made an unbeaten 39, which was the second-highest score of the innings, the next highest being 19, and he put on 98 in 35 minutes with W.J.H. Curwen. Later, opening against Hawke's Bay, he made 85, which was his highest score of the tour, in which he played in seven of the eleven-a-side matches, scoring 203 runs at an average of 23.

He did not play in either of the unofficial tests, R.H. Fox keeping wicket. Fox also found time to head the tour bowling averages, with ten wickets at an average of 7.50, relegating J.W.H.T. Douglas, with 84 wickets at 10.58, into second place. Tufnell also did some bowling, and would do so throughout his career, bowling slow right arm. His father, Carleton Fowell Tufnell, had been an all-rounder, batting in the middle order and bowling right-arm medium-slow, round-arm deliveries. He played eight first-class games, seven of them for Kent in 1878 and 1879, averaging 10.80 with the bat, with a highest score of 26, and took 15 wickets at 19 apiece.

In 1908, Neville Tufnell, then at Cambridge University, made 51 and 13 in the Freshman's match. He played one game for the university that season, and became established in the side in the next year.

At the end of August the MCC committee met to select a party to tour South Africa that winter. Their selection did not include a second wicket-keeper: it was anounced that one would be chosen later. This seems to have been done in mid-October, judging by a report in *Cricket* of 28 October which announced that Tufnell had been picked as the second wicket-keeper. That year he had stumped sixteen batsmen in seven matches for Cambridge, including seven Yorkshiremen, five of them in one innings, all off the bowling by J.H. Bruce-Lockhart. *Wisden* in 1909 wrote of his 'keeping as "on nearly all occasions being very smart indeed".

On the tour he had an unhappy time as a batsman: his seven first-class innings brought 37 runs at 5.21, with a top score of 16, and in all matches he averaged 4 from 11 innings. However, he made history by becoming the first substitute to make a test match stumping, when he replaced Strudwick, who had been hit in the face by a ball from one of his own bowlers. It was also on the tour that he played in his test match, replacing the injured Strudwick for the final match, which England won by nine wickets, resulting in a final 3-2 scoreline to South Africa.

In 1910, now Assistant Treasurer of Cambridge University Cricket Club, he scored his only first-class century, making 102 for the university against the Gentlemen of England at Eastbourne. That season he scored 268 runs at 19 to come seventh in the university averages. He also played in the Varsity match, which became known as Le Couteur's match, of which *Cricket* said: "From the Cambridge point of view the match was little less than a fiasco." Despite play not beginning until 3.50pm on the first day, the match was over in two days as Le Couteur scored 160 and took 6-26 and 5-46.

In February and March of 1912 Tufnell went with the MCC's all-amateur party to Argentina, under Lord Hawke. It was the first tour to Argentina from anywhere outside of their continent. In one of the matches, against a team of Argentinian-born cricketers, Tufnell and MacLaren put on 314 for the third wicket.

Tufnell served with the Grenadier Guards during the First World War, and after his discharge from the army in 1920 he became a member of Lloyds. In 1922 he played his only county game, representing Surrey against Oxford University at the Oval. Surrey were without Hobbs, Fender, Ducat and Sandham, and Oxford also had about half of their side missing. Strudwick also played for Surrey, and Tufnell, batting at number eight in the first innings, made 7, following this with 2 in the second. He bowled one over for 5 runs.

A gentleman usher to the king from 1937–1945, in the early part of the Second World War he commanded a battalion of the 60th King's Royal Rifle Corps – now the Royal Greenjackets – before becoming an AAG at the War Office from 1941–45. He retired from the army with the rank of colonel.

First-Class:

| Matches | Inns | NO | Runs | HS | Aver | 100 |
|---|---|---|---|---|---|---|
| 71 | 121 | 14 | 1514 | 102 | 14.14 | 1 |

| Wkts | Average | SR | Best | 10wm | 5wi | ct | st |
|---|---|---|---|---|---|---|---|
| 1 | 118 | 84 | 1-54 | – | – | 59 | 40 |

Gents: 3 appearances

| Inns | NO | Runs | HS | Aver | ct | st |
|---|---|---|---|---|---|---|
| 5 | 0 | 64 | 25 | 12.80 | 2 | 1 |

# 7   *S.P. Kinneir (Warwickshire)*

Born: 13 May 1871, Cosham, Wiltshire. Died: 16 October 1928
1st Test, 1911–12 v. Australia
Batting: 1st Inns: (No.2)   22   2nd Inns: (No.2)   30

Paul Kinneir was a neat, left-handed opening bat who was, in the main, happy to rely on defence and orthodox stroke play in which the cut and off drive were most prominent. He also bowled a bit of medium pace. He was a consistent scorer for Warwickshire over seventeen seasons and contributed more runs than anyone else in their first championship-winning season of 1911.

That year he scored 1,418 runs at 44 for the county, topping the championship averages. His 268 not out, made in 430 minutes with 27 boundaries, against Hampshire at Edgbaston was the highest score in the championship that season. Only F.R. Foster, who made 305 not out against Worcestershire at Dudley, and Brian Lara who made the world record score of 501 not out against Durham at Edgbaston in 1994 have played bigger innings for Warwickshire. Kinneir made hundreds in both innings – the first Warwickshire batsman to do so – against Sussex at Chichester. Such form led him to be selected for the Players at the Oval, where he scored 158 and 53 not out. This resulted in selection for the forthcoming tour to Australia, the eighth man to join the party. As *Wisden* wrote: "His play made a great impression. It was thought that with his strong defence and extreme steadiness he would be just the man for the Sydney and Melbourne wickets [...] but I doubt if Kinneir would have been asked if Mead had, in the first half of the season, obtained the big scores that he afterwards made. Kinneir had been the soundest and most consistent of all left-handed batsmen, knowing no serious rival until Woolley and Mead appeared on the scene."

At a meeting of the Imperial Cricket Conference on 15 June 1909, it was agreed for England to visit South Africa in 1909–10, and for South Africa to visit Australia in 1910–11. It was also decided that "an effort should be made to have the first Triangular Cricket Contests in 1912, subject to South Africa waiving its claim to come alone that year [...] to further this object, England pledges herself to visit Australia in 1911–12." This was the rider to their agreement, "that the principle of Triangular Tournaments is approved".

About the end of June the MCC began to gather a team. At first eight were invited: C.B. Fry, who was to be captain, Spooner, F.R. Foster, Rhodes, Hobbs, Barnes, Strudwick and Warner. R.H. Spooner declined the invitation and Fry, after much hesitation, opted out of the tour due to his responsibilities to the training ship *Mercury*. By the end of July the other six had accepted.

After the Gentlemen versus Players match in which he scored 72 and 22 not out and took 7-91, J.W.H.T. Douglas was invited to the side. shortly afterwards invitations were sent to Kinneir and Ironmonger and later to George Gunn, Woolley and Mead around 10 August. Significantly, all were good fielders – the previous selections had lacked either good slippers or outfielders. On 16 August, Fry having announced he could not tour, Warner was appointed captain. Towards the end of August Hitch and Vine were selected, Jessop having already been invited but declined. On 14 September the last man, Hearne, was picked because of promptings from Warner.

Eleven of the side had scored a thousand runs in the previous season. Kinneir with 1,622 runs at 49.36 had finished higher in the averages than everyone except Mead, with 2,562 at 54.51. The side was generally held to be a strong one, though some questioned the quality of the fielding.

Kinneir did not play in the match in Colombo, nor in the opening game in Australia against South Australia. In this match Warner played his only game of the tour, but had to withdraw owing to injury, although he remained with the party. This had significance for Kinneir in two ways. Warner had played all bar five of his twenty-five test innings as an opener, so there was now a vacancy for Hobbs' opening partner. Warner had been left by the MCC to choose a vice-captain. Amongst the tourists was Kinneir's county captain, Foster who, in his first season as captain, had led Warwickshire to the championship.

Instead, Warner chose Douglas – who had also been appointed

captain of his county at the beginning of the previous season – on the grounds that he was senior in age and cricketing experience. Douglas' captaincy in the first test was criticized; he came under fire particularly for his decision to open the bowling himself. Warner admitted after the tour that "it is possible that Douglas did not have his side in hand by the time the first test match was reached, but the experience gained in that match was invaluable to him."

Kinneir did not play in many matches leading up to the test. He played in the second match, against Victoria, making 32 and 12, but missed the next two. He played in two matches immediately prior to the first test; in the second, against an eleven of Australia, Hobbs was unwell and unavailable for selection. Kinneir chalked up a first innings of 63, full of well-timed shots and was consequently selected as Hobbs' opening partner for the first test, (for which Hitch was unavailable through injury). Aged 40 years and 216 days, he was then England's second oldest debutant, following James Southerton, who, at 49 years and 119 days, had played in the first-ever test match. Subsequently, E.R. Wilson was older than Kinneir on debut, by 121 days.

In the first innings of the test, Kinneir helped Hobbs put on 45 for the opening wicket and, batting well, looked to be set when Kelleway clean bowled him. In the second innings England were chasing 438 for victory. Hobbs started in good form, whereas Kinneir was leading a charmed life. For his first run, he snicked a ball from Cotter; Carter jumped for the chance and cut off Armstrong's view, so that he in turn missed it. With the total on 8, Kelleway missed Kinneir in the slips – a hard one-handed catch off Cotter's bowling – and, at 17, Horden dropped a relatively straightforward caught and bowled. Yet it was Hobbs who was the first to go, having contributed 22 to their partnership of 29. At the close of the fifth day – these were timeless tests – England were 65-1 with Kinneir on 27. Kinneir was soon out next day, caught at short leg by Trumper, who, by throwing himself full length forward on the turf, was just able to take the catch.

England lost the match by 146 runs. In both Australian innings England's fielding had been patchy. Hobbs, at cover, Rhodes, and Barnes at point, had distinguished themselves, but, as a whole, the side was slow in the field, several runs being given away in the outfield and many boundaries almost, but not quite, cut off. Of England's bowling Warner wrote, "We missed a bowler of real pace like Hitch".

After the test the match against the Combined Universities was cancelled owing to the test match going on to the Thursday. On Boxing Day and 27 December the MCC played a fifteen of Bendigo. Kinneir did not play, but Hitch did, and took 7-47. For the second test Hitch came in for Kinneir and Smith replaced Strudwick behind the stumps. England won this test by eight wickets and picked an unchanged team for the third test, which they won. Hitch had a strain for the fourth test and was replaced by Vine, an all-rounder also good in the outfield. When Hitch returned for the final test it was at Mead's expense.

Reflecting on the tour, Warner wrote that "Kinneir would, I am sure, have made a lot of runs had he played regularly, but there was no room for him in the best eleven, as he is very slow in the field."

Kinneir had joined Warwickshire in 1898 at the advanced aged of 27, though he had claimed to be 25. Previously he had played for Wiltshire for many seasons and, helped by this experience, he took readily to first-class cricket before the First World War ended his career.

Against Lancashire at Edgbaston he took part in two record stands for Warwickshire. In 1901 he put on 327 with W.G. Quaife for the third wicket, which remains the record, where he made 215 not out – the first of his two double-centuries – and in 1905 he put on 333 with J.F. Bryne for the first wicket. In 1907 he carried his bat throughout both innings against Leicestershire at Leicester, scoring 70 out of 239 and 69 out of 166. He also carried his bat against Somerset at Taunton in the next season, making 65 out of 164. One of *Wisden's* Cricketers of the Year in 1912, he was killed in a motorcycle accident in 1928, returning home from a game of golf.

First-Class:

| Matches | Inns | NO | Runs | HS | Aver | 100 |
|---|---|---|---|---|---|---|
| 312 | 525 | 47 | 15641 | 268no | 32.72 | 26 |

| Wkts | Average | SR | Best | 10wm | 5wi | ct |
|---|---|---|---|---|---|---|
| 48 | 31.08 | 78 | 3-13 | – | – | 181 |

Players: 2 appearances

| Inns | NO | Runs | HS | Aver |
|---|---|---|---|---|
| 4 | 0 | 264 | 158 | 52.67 |

# 8   *A. Dolphin (Yorkshire)*

Born: 24 December 1885, Wilsden, Yorkshire. Died: 23 October 1942
4th Test, 1920–21 v. Australia
Batting:   1st Inns: (No.9)   1   2nd Inns: (No.7)   0
Fielding:   1st Inns: 1ct         2nd Inns: –

Wicket-keepers are prime candidates for the ranks of the one test wonder. The scenario is easy to imagine: regular wicket-keeper is injured, replacement steps in for one match, regular wicket-keeper gets fit again and resumes his place in the team. The next time the wicket-keeping berth becomes vacant, either through injury or form, maybe a few seasons later, others will have established their credentials for the vacancy. Unlike other positions, there can be nowhere else for the wicket-keeper to go, unless he plays as a specialist batsman. If the team's star fast bowler is injured, and his replacement does well, it is probable that both will play, fitness permitting, in the next match. This is an option not available with wicket-keepers. 17% of England's specialist wicket-keepers are one test wonders – the figure drops to 13.7% for other team positions.

Eight wicket-keepers have become one test wonders; in addition Moon 'kept in one test, although, either side of this test, he played in three others as a batsman. In her 761 tests to the end of 1999 season, England had only used 59 wicket-keepers, and only 49 specialist wicket-keepers, as the other ten have spent part of their careers as specialist batsmen, three for the majority of their career, seven for the minority. Indeed, between them, England's eight most capped wicket-keepers – Knott (95 caps), Taylor (57), Russell (54), Ames (44), Parks (43), Stewart (40), Lilley (35) and Downton (30), have 'kept in over half of England's tests. The three most capped in nearly a third of them. Ames, Parks and Stewart have also played in test matches in which they did not keep wicket.

Arthur Dolphin first kept wicket for Yorkshire in 1905 – becoming the first Bradford league player to play for Yorkshire – but it was not until 1910 that he was established as Yorkshire's wicket-keeper. Yorkshire rarely change their wicket-keepers. Between 1868 and 1946 they had only five regular wicket-keepers: Joe Pinder (1868–80), Joe Hunter (1881–88), his brother, David Hunter (1888–1909), Arthur Dolphin (1910–26) and Arthur Wood (1927–46). The trend has continued since the war, with Jimmy Binks, who 'kept for the county between 1955 and 1969, missing only one of the 492 matches played by Yorkshire in his career. When he retired at the end of 1969 David Bairstow took over, keeping wicket regularly until he was eased from the position in 1988 in favour of Richard Blakey, who has 'kept since.

A wicket-keeping contemporary of Dolphin, Herbert Strudwick, described Dolphin's technique: "He stood with his right leg a little further back. This helped him to take the ball that is going away from the leg to the off which Rhodes and Kilner served up on sticky wickets – giving him a quarter sweep to the wicket. In my opinion Dolphin moves to the bails more quickly than any other 'keeper."

His team-mate Herbert Sutcliffe wrote that "his quick brain and exceptionally keen eyesight were responsible for disposing of a large number of batsmen from chances which many wicket-keepers would have missed without even affecting their reputations." George Macaulay said, "I never saw a man with such quick hands."

Dolphin's lack of test recognition is often attributed to him being a contemporary of Strudwick and E.J. Smith. But this is not the full picture. Of the 45 tests England played between 1910 and 1926 Strudwick 'kept in 23 of them, and Smith in eleven. Between the 1911–12 series with Australia and 1924, England selected seven different wicket-keepers; Livsey also toured South Africa in 1922–23, as understudy to Brown, but did not play test cricket.

Herbert Strudwick and E.J. Smith went on England's tour of South Africa in 1911–12. Strudwick 'kept in the first test, before Smith took over for the remaining four, on the basis that he was more familiar with the bowling and signals of F.R. Foster, his county captain and England's leading bowler. Smith remained behind the stumps for the triangular series of 1912, and toured South Africa with Strudwick in 1913–14, where Strudwick 'kept in all the tests; Smith played in the second test as a batsman – his last test appearance although he continued to play county cricket until 1930.

Dolphin's test came on England's first post-war tour to Australia in 1920–21. In 1920 George Wood had captained one of Cambridge University's strongest-ever teams, whilst also keeping wicket, standing up to all bar the fastest of bowling. He was invited to tour with England, but declined. As a result Dolphin understudied Strudwick on this tour. He played in the second innings of the third test, becoming one of Mailey's nine victims – so far the only occasion an Australian has taken nine wickets in an innings.

Strudwick continued as England's wicket-keeper for the beginning of the 1921 series before being ousted by the superior batting skills of Hampshire's part-time wicket-keeper George Brown. Brown's skills as a batsman were illustrated at Southampton in 1926 against Warwickshire. Disgusted to be placed at number ten, he hit a six over the wicket-keeper's head, splitting his bat in two; he threw the broken piece to the umpire and carried on batting with the remaining half for some time. Brown 'kept for the tour to South Africa in 1922–23, understudied by Livsey, the main Hampshire wicket-keeper. When Livsey was incapacitated, Street joined the tour, playing one test. For the 1924 series with South Africa, Wood 'kept for the first three tests, Duckworth for the fourth and Strudwick for the fifth, continuing as England wicket-keeper until Dolphin's retirement in 1926. That year *The Cricketer* wrote of Dolphin's 'keeping as being "inferior to none ... except Strudwick."

Dolphin's county career brought him eight championship winners' medals. In three consecutive seasons – 1914, 1919 and 1920 – he was the most successful 'keeper in the championship, with 68, 67 and 55 dismissals respectively; in the first of these years Street and Strudwick also took 58 dismissals, though Dolphin, with 16, had the higher number of stumpings. In 1919, Yorkshire won the championship. That year Dolphin's resolute batting had come to Yorkshire's aid at Leyton when he scored an unbeaten 62 – one of six half-centuries in his career – to put on 103 for the last wicket with E. Smith, to avoid the follow on. That season he also took the concurrent Yorkshire record of 82 dismissals in all matches, and against Derbyshire at Sheffield he equalled Yorkshire's 'keeping record of dismissals with eight catches and a stumping. He shared this record with Joe Hunter, who had caught nine Gloucestershire batsmen in 1887, until David Bairstow equalled the world record by catching eleven Derbyshire batsmen in 1982.

In 1921 Dolphin fractured a wrist in a dressing-room accident and it appeared that his career might be over, as he was 35 and Yorkshire had a capable deputy in W.R. Allen. But he returned the next season and kept wicket with all his previous ability, winning another championship medal.

E.R.T. Holmes described Dolphin as "a thoroughly cheerful character". He is also described as having had a 'presence' about him, which worked to his advantage one evening in a Midlands pub. The Yorkshire team were coming in for some unwelcome attention from a rough group of locals who were seeking trouble. Dolphin moved over to the group and sat down with them and placed his hands, knuckles up, on the table. The local trouble-makers looked at his gnarled joints and, thinking that he must be a celebrated bare-knuckle boxer, quickly departed.

He had a number of habits. When changing for a match he would slip his feet into his boots as they stood, without moving them, rather than pick them up to shoe himself. Macaulay noticed this and one day nailed his boots to the floor. Dolphin dressed as usual, but when he tried to move off he remained rooted to the spot, and fell flat on his face. When eventually he retired and became an umpire, he was soon noted for yet another custom, of standing bare-headed, whatever the weather.

First-Class:

| Matches | Inns | NO | Runs | HS | Aver | | |
|---|---|---|---|---|---|---|---|
| 449 | 465 | 164 | 3402 | 66 | 11.30 | | |

| Wkts | Average | SR | Best | 10wm | 5wi | ct | st |
|---|---|---|---|---|---|---|---|
| 1 | 28 | 66 | 1-18 | – | – | 609 | 273 |

Players: 5 appearances

| Inns | NO | Runs | HS | Aver | ct | st |
|---|---|---|---|---|---|---|
| 6 | 2 | 27 | 21 | 6.75 | 12 | – |

# 9   *E.R. Wilson (Yorkshire)*

Born: 25 March 1879, Bolsterstone, Yorkshire. Died: 21 July 1957
5th Test, 1920–21 v. Australia
Batting:    1st Inns: (No.9)   5    2nd Inns: (No.4)   5
Bowling:    1st Inns: 14.3-4-28-2   2nd Inns: 6-1-8-1

Rockley Wilson was educated at Rugby, where he played in the eleven from 1905 to 1907. In the final of these years he captained the side, and headed both batting and bowling averages, and played an innings of 206 not out. He went up to Cambridge and made his first-class debut against the university when he was drafted into A.J. Webbe's team at the final moment. He scored 117 not out. That year, 1899, he won a Blue, as he did in three following seasons. In 1901 he made 118 against Oxford – to give him the distinction of scoring centuries against both universities whilst in residence – and took 5-71 in the first innings. He was captain in 1902, taking 5-23 in Oxford's first innings, and Cambridge won by five wickets.

He was one of the best slow right-arm bowlers of his generation. Bowling with a low action, he had immaculate control of length. He coupled this with disguised variations of pace, believing that only a little amount of spin was required to beat the bat. A man of gentle, self-deprecatory humour he once said of his success, "I have always been a lucky bowler, as my best ball has been the ball which broke from the off when I meant to break from leg. I bowled far more of these as a man of 40 than as a young man."

Rockley was the youngest of five brothers. His elder brother, C.E.M. Wilson, had attended Uppingham, where, in 1893, he scored 722 runs in the season, including consecutive innings of 117, 145 and 183, the last of these carrying his bat. He gained a Blue at Cambridge in each of his four years, and was captain the year before Rockley went up to university, scoring a century in that year's Varsity match. He played a handful of games for Yorkshire, and a couple of times for England, before retiring from first-class cricket upon his ordination. Another brother, C.R. Wilson, was on the Yorkshire committee for thirty-two years.

Between 1899 and 1902 Rockley Wilson played nine times for Yorkshire. He had intended going to Winchester after university, to become a master, but he had promised Lord Hawke that he would play for Yorkshire for the whole of the 1903 season. However, a serious illness to the master in charge of cricket lead to Wilson heading for Winchester earlier than planned. He taught French, and held the post of cricket master for twenty-four of his forty years at the school.

Lord Hawke again asked Wilson if he would turn out for Yorkshire in the school holidays in 1903 and 1904. Wilson declined, saying that since he would have only a month's cricket a year he preferred to play as many games as possible, and favoured three two-day country-house games a week rather than two three-day county matches.

In 1901 he had gone with B.J.T. Bosanquet's side to America and in 1902 went with a team of amateurs to the West Indies, where he topped the bowling averages with 78 wickets at less than 11 runs each. In 1912 he went with an MCC team, under Lord Hawke, to Argentina. Having had a successful tour, he was asked by Hampshire if he would play for them, as he had a residential qualification through living at Winchester.

Wilson related that he accepted "as I did not think Yorkshire would mind, but they very kindly asked me to play again, and I did so – and very much enjoyed it. My real reason for wishing to play first-class cricket again was to see for myself the changes in the game caused by swerves and googlies."

So in 1913 he resumed his Yorkshire career, now aged 34. That year he took 18 wickets at 19.66 and scored his only century for Yorkshire. This came against Essex at Bradford when his undefeated 104 included a six over the wicket-keeper's head. The following year he hardly featured but, in the years after the war, he became an important member of Yorkshire's side for the conclusion of the county programme. Two of Yorkshire's top bowlers, Drake and Booth, had died in the war years, and Wilson added freshness to the bowling attack at a time when it was most welcome.

In 1919 he finished second in the Yorkshire averages – behind Rhodes – and seventh in the national averages. He took 36 wickets at 16.58. He played for the Gentlemen at Lord's and took a hat trick.

Yorkshire won the county championship that year, and came extremely close to doing so again the following year. Against Middlesex at Bradford, Wilson and Waddington came together in a ninth, and last, wicket stand – Kilner was ill and unable to bat – with Yorkshire needing 58 for victory. 53 runs into the partnership, Waddington drove a ball from Stevens hard, back past the bowler straight into the stumps. Had it evaded them a four was the only possible consequence, such were the fielding positions. Later that over Waddington was bowled. Middlesex went on to win the county championship. Had Yorkshire won this game, they would have been champions.

In 1920 Wilson again trailed Rhodes at the head of Yorkshire's averages, with 49 wickets at 14.20. His season included returns of 6-62 from 44 overs against Middlesex, 5-29 against Surrey, 5-20 versus Hampshire and 4-63 and 6-29 for his county against the MCC at Scarborough.

That winter the MCC were sending a test team to Australia. Spooner had been offered the captaincy, but had declined. The selectors thus needed an extra player for their party. Ideally they sought an amateur, and this resulted in Wilson being selected. He was 41 years old. Wilson, appointed vice-captain, jokingly called himself 'the discovery of the season'.

He bowled with his customary accuracy throughout the tour, and his 30 wickets at 14.50 apiece saw him to third in the averages. But he was not an original selection for the tour and only played in the final test, becoming the ninth debutant to play for England in the series. This meant that for most of the series he was a spectator – and a reporter. Both he and Percy Fender were writing on the tour and *Wisden* said that "a good deal of friction was caused by cable messages sent home to the *Daily Express* by Mr E.R. Wilson. This led to a resolution passed at the annual general meeting of Marylebone Cricket Club in May deprecating "the reporting of matches by players concerned in them".

In 1921 he topped the national averages with 51 wickets at 11.19. In 1922 and 1923 Yorkshire again won the county championship with Wilson contributing 16 wickets at 17 to the first success and 10 at 26 to the second. At the end of the 1923 season he retired. Only Rhodes' Yorkshire career had spanned more years.

His love of cricket was immense. Even his lavatory had W.G. painted on the door. He was able to quote facts and figures with ease – many of these were culled originally from his extensive cricket library, which he bequeathed to Lord's.

First-Class:

| Matches | Inns | NO | Runs | HS | Aver | 100 |
|---|---|---|---|---|---|---|
| 135 | 190 | 28 | 3565 | 142 | 22.00 | 4 |

| Wkts | Average | SR | Best | 10wm | 5wi | ct |
|---|---|---|---|---|---|---|
| 467 | 17.63 | 51 | 7-16 | 5 | 26 | 106 |

Gents: 4 appearances

| Inns | NO | Runs | HS | Aver | O | M | R | W | Aver | BB |
|---|---|---|---|---|---|---|---|---|---|---|
| 7 | 3 | 64 | 23 | 16.00 | 160.5 | 40 | 416 | 17 | 24.47 | 4-102 |


# 10 *T.L. Richmond (Nottinghamshire)*

Born: 23 June 1890, Radcliffe on Trent, Nottinghamshire. Died: 29 December 1957
1st Test, 1921 v. Australia
Batting: 1st Inns: (No.11)   4   2nd Inns: (No.11)   2
Bowling: 1st Inns: 16-3-69-2   2nd Inns: 3-0-17-0

In 1921 England embarked upon a test series with Australia, having just lost 5-0 to her the previous winter. The captain for this series had been J.W.H.T. Douglas, and it seemed that the summer's selectors did not have confidence in him. One of them – Harry Foster – wrote a letter to C.B. Fry on 25 April enquiring about his form and whether he felt inclined towards the England captaincy. On that day Fry, who had not played test cricket for nine years, was celebrating his 49th birthday. He declined the offer, at least temporarily, citing the possible inability "of a man of fifty to lion tame two of the finest fast bowlers ever known". But he declared that he would reconsider for the Lord's test "if they were really bunkered for a captain".

   The series had already begun badly for England with uncertainty over the captain. The selectors wanted Douglas out, but did not know if they could have their preferred choice; consequently Douglas remained captain for the first test. The appointment of a captain was the first resolution the selectors had to make, and the first of their many more clumsy decisions. During the summer the selectors were to pick 30 players in a staggering display of muddled selectorial judgement never again equalled. The nearest comparison was in 1988 when, for five tests against the West Indies the selectors picked 21 players, then bringing in another seven new players, including four new caps, for the final test of the season against Sri Lanka. In 1950, for four tests against the West Indies, England used 25 players. Against these opponents in 1976 and 1984, 21 players were called upon, whilst in 1948 the Australians were pitted against 20 players at various times.

   It is a feature of all these series that England were doing badly: something of the adage 'never change a winning team' working in reverse. There seems to be genuine confusion as to who England's best players were in 1921. The selectors seem to have consulted a wide variety of people as to whom they should choose; it is said that they even approached strangers, soliciting their views. This process, far from helping them make up their minds, merely seems to have added even more names to the melting pot.

   Test cricket had been interrupted by the war, and this hindered the natural development of the national side; normally players emerge and develop over time, the cream gently rising to the top. With only two full seasons played since the war, this process had little time to bear fruit. England started her first test after the war on 17 December 1921. The previous test – South Africa versus England – had finished on 3 March 1914. Australia had not played since 22 August 1912. Old talent had aged and, in some cases, died, and the new talent had little opportunity to establish itself.

   For the first post-war test Australia gave debuts to seven players – England to four. Australia settled quickly upon their side. They won the first test by 377 runs and eight of this team played in all of the subsequent tests; only fourteen players were used in the rubber. Roy Park was given a debut in the second test and, bowled first ball in an innings victory, he never played test cricket again. A doctor, the previous night he had been called out to attend a difficult birth, which had resulted in an all-night vigil. Debutant Ted MacDonald took his place in the third test, and with Gregory at the other end thus was formed one of Australia's great fast-bowling partnerships. England, on the other hand, were constantly adding players; it was not until her fourteenth post-war test that she put out a side which did not contain at least one debutant.

   In this respect it is worth considering views expressed about selection in the summers of 1966 and 1988. In the 1967 *Wisden* the editor commented, "One must remember that compared with other countries England have many more first-class players on the fringe of test standard, yet few who can be termed automatic choices." In an interview with *The Cricketer,* Peter May, Chairman of Selectors in 1988 – also a selector in 1966 – said, "We have more players of a certain standard than any other country [...] it is often easier to pick a team if you have fewer players to choose from."

Test teams normally contain a few automatic choices, which, injuries apart, limit the number of places in the team which need to be selected, thereby restricting possible changes. In 1921, with so little recent test cricket, there had not been the chance for people to establish a claim to a test place over a reasonable period. One player who was an automatic choice was Hobbs, who had averaged 50 in the 1920–21 series and scored two centuries. Yet illness kept him out of all but one test, and in that he was too ill to bat. Hobbs, and J.W. Hearne, *The Cricketer* declared, were "the two best batsmen in England against high-class bowling." Hearne, like Hobbs, was fit enough to take part in only one test in the summer. A fit Hobbs would have been expected to open for England in all the tests. As it was, England used seven different openers.

Had these two been fit they could have combined with Frank Woolley, who played in 52 consecutive tests from his debut in 1909 to 1926, to form the basis of a solid batting line up. Woolley – with J.W.H.T. Douglas, England's only ever-present that summer – scored 343 runs at 43 in the series. Another batting great, Patsy Hendren, played for England in the first two tests of that series, making scores of 0, 7, 0 and 10. Having played in the last seven tests, making 346 runs at 24.71 in them, he did not play test cricket again until 1924–25 when he scored two centuries and two half-centuries in his four innings in the series with South Africa.

Unlike Australia, England did not have an established bowling attack, and, as so often with desperate teams, the wicket-keeper was jettisoned in favour of one who could score more runs, in this case Hampshire's reserve 'keeper.

A feature of the press coverage of the series seems to be the lack of blame apportioned to the selectors, certainly in the cricketing press. The selectors' feckless performance of 1988, which saw four official captains appointed and a fifth captain England in the field, was justly criticized. Of 1966 *Wisden* noted, "Before the summer ended the selectors themselves came in for adverse criticism."

In contrast, after England had lost the first test by ten wickets *The Cricketer* had this to say: "Owing to our unfortunate habit of leaving everything to chance, and of not organising properly for war or for games, the Selection Committee were faced with an extraordinarily difficult task in picking the England eleven for the first Test Match. There had been no trial game of any sort, and, moreover, the fixtures this season were so badly arranged that there were no semi-representative matches such as there used to be in former years. Therefore it would be absurd to blame in any way the Selection Committee for the downfall at Nottingham."

This said, somewhat incongruously, *The Cricketer* went on to say that "for ourselves we would make a clean sweep of the side that played at Nottingham, with the exception of J.W.H.T. Douglas, D.J. Knight, Woolley and Hendren."

That *The Cricketer* can absolve the selectors from any blame, and then proceed to announce that they would have little to do with the team those selectors had picked, suggests an acceptance that no one could be sure who should be playing for England.

That said, it is hard to imagine that one selection of eleven names could approximate to the best team England could field, if a fortnight later a very different collection of players could somehow be the best team again. One has to question the selectors' analytical powers and their confidence in their own judgement. They certainly were not ready to stand by their selections. There were six changes for the team for the second test, seven for the third, six for the fourth and two for the final.

The selectors in 1921 were H.K. Foster, R.H. Spooner and J. Daniell. Foster had been on the last selection panel, for the Triangular Tests of 1912 but Jack Daniell, Somerset's captain and Reg Spooner from Lancashire were county cricketers and new to the panel. Spooner had been offered the captaincy of the previous winter's tour, but business commitments had prevented him from accepting. *The Cricketer* had applauded the appointment: "Their selection will give universal satisfaction [...] There can be no doubt that our selectors have a difficult task before them, but the cricketing public may rest well assured that the interests of English cricket are in thoroughly safe hands."

The selectors met to decide the team for the first test on Sunday 22 May, for a test beginning on the 28th. 'Discuss' might be a more appropriate word, as at the end of a full day of deliberation they had only decided upon nine names, which were duly released to the press, with the promise that the remainder would be announced the next day. In fact the rest of the party was announced some days later.

Richmond was one of five in the final eleven who had not played in the winter series. Richmond, reported *The Cricketer*, "bowled well on the whole, if occasionally sending down a loose ball," and he took the first wicket of the series when Collins was 'palpably' lbw.

Of England's defeat *The Cricketer* declared, "There is no need to be unduly pessimistic, for the absence of Hobbs and Hearne made a great rent in our armour. It is probable that both of them will be able to play at Lord's, and in any event, there are certain to be four or five changes in the team that represented us at Nottingham." Richmond was not selected in the party for Lord's.

Often articles about Richmond explain that he did not receive more test honours due to being a contemporary of another leg break bowler, 'Tich' Freeman. Though they were in competition to be the best leg break bowler of the day, Freeman did not block Richmond's way into the test team. Freeman only played in a dozen of the hundred tests England played during Richmond's career, the first of them in 1924–25. His last three tests were played after Richmond had retired.

Richmond bowled more quickly than Freeman and with more spin but to a less consistent length. Whereas Freeman's bowling improved the older he got – indeed he made his first-class debut at 26 – Richmond's bowling fell away as his weight increased. As soon as his bowling lost its penetration he was dropped from the side, as he added little to the team's batting and fielding abilities, and Nottinghamshire had a promising fast bowler in Bill Voce coming through to take his place.

Richmond's batting was such that the runs he made exceeded his wickets by only 468. Viewed in context, therefore, it can be understood how his performance at Worksop in 1922 when he scored 70, adding 140 in 65 minutes with S.J. Staples against Derby for the last wicket, caused much remark. It was one of two half-centuries he made, the other being an innings of 59 against Cambridge University. Of his fielding, *The Cricketer*, commenting on the 1921 season, remarked that Nottinghamshire's captain "has found a place for him in the field – deep third man – where he is not likely to have a catch, and where he fields well on the ground and can throw hard. It is a most unusual position for a bowler to occupy, for as a rule bowlers should throw as little as possible, and should occupy a position somewhere near the wicket so as to avoid running, but in this case a novel experiment in placing the field had turned out a great success. Certainly, so far from injuring him, Richmond bowled better last summer than ever before in his career."

That summer Richmond, playing in a championship-winning side, had taken 169 wickets at 13.48 runs each. In returning figures of 15.1-8-21-9 against Hampshire at Trent Bridge in the final innings of the season he exceeded the Nottinghamshire record of 163 wickets set in 1907, the last year in which they had been champions. In 1954 this record was broken by another leg break bowler, the Australian, Bruce Dooland. *The Cricketer* wrote of Richmond's achievement that "he was unlucky in not being chosen for the MCC's tour in South Africa. The matting wickets might have been very much to his liking."

Richmond first appeared for Nottinghamshire in 1913, and in 1914 he played a few matches. In 1919, after war service in the Sherwood Foresters, he began to be talked about as a possible England player in taking 60 wickets at an average of 20.83. In 1920 he took 145 wickets at 19.20. In the next seven seasons he was again to top the hundred wicket mark. In 1925 he took nine wickets in an innings for the second time, taking 9-55 against Northamptonshire at Trent Bridge. That season he captured 14 wickets in a day – 7-30 and 7-53 – at Cheltenham against

Gloucestershire. In 1926 he took a hat trick against Lancashire at Trent Bridge in amongst the thirteen wickets he took for 165. For Pudsey St Lawrence in 1920 he took all of Lowmoor's wickets for 39 runs.

During his career his action involved so much strain that, after a heavy spell of bowling, he often found it necessary at night to have his arm tied in a more or less vertical position to the bedpost.

On leaving Notts he became the bowling mainstay of Sir Julien Cahn's XI, taking a hundred wickets for them in 1929 and 1930. In 1929–30 he toured Argentina, playing three first-class matches. His last first-class match was for Sir Julien Cahn's XI against the South Africans in June 1932.

First-Class:

| Matches | Inns | NO | Runs | HS | Aver |
|---------|------|-----|------|-----|------|
| 252 | 281 | 116 | 1644 | 70 | 9.96 |

| Wkts | Average | SR | Best | 10wm | 5wi | ct |
|------|---------|-----|------|------|-----|-----|
| 1176 | 21.22 | 41 | 9-21 | 19 | 90 | 39 |

Players: dnp

# 11   A.E. Dipper (Gloucestershire)

Born: 9 November 1885, Apperley, Gloucestershire. Died 7 November 1945
2nd Test, 1921 v. Australia
Batting: 1st Inns: (No.2)   11   2nd Inns: (No.2)   40

An opening bowler in the second eleven of the Devon side, Plympton, had a most idiosyncratic run-up. He began by thrusting out his left arm behind him before taking two paces forward, then stopping with knees bent; he straightened up as a preliminary to two more paces forward, then, taking very small steps, he turned a complete circle until he faced the bowling crease, which he approached in a zig-zag fashion. He bowled medium-pace deliveries noted for their accuracy. He had learnt to bowl in his grandfather's cramped back garden, where, in order to manage a run-up, he had to push himself off the wall of the garden shed, duck under the washing line, circle past a tub of flowers and then weave in and out of a row of flower-pots. When he tried a more normal run-up, encountering a cricket field without these constrictions, his bowling went all over the shop.

Geoff Boycott's trademark shot of the back-foot square drive owed a lot to his early cricket in the streets, where the wicket was at the right-angled junction of two roads and square of the wicket on the off side provided one of the few run-scoring areas.

Alf Dipper played almost everything to leg; one commentator estimated that ninety per cent of his shots were played to this side. To enable him to favour the leg side to this extent he would shuffle across his stumps as the bowler was running in so that, when the ball was delivered, the stumps were obscured from view. E.M. Wellings remembered the first time he bowled to Dipper: "As I started the run I looked down at the ground until I was a couple of paces short of the crease. When I looked up on this occasion, the stumps had disappeared. My immediate thought was that the wicket-keeper had taken leave of his senses and whipped the stumps out of the ground. I stopped, Dipper moved back, and the stumps were revealed again […] Unless you kept an eye on him all the time it was difficult to know where the target was."

When Dipper began playing cricket in Deerhurst it was in a field where, so the story goes, a bed of nettles lay under the hedge on the leg side.

The nettle-seeking batsman joined Tewkesbury Cricket Club, from which he was plucked to make his first-class debut for Gloucestershire. Finding themselves a man short for the game against Kent in June 1908, the county contacted Tewkesbury, who sent the 22 year-old Dipper. The newcomer's style, or lack thereof, caused much interest and amusement. Gilbert Jessop recalled in his *Cricketer's Log*: "A more unlikely-looking batsman than Dipper appeared to be, when he took his stance that day, was never seen outside the pages of a boy's cricket story. The hind part of him stuck out almost at an angle of ninety [degrees] – arms so stiff that they looked as if they had been nailed onto the handle of the bat – a pleading, anxious expression, as if to say, 'Don't hit me – I'll be good'. And then, as the ball delivered by Blythe came within his reach, his feet moved in the crease and the ball found the middle of the bat."

Coming in at number nine, he made the highest score of the innings, an undefeated 30. A first-class career was underway, although it was not until 1911, the first season in which he scored a thousand runs, that he could be sure of a place.

Dipper became the sheet anchor at the head of the Gloucestershire innings. For several years, lacking strong support from the rest of the batting line-up, he often resorted to a defensive role, keeping up one end whilst ticking the score along through on side nudges and drives. Some contemporary commentators argued that he could be too defensive, although that he eleven times carried his bat for Gloucestershire is testimony to the extent to which he underpinned the Gloucestershire batting. Although inclined to concentrate on defence, he was able to play most of the attacking strokes and, though rarely becoming aggressive, many times made more than half the runs put on during his stay.

When Hammond established himself in the side Dipper was no longer the main batsman on the team, and this afforded him greater freedom to play a more expansive game. A notable occasion was at Trent Bridge in 1926 when he took on Larwood, who was getting lift from the wicket, and scored 50 in half an hour, frequently pulling and hooking the fast bowler behind square on the leg side.

When he retired after the 1932 season Dipper had made more runs for Gloucestershire than any other player; subsequently only Wally Hammond and Arthur Milton have scored more. In fifteen of the 21 seasons of his first-class career Dipper reached a thousand runs, five times scoring over 2,000. Although mainly a batsman, he also bowled slow medium-paced deliveries which were good enough for him to be able to return 14-104 against Leicestershire at Cheltenham in 1919.

He was not a glamorous player – anchormen rarely are – and his style was clumsy. It might also be argued that he suffered from playing for Gloucestershire: not that one could imagine him being associated with another county, as there had been Dippers farming in Gloucestershire since the 1700s. Being an unglamorous player in an unglamorous team could have hindered his chances for wider recognition, a point *The Cricketer* recognized in an article on 11 June 1921: "It has been said, and with a great deal of truth, that a cricketer who does not happen to play at Lord's or the Oval is apt to be lost sight of when the selection of representative teams comes up for consideration. Gloucestershire, once the most famous of county teams, have not been seen on either of the two great London grounds for many years; but in Dipper and Parker they possess two players who, in match after match, perform redoubtable feats. [...Dipper] must surely be one of the most consistent scorers in the county, and when it is remembered that he is playing on a comparatively weak side, his success is all the more notable. He must be a strong candidate for a place in the Players XI, and possibly in the England XI, for apart from his batting, he is a very fair bowler and a good field. Moreover, he has imperturbable temperament, and, as the Americans say, plenty of sand and grit."

Dipper was, in fact, anything but a good field. Perhaps it was not solely selectors who were apt to lose sight of players if they did not appear at Lord's or the Oval! The Gloucestershire side of the period was one of the more interesting fielding sides, containing one of the best slip fielders in the world in Wally Hammond but also some extremely immobile fieldsmen, of which Dipper was one.

Dipper was not selected for the Players in 1921, his sole appearance coming in 1926, but he was picked in the party of fourteen for the Lord's test. This did not originally guarantee selection because the side was top-heavy with batsmen, as *The Cricketer* noted: "There are eight good batsmen in the team, and plenty of bowlers, but although the slip fielding is well provided for, there is, with the exception of Hendren, a conspicuous lack of 'country' fielders. [...] Mr Douglas will not have an easy task in placing his men, especially when the slow bowlers are on. But it is an infinitely better side than that which represented us at Nottingham. The selectors have had a difficult task, but they have taken the greatest possible pains, and they have picked a good batting and bowling side, though, as we have said before, the fielding is of very doubtful quality."

In the end Dipper's selection became certain as four of the batsmen dropped out, leaving the selectors having to summon the Hon. Lionel Tennyson at the final hour to ensure a quorum. Dipper had impressed the Australians in making 24 and 70 not out for Gloucestershire in their drawn match with the Australians just prior to the test.

*The Cricketer* reported that the test began "before an enormous crowd of spectators – certainly the largest that has ever been seen at Lord's [...] Dipper impressed with the bat in the match, particularly with his 40 in the second innings." Of his innings, the third highest of the innings, *The Cricketer* commented: "Dipper played splendidly. [...] Dipper's was an excellent innings. He is very good at playing the ball off his legs, and he gets well forward to the fast bowlers, and he plays his strokes with certainty and confidence. [...] Dipper had played exceedingly well, and is to be congratulated on his successful first appearance in a test match."

However Dipper had not performed well in the field, an impression heightened by the selectors picking a poor fielding side in the first place, and it was this, rather than his batting, that lead him to be dropped.

In 1921 Dipper passed a thousand runs for the fifth time, and, having been discarded by England, his batting became even more successful. In 1922 he again reached a thousand runs and in 1923 he reached 2,000 runs for the first time, making 2,048 runs at 40 and scoring the highest of his three double centuries in compiling an undefeated 252 against Glamorgan at Cheltenham. With Hammond flowing at the opposite end, Dipper went on to reach two thousand runs in the seasons 1926–1929, 1928 being the most productive with 2,365 runs at an average of 55. In 1925 they put on 330 against Lancashire at Old Trafford, which remains the third wicket record for the ground.

When he retired in 1932, just before his 47th birthday, Dipper became a first-class umpire. He was also a noted billiards and bowls player.

First-Class:

| Matches | Inns | NO | Runs | HS | Aver | 100 |
|---|---|---|---|---|---|---|
| 481 | 865 | 69 | 28075 | 252no | 35.27 | 53 |

| Wkts | Average | SR | Best | 10wm | 5wi | ct |
|---|---|---|---|---|---|---|
| 161 | 30.45 | 56 | 7-46 | 1 | 5 | 210 |

Players: 1 appearance

| Inns | NO | Runs | HS | Aver |
|---|---|---|---|---|
| 2 | 1 | 75 | 75no | 75.00 |

# 12    F.J. Durston (Middlesex)

Born: 11 July, Clophill, Bedfordshire. Died: 8 April 1965
2nd Test, 1921 v. Australia
Batting:   1st Inns: (No.11)   6 no    2nd Inns: (No.11)    2
Bowling: 1st Inns: 24.1-2-102-4      2nd Inns: 9.3-0-34-1

Jack Durston progressed from club cricket to the Lord's groundstaff, which he joined in 1914. After serving with the Royal Engineers during the Great War he made his county debut in 1919. In five matches that season he took five wickets at a cost of 74.2 each. In the next two seasons he bowled Middlesex to the county championship.

In 1914 Middlesex's batting had taken them towards the championship; their bowling took them away from it. But by 1920 they had a bowling attack to back up their batting strength. Durston provided them with 103 championship wickets at 19.93 and J.W. Hearne gave 110 at 16.82. G.T.S. Stevens was the third highest wicket-taker with 44 at 18.93. Durston's hundred wickets were a product of hard work and determination rather than unplayable brilliance; he was 58th in that season's first-class averages. Middlesex were still a batting-orientated side – their highest bowler in the first-class averages was only at number 42.

In 1921 Durston became the county's highest wicket-taker with 103 championship wickets at 19.91, to head the county averages. His opening partner, Haig, was close behind with 96 wickets at 20.32.

T.C.F. Prittie, cricket correspondent of *The Manchester Guardian*, wrote in *Mainly Middlesex* that Durston and Haig were "honest, straightforward attackers, who made up for their shortcomings with an abundance of energy and concentration, and replaced genius by a sturdy, fighting spirit." Prittie had written this book whilst a POW in Germany. He had also written an article on playing cricket in a 30-foot medieval moat which he sent to *The Cricketer*, but not before the German cypher experts had spent a long time with it, convinced from its language that it must be in an elaborate code.

Durston started off as a quick bowler but, increasingly required to bowl long spells in a side lacking bowling strength, his pace gradually declined, until he ended his career bowling off breaks. Tall and powerfully built – fifteen stone and six foot three – his action lacked grace but he could bang the ball into the pitch from a height.

*Wisden* recorded that Durston "showed greater control of length as his career progressed and he took many wickets on the hard pitches of Lord's with a speedy break back." His batting also increased in usefulness during his career and in 1927 he and Patsy Hendren, who made 201 not out, set up a Middlesex ninth wicket record which still stands, taking

160 runs off the Essex bowling in 80 minutes. Durston's batting method involved making maximum use of his strength and reach. Robertson-Glasgow recorded in *More Cricket Prints* that "his batting, without violent variation in result, developed from the painstaking to the eccentric, and he once answered my inquiry on his progress with 'gave up style this year, and jumped to 13th for Middlesex'."

In 1932 *The Cricketer* commented, "As long as he tries to hit the ball hard and does not try to imitate Hearne, Durston is an admirable forcing batsman. His reach is so enormous that he can get to the pitch of the average good length ball. His driving is as powerful as one would expect from such a magnificent physique [...] his batting, if not bringing him much reward, generally provided the spectators with a few minutes' amusement." That season he scored 434 runs at an average of 10 with a highest score of 40.

With the selectors casting around for a bowling attack, it is not surprising that the men who led the attack for the county champions who were again going well in the championship, were called up for England. Durston's case for inclusion was also considerably strengthened by returns of 7-84 and 4-65 against the Australians at Lord's. Haig and Durston were both chosen to make their debuts in the Lord's test. *The Cricketer* welcomed Durston's involvement: "Durston has fairly earned his place, and has the great advantage, to a fast bowler, of being very tall."

After England had scored 187, Durston opened the bowling. Australia began well, bringing up the hundred in 55 minutes and scoring 191 for the loss of three wickets in the two hours left of play on the first day, Durston taking two of the wickets, both caught behind. On the second day he added two more wickets, and could have had a 'five for' return had Evans not dropped Gregory from a difficult chance. Australia went on to win by eight wickets. Durston's last ball in test cricket was an unusual one. The ball slipped out of his hand and landed in the middle of the pitch and rolled to a halt. Both batsman and – illegally – bowler ran towards the ball. Bardsley won the race and hit the stationary ball for the winning four.

Durston had led England's attack, bowling 33.4 of the 104.4 overs, and taking five of the twelve wickets to fall. Haig, with figures of 2-61 and 0-27 from three overs was dropped from the party for the next test.

Nigel Haig was a good all-round sportsman, adept also at lawn tennis, golf, and racquets. "Seemingly built of whipcord" according to *Wisden*, he was a nephew of Lord Harris and had won the M.C. in the First World War whilst serving with the Royal Field Artillery. In 1921 he went on to record the double of a thousand runs and a hundred wickets. Whereas Durston's career and achievements tailed off slightly around 1927–28, Haig's continued to rise. In 1927 and 1929 he again obtained the double – he was to take a hundred wickets in a season five times and score a thousand runs six times. He toured the West Indies under Calthorpe in 1928–29 and played in all four tests.

Durston was included in the party of thirteen for the third test but he and the then uncapped Charlie Hallows were left out, leaving England to go into the test without a quick bowler. Hallows, an elegant left-handed Lancashire batsman, was to make his debut in the fourth test, and was then dropped. However, he reappeared for England in one more test in 1928, playing the first test of that rubber.

Durston, though, was again to take part in a test, thanks to appendicitis. He fielded as substitute for Hobbs, who was absent ill. On the Sunday it was reported that Hobbs was better and would play on Monday. On Monday Hobbs was feeling ill again and an examination found that he was suffering acute appendicitis. On Monday Hallows fielded in Hobbs' place instead, but on the morning of the third day news was received that Johnny Douglas' wife also had appendicitis and so Douglas left and Durston fielded for him. The party for the fourth test was fifteen-strong, causing one wag to remark that perhaps John Daniell, an England rugby selector since 1913, had forgotten what type of team he was choosing. Left out, Durston again acted as twelfth man.

In 1926 he was selected for the Rest against England in the test trial. The Rest made 211 and England at the close of the first day were 38-3. It could have been 38-4 as Hobbs, on 9, was missed off Durston. Durston's opening partner, the uncapped Harold Larwood, took all three wickets. Hobbs went on to make 85 of England's 250. Durston in the first innings returned figures of 30-8-73-2, and 7-0-18-1 in the second innings. Larwood returned figures of 29-2-57-3 and 10-2-22-2, and, with the all-rounder J.W. Hearne, who had played in seven of the previous eight tests, was the only member of the Rest's attack to play for England that summer. He made his debut in the second test, coming on as second change, and was then dropped, reappearing in the final test.

In his younger, slimmer days he had kept goal for Brentford but, as a cricketer, Durston took a hundred wickets in a season six times, and performed the hat trick twice – once against Cambridge University in 1922, and later against Oxford University the following year, in a second innings analysis of 8-27.

First-Class:

| Matches | Inns | NO | Runs | HS | Aver |
|---------|------|-----|------|------|-------|
| 386 | 473 | 144 | 3918 | 92no | 11.90 |

| Wkts | Average | SR | Best | 10wm | 5wi | ct |
|------|---------|----|------|------|-----|-----|
| 1329 | 22.03 | 54 | 8-27 | 11 | 72 | 257 |

Players: 7 appearances

| Inns | NO | Runs | HS | Aver | O | M | R | W | Aver | BB |
|------|-----|------|------|------|-------|-----|-----|-----|-------|------|
| 6 | 2 | 46 | 25no | 7.67 | 228.4 | 47 | 632 | 33 | 19.15 | 4-49 |

# 13   A.J. Evans (Kent)

Born: 1 May 1889, Newtown, Hampshire. Died: 18 September 1960
2nd Test, 1921 v. Australia
Batting: 1st Inns: (No.6)   4   2nd Inns: (No.6)   14

John Evans, a gifted all-round sportsman from a sporting family, owed his fame more to his escapes from enemy prison camps in World War I than as a result of his sporting prowess. At Winchester, where his father, an Oxford Cricket Blue, was a master, he was in the eleven for three years and won the school's racquets and golf competitions three years in succession. In 1909 he went up to Oxford, just after his cousin W.H.B. Evans, who was a Cricket Blue from 1902 to 1905. It was at Oxford that he played the bulk of his first-class cricket – he had already played for Hampshire, for whom his father and brother also played, whilst at Winchester – as well as representing the university in racquets and golf.

Evans was a classical bat with a punishing off-drive and a habit of pulling the ball from outside off stump, wide of mid on; he was also a medium-paced inswing bowler and a good slip fieldsman.

He gained his Cricket Blue in his freshman year. Oxford batted first and he and M.G. Salter put on 115 for the opening wicket in an hour and a half before the innings fell away against the leg spin of Lockwood to close at 267. Evans played the leg spinner better than most, going down the pitch and hitting him on the full before he, too, fell to Lockwood, stumped by Tufnell for 79. In Oxford's second innings of 191-8 declared he made 43 before falling again to Lockwood, this time lbw. He took 2 wickets for 27 in the match.

That season he came fourth in Oxford's batting averages with 417 runs at 28; he also took 11 wickets at 26. The next season was markedly less successful: 16 first-class innings brought 240 runs at 15, and his twelve wickets cost 35 each. The Varsity match finally got underway at four o'clock on the first day. Cowie opened with two wides, and the first legitimate delivery of the day saw Evans slicing a catch to slip. His high spot of the summer came in Cambridge's second innings: not having bowled in their first innings he returned figures of 4-2-7-4 as Oxford won by an innings. This spell also rather redeemed his season's bowling figures as without it he would have had 8 wickets at 52.

In 1911 he captained Oxford. The All India team opened their tour at the Parks and he took 4-17 and 5-32. In the Varsity match he again made a first innings duck, before scoring 42 second time around. By this stage he had moved up to take the new ball, bowling 29 overs in the match for four wickets, conceding 76 runs. His batting again was mediocre – 241 runs at 20, to come sixth in the averages – but his bowling

brought him 32 wickets at 13.81 to top Oxford's averages. That season
he also turned out for Hampshire.

The following year, no longer captain, he again excelled against the
tourists when in the second innings against the South Africans he made
107 – the only century score by an Oxford bat that season – after making
56 in the first. He also took 5-73. He again won his Blue. Coming in at
four against Cambridge he made 4 and 46; opening the bowling he took
3-65 and 1-37. His seasonal total was 275 runs at 30.55 and 21 wickets
at 24, placing him third and second respectively in the Oxford averages.

In World War I he served in the Royal Flying Corps and was captured
at the Battle of the Somme after his engine stopped dead at 4,000 feet,
ten miles behind enemy lines. Because he knew he would not have time
to set fire to the aircraft before he was captured, he deliberately crash-
landed the machine. The first of his many excursions from captivity came
from his second camp, Clausthal, where he and a German-speaking
Belgian, dressed in civilian garb, cut through the wire fence of the kitchen
gardens and escaped by train. His fellow escapee was caught on the train,
Evans was caught on foot, only yards from the border,

As a result he was sent to Fort 9 at Ingolstadt where difficult POWs
who had previously escaped were imprisoned – one of their number had
apparently painted his face green to look like a water lily, and swum the
moat in daylight. Evans' first attempt at escape from this camp was by
making a break for it over the frozen moat during a roll-call. The sentry
spotted him only when he was already well onto the ice. He fired at Evans,
and missed, before his rifle jammed. But Evans was quickly recaptured
on the other side by the unlucky passing of a group of civilians in a
wagon. He later escaped again over the ice which he accessed through a
gap cut in the bars of the latrine window only to be recaptured in the
woods by a pursuing guard.

Whilst being transferred from one camp to another by train, he again
escaped with a fellow German-speaking prisoner by hopping out of the
train window while the other prisoners caused a commotion. Seventeen
nights later they made it into Switzerland, eleven months after he had
first been captured.

He was then sent to command a bomber squadron in Palestine. A few
months into his command he once again came down over enemy lines
through engine failure. He escaped his Turkish captors by running away
on a visit to an outside latrine but, footsore, lost and weak he eventually
gave himself up. Later he obtained passage out of Smyrna on an exchange
ship that took him to freedom. "Technically, I think I may claim to have
escaped from Turkey as well as from Germany, but I am not particularly
proud of the Turkish escape," he wrote in his book *The Escaping Club*,
published in 1928.

In 1921 he made his first appearance for Kent, qualified to do so by
residence at Sittingbourne since 1913. In his very first match for the

county, at Northampton, he scored 102, taking his total from 50 to 100 in 25 minutes. Previous to this he had made 69 for the MCC against the Australians. These performances, but particularly his performance against the tourists at Lord's, brought him good notices. *The Cricketer* advocated his selection for the next test, and Evans was selected in the party of fourteen for the Lord's test. This didn't guarantee selection – anything but, originally – as there were eight batsmen in the party.

In the end his selection became certain as four of the batsmen dropped out. C.B. Fry stood down at his own request, thinking his recent form not good enough, and Hobbs, Hearne and Mead were declared unfit. After Fry had withdrawn he had, in his own words, 'a brainwave' and travelled to London by the evening train to suggest to the selectors that the Honourable Lionel Tennyson should be called up. Tennyson had toured South Africa in 1913–14, playing in all five tests against the somewhat weak hosts, averaging 17. Tennyson received a telephone call at his London club where he was chatting with friends, at one o'clock on the morning of the match, inviting him to play. Tennyson replied that he would be honoured to play, but had the selectors informed him of their intentions earlier he would have knocked off a cigar or two and gone to bed at a more suitable hour. Dismissed later that day for five he passed the selectors on the pavilion steps as he returned; "Never mind," he told them breezily, "next time I'll get fifty for sure." He did, and by the time the next test arrived he was England's captain.

Evans made four in the first innings of the test, and began his second innings shakily. On 9 he snicked a ball from Gregory between his legs and stumps for four and, one run later, was lbw to a yorker. He missed two catches, one of them a hard, low chance to his left at second slip. He was not called upon to bowl. Evans' selection had been a gamble which, had it come off, would have proven his selection an inspired choice, just as, in its conception, the more bizarre selection of Tennyson had become.

After this, Evans played little first-class cricket before taking over the captaincy of Kent in 1927. That season he scored 143 against Lancashire, the county champions, and was selected for The Gentlemen at Lord's. His remaining appearances in first-class cricket came in a few matches in 1928. His first game that season was at the end of June against his old county, and quite schizophrenic in style. In the first innings he took half an hour to get off the mark, and was dismissed for four, the product of his only scoring stroke, after three-quarters of an hour. In the second innings he scored 78, at the rate of a run per minute. *The Cricketer* commented, "He played a most beautiful game. […] His off-driving, square-cutting, and pulling the short ball on the off just wide of mid on, were the features of a really high-class display of batsmanship. […] in form there are few batsmen who exhibit such care, power, and real class as Evans; it is doubtful if he can ever have been seen to better advantage than he was in his second innings at Dover."

First-Class:

| Matches | Inns | NO | Runs | HS | Aver | 100 |
|---|---|---|---|---|---|---|
| 90 | 148 | 6 | 3499 | 143 | 24.64 | 6 |

| Wkts | Average | SR | Best | 10wm | 5wi | ct |
|---|---|---|---|---|---|---|
| 110 | 27.83 | 55 | 7-50 | 1 | 4 | 94 |

Gents: 4 appearances

| Inns | NO | Runs | HS | Aver |
|---|---|---|---|---|
| 7 | 1 | 169 | 64no | 28.17 |

# 14   A. Ducat (Surrey)

Born: 16 February 1886, Brixton, Surrey. Died: 23 July 1942
3rd Test, 1921 v. Australia
Batting: 1st Inns: (No.4)   3    2nd Inns: (No.6)    2

Andy Ducat – known as Mac – joined Surrey in 1906, but he took time
to get onto the first team, Surrey being well endowed with batting talent.
By 1909 he had made for himself a place in the side, scored a maiden
century against Somerset and reached 1,000 runs. In his second full
season he made 153 against Yorkshire at the Oval, the best score by a
Surrey bat that year. He and Jack Hobbs put on 121 in an hour and a
quarter; then Hitch joined Ducat, and they put on 127 in the next hour.

By nature Ducat was a forcing bat. Motionless at the crease when the
bowler ran in, he was quick to get into position, his rapid scoring a result
of innate timing rather than violent intent. He possessed shots all round
the wicket and particularly favoured pulls and cuts, and a fluent drive.
He was fearless against fast bowling and used his feet to the spinners.
Athletic, he was quick between the wickets and a good outfielder. Andy
Sandham would pant, "you'll be the death of me," as he crossed with
the racing Ducat. Once, against Hampshire, Ducat ran seven without
the benefit of overthrows. Hampshire's fast bowler, Jacques, was bowling
leg theory to a packed leg side field. The sole off side fieldsman was C.B.
Fry at mid off. Ducat cut one to third man, and ran seven before Fry
could retrieve the ball. On top of this he was something of a fitness
fanatic, and fussy also with his food, something which led him at one
stage to become a vegetarian. A keen sportsman, he played international
football and was a good golfer and an even better table tennis player.

Cartilage trouble limited his appearances in 1912 and a broken leg
prevented him playing in 1913. Both injuries were legacies from the
football field and it was feared he might never play sport again. A silver
plate was inserted in his shin-bone, and he used crutches for a long time.

But he built up his leg muscles again through taking long walks, and in 1914 he resumed his county career, making four centuries.

In 1919 he had a tremendous season. Against Oxford University at the Oval he made 306 not out, in four hours and fifty minutes. The first hundred took two hours, and then he accelerated further. At one stage he hit ten consecutive deliveries for nine fours and a five. The previous week he had taken 190 from the Sussex attack in three and a half hours; a month later he made 271 against Hampshire at Southampton, including a hundred before lunch, and a Surrey third wicket partnership of 353 with Ernest Hayes, who had also scored a pre-lunch century. In his career Ducat made seven double-centuries in addition to his triple century. He finished the year with 1,695 runs at 52.96, placing him sixth in the national averages. In 1920 he was one of *Wisden's* Cricketers of the Year.

1921 was another successful year, which would eventually bring 1,881 runs at 47 and ninth place in the national averages. In Surrey's eighth match, against Essex at Leyton, he made an undefeated 290 in four hours and forty minutes, including two sixes and 35 fours. Andrew Sandham, Surrey's usual opener, had been prevented from batting earlier due to a slight illness, but came in at the beginning of the second day, at number eleven, to join Ducat. They added a Surrey record of 173 for the last wicket, before Sandham was run out for 58, with Ducat moving on from his overnight 184, to record a hundred runs before lunch. In the second of the Australians' five games between the second and third tests, he made a respectable 47 and 30, top scoring in both of Surrey's innings.

His seasonal form, together with his reputation against pace bowling probably helped him to get into the test side, struggling as England were against the Australian pace bowling. In the first innings he contrived to get out twice to the same delivery. A fierce delivery from McDonald broke the shoulder of his bat and the ball flew to Gregory in the slips, meanwhile a splinter from the broken bat dislodged a bail. His dismissal was recorded as 'caught'. The wicket-keeper, Hanson Carter, handed him the sliver of bat "as a souvenir", and in the second innings stumped him for two.

Later that season Ducat hit an undefeated 204 off the Northampton-shire attack, moving to his century before lunch, taking less than three and a half hours over an innings, having hit two sixes and 15 fours.

In 1928 he hit another purple patch, scoring 649 runs in seventeen days, whilst only being dismissed twice. The sequence involved centuries against Lancashire, Warwickshire and Sussex, and a double-century against Essex, all in consecutive matches. In 1931 he made 2,000 runs in the season for the first time, scoring 2,067 runs at 49.21 with five centuries. The following season he made the last of his centuries for Surrey, by which time had already been informed that the cost-cutting county would be jettisoning him at the end of the season.

His football career had started in Southend, where he graduated from schoolboy level to play for Westcliffe Athletic and then Southend Athletic. In February 1905 he joined Woolwich Arsenal and it was with them that he won the first half of his six caps, playing in the home internationals of 1910. In June 1912 he was transferred to Aston Villa for £1,500. It was with them that he won the remainder of his caps, playing two matches in 1920 and one in 1921. But his proudest football moment was captaining the victorious Aston Villa side in the 1920 FA Cup Final. He led by deed rather than word. Possessed of immense stamina, he was eager to get forward in attack whilst still being able to get back to defend. A clean tackler who would not retaliate for the bruisings others would sometimes give him. He was described as "cultured and unflurried, a master of positional play". In May 1921 he was transferred to Fulham for £2,000, and in May 1924 he retired as a player and became their manager. He was to have played county cricket that summer, but had broken his arm in pre-season nets, and was out for the year.

A quiet, shy man, seldom motivated to voice his opinions, he was not a typical choice for a football manager. In *Beyond Bat and Ball*, David Foot quotes Ducat's daughter: "People would come to the house and stay for a couple of hours. When they left, they would turn to Mum at the door and say what a charming chap Dad was. Yet he would probably not have said more than a couple of words all evening." Robertson-Glasgow wrote of him: "The character was gentle and kind. Nothing showy, insincere or envious came near to his nature."

Fulham just avoided relegation and he gave up the post of manager, telling his wife that he would stick to cricket "without the worries". Football management, anyway, would not have fitted in easily with a full-time county career. After retiring from cricket he became Eton's cricket coach and covered football and cricket for the *Daily Sketch*. He died of a heart attack, whilst batting at Lord's for the Surrey Home Guard. Claude Taylor, a former Oxford Blue and master of cricket at Eton wrote in an obituary, "He had won the affection of cricketers by the rare qualities of enthusiasm and modesty which he combined with great cricketing skill."

First-Class:

| Matches | Inns | NO | Runs | HS | Aver | 100 |
|---|---|---|---|---|---|---|
| 429 | 669 | 59 | 23373 | 306no | 38.31 | 52 |

| Wkts | Average | SR | Best | 10wm | 5wi | ct |
|---|---|---|---|---|---|---|
| 21 | 43.00 | 94 | 3-12 | – | – | 206 |

Gents: 3 appearances

| Inns | NO | Runs | HS | Aver |
|---|---|---|---|---|
| 5 | 0 | 151 | 80 | 30.20 |

# 15 H.T.W. Hardinge (Kent)

Born: 25 February 1886, Greenwich, Kent. Died: 8 May 1965
3rd Test, 1921 v. Australia
Batting: 1st Inns: (No.2)   25   2nd Inns: (No.2)   5

Wally Hardinge was introduced to cricket early in life – his pram was used as the wicket for a 'test match' for small boys. From being ensconced in one of the items of equipment for the game, he graduated to playing it and, aged nine, made his debut for the school side. His elder brother played for a Blackheath club but, although he knew his brother was good, thought him too young to be put forward. However, at the age of eleven he was spotted by Dulwich Ormonde and joined them. When they played the Blackheath club, Wally took many wickets – including his brother's.

Aged thirteen, he was taken on at Tonbridge as a net bowler. A friend of his was going to the Rectory field at Blackheath and Hardinge was invited. The friend did not turn up; there was only one man at the nets, with a pro bowling to him. Hardinge asked if he could bowl at the batsman, who consented. The impression he made led on to him eventually joining the groundstaff.

In 1902, aged sixteen, Hardinge played for Kent against Lancashire as a bowler. In that season, in club matches, he took 152 wickets at nine runs apiece, but always went in at number eleven. Then at end of season, he played for Club and Ground versus Lord Harris' Band of Brothers. He was put in at number five and made 86. In July 1903 he was selected by Kent for his bowling and scored 62 not out against Somerset, having come in on a hat trick. Since then he was played for his batting as Kent was already rich in left-handed bowlers.

Hardinge was an adept player of medium and fast bowlers, also of finger-spinners. He would play with the bat close to pad, and was a good defensive batsman who also possessed shots all round the wicket and, quick on his feet, would use his feet to slow bowling. His favourite shots were the cut and the off-drive. Though normally acting as the sheet anchor, he was capable of scoring quickly.

He bowled slow left-arm spin to a good length with variations of flight, and was almost invariably used by Kent as a change bowler. He was also an exceptionally fast outfielder, who retained his athleticism into his forties, and had a safe pair of hands and a flat throw.

Hardinge was a most successful player for Kent. Only Frank Woolley has scored more runs for the county, and Hardinge was a member of the first four Kent teams to win the championship. Eighteen times he made a thousand runs in the season, five times passing two thousand runs. His most successful season was in 1928 when he made 2,440 runs at 59.65 and came eleventh in the averages. That season he made his highest score, an undefeated 263 against Gloucestershire. This left him seven runs behind Kent's then highest score: Frank Woolley's 270 against Middlesex at Canterbury in 1923. This is a record he had taken from Hardinge. In 1922 Hardinge had made 249 not out against Lancashire. During the course of the innings he had put on 88 for the first wicket with Ashdown, of which Hardinge made 80 and Ashdown 4. When Ashdown spent 55 minutes to make his last run Hardinge scored 78. He was on the field for the whole match, a feat he repeated later in the season at Tunbridge Wells against Northamptonshire.

That double-century involved carrying his bat throughout the innings. He had first batted throughout an innings in 1911 when making 113 out of 220 for the Rest against England at Lord's. He carried his bat again later in the season for his county against Essex at Tonbridge, making 123 out of 203, one of ten occasions he carried his bat for the county. Four times he made centuries in both innings of a match: 153 and 126 versus Essex at Leyton in 1908; 175 and 109 versus Hampshire at Southampton in 1911; 117 and 105 not out against Hampshire again, this time at Dover, in 1913, and 207 and 102 against Surrey at Blackheath in 1921. In 1913 he made centuries in four successive innings scoring 154 not out against Leicestershire at Canterbury in an innings before the Southampton game at Hampshire, and 107 off Northamptonshire at Dover after it.

Carrying his bat for 118 at Lord's for Kent in their thirty-run victory over the MCC in the first game of the 1921 season, helped to draw attention to his batting, and he was brought into the test side at Headingley as one of eight changes. Hardinge and Ducat impressed in the field when Australia batted after winning the toss. *The Cricketer* reported, "Ducat and Hardinge deserve high praise for their magnificent work at deep third man and in the long field. They saved any number of runs by their speed and clean pick-up, while their throwing was delightful to watch, the ball coming in fast and hard from a low and hard trajectory."

Australia scored 407, leaving England an awkward period of batting at the close of the day. Having nibbled at a few balls early on, Hardinge settled down and "made two fine shots on the off side," before a second appeal for bad light was allowed, letting England leave the field at 22-2, with Hardinge on 11. On the second morning he again nibbled outside off stump early before settling down and, according to *The Cricketer,* "was batting well when he was dismissed."

Almost invariably any reference to Hardinge's batting one comes across is laudatory but with a caveat about limitations. A typical example comes from *The Cricketer* of 9 May 1931: "One can think of no batsman, with the possible exception of Mead, of Hampshire, who is such a past master of knowing his limitations, except possibly on a very fast wicket, as Hardinge."

Ian Peebles expounds upon this in *Woolley: The Pride of Kent*: "The enquiring mind may wonder why such a successful county player played but once for England. The answer must surely be that which applies to a number of similarly successful domestic cricketers. He was a very fine county cricketer but ill at ease beyond his limits. As a batsman he was notoriously uncertain against real pace and, from my own observations, harassed by wrist spinners. Such flaws are fatal in the top class where there is usually the means to penetrate them. As a bowler he was useful, but again would have fallen short of the standards to disturb batsmen of international calibre. [...] As in many things of life, the margins in such matters can be, at the same time, very small and wholly decisive. It is the difference in what is aptly but inelegantly called class."

Wally Hardinge was a double international, and a double one test wonder. He made his football league debut for Newcastle, against Sunderland, in 1905 playing at centre forward. Later in his career he was to play at inside-left dropping back into midfield in a tactic which was to become popular after he had retired. He was unable to secure a regular place in the strong Newcastle team – they won the first division in 1906–07 – and so moved to Sheffield United in December 1907. It was with them that he earned his cap, playing against Scotland at Hampden Park. In May 1913 he moved to Woolwich Arsenal for £500. He retired at the end of the 1933 season. He later had a spell as Spurs' reserve team coach.

After retiring from cricket, having played thirty-one seasons for Kent, he went on to become a manager at John Wisden and company. One of the men under him was a bat-maker called Yates, who had been Hardinge's captain at Dulwich Ormonde.

First-Class:

| Matches | Inns | NO | Runs | HS | Aver | 100 |
|---|---|---|---|---|---|---|
| 623 | 1021 | 103 | 33519 | 263no | 36.51 | 75 |

| Wkts | Average | SR | Best | 10wm | 5wi | ct |
|---|---|---|---|---|---|---|
| 371 | 26.48 | 66 | 7-64 | 1 | 8 | 297 |

Players: 6 appearances

| Inns | NO | Runs | HS | Aver |
|---|---|---|---|---|
| 10 | 3 | 257 | 127 | 36.71 |

# 16   C.W.L. Parker
## (Gloucestershire)

Born: 14 October 1882, Prestbury, Gloucestershire. Died: 11 July 1959
4th Test, 1921 v. Australia
Batting:   1st Inns:   –                     2nd Inns: (No.3)   3 no
Bowling: 1st Inns: 28-16-32-2

Charlie Parker took 3,278 wickets at an average of 19.46. In a purely
statistical sense he could be said to have had to work two and a half times
harder than any other bowler to achieve his level of test caps. Parker
received one test cap for every 3,276 wickets he took. The next highest
ratio is Frederick Durston's 1329:1. In contrast, Fred Trueman, Jon Snow
and Phil Edmonds, all left out of touring parties and test teams for what
might be termed not strictly cricketing considerations, still received a
test cap every 34, 24 and 24 wickets respectively.

Other bowlers, of course, who never played test cricket can be
considered to have had even less recognition for their achievements. D.J.
Shepherd, with 2,218 wickets at 21.32, and 668 first-matches, holds the
record both for the most first-class wickets taken, and most first-class
matches played by someone who did not play test cricket. Second in
this bowling list is Parker's team-mate George Dennett; third is Jack
Newman. Newman played for Hampshire, bowling medium-pace; as
well as taking 2,054 wickets, he made 15,000 runs and achieved the
double five times. In 1921 only one man took more wickets than his 177
at 21.56, and Newman was the first to the double that season, doing so
on 31 July.

Parker was a difficult, temperamental man, yet one who could be good
company and warm-hearted off the field. He did not like the establishment and the feeling was mutual. He had a strong class consciousness
and disliked many of the amateurs. When asked by a fellow professional
why he invariably rubbed the amateurs up the wrong way, he replied
"because of their privileged backgrounds. What do these buggers know
about life?" Parker was keen that professional cricketers were given more
status and self-respect: 'dignity of labour' was a phrase he used. He
campaigned for salary cheques and for a fairer deal for those not in the
team. He studied the Russian Revolution as part of a systematic process
of self-education which saw him able to learn the classics, quote the bible
and hum classical music.

He made little secret of his belief that he would not get test recognition
with Plum Warner as a selector. Warner was guest speaker at the 1926
Gloucestershire County Cricket Club annual dinner. In his speech there
was not even a cursory mention of Parker when he praised Gloucestershire cricketers past and present. In his speech at the 1929 dinner, dealing

mainly with his admiration for certain West Country players, he also ignored Parker. Parker later, it appears, manhandled him in the lift, when the lift attendant was busy making people give way for Mr Warner – Parker's class consciousness and personal antipathy simply boiled over. In *Lord's*, Geoffrey Moorhouse writes that someone who knew Plum Warner well described him as "a rather vicious enemy if you fell out with him."

There was also a feeling that Parker could not bowl on plumb pitches. This seems slightly at odds with his record, although his chief fame was being a demon on a 'sticky'. Cheltenham was favourable to spin but Gloucestershire played most of their games at Bristol which was considered too slow a pitch for bowlers. But Parker could shrink when under attack from batsmen. *The Cricketer* remarked that "the great weakness about Parker as a bowler is that if he fails to pitch the ball far enough up and gets a four hit off him he thinks he must at once change his tactics and this is always fatal. Parker can bowl 'flighty' balls like Wilfred Rhodes – he can also bowl fast medium, and when bowling the latter on a sticky wicket or a crumbling one, [is] almost unplayable."

Parker's lack of test recognition is shared by the other major Gloucestershire spin-bowlers. Tom Goddard lies fifth in the list of all-time wicket-takers – J.T. Hearne, fourth, separates him and Parker – with 2,979 wickets at 19.84, which brought him only eight caps. George Dennett took 2,151 wickets at 19.82; Cecil ('Sam') Cook took 1,782 wickets at 20.52 and received only one cap. These four are Gloucestershire's leading wicket-takers.

For someone who was to become the third highest wicket-taker of all time – only Rhodes, with 4,187, and Freeman, with 3,377, have exceeded his wicket tally – Parker's career had an unusual beginning: in the first four years of his career he took one wicket. He made his debut against London County in 1903. It was the only game he played in 1903 and he did not play in 1904. Against Lancashire at Old Trafford in 1905 he collected his first wicket with his second ball, that of one of the most notable amateur bats of the period, Reg Spooner. Parker didn't play in 1906, so in four seasons he had played twice for that solitary wicket. It was 1908 before he gained a regular place in the Gloucestershire side, and between 1908 and the outbreak of war he took 454 wickets. His penchant was to spin the ball, but with Dennett established in the side, it was thought that there was no place for a second slow left-armer, so Parker bowled fast medium inswingers instead.

After the war, in which he was twice turned down by the army and ended up in the Royal Flying Corps, he was invited to rejoin Gloucestershire. He agreed to do so only on the understanding that he could be a spin-bowler. He was then 35 years old. With Dennett still away, Gloucestershire had a vacancy for a spinner and Parker filled it. That season he took 92 wickets at 24.55. In 1920 he took 100 wickets for the first time.

A leisurely run-up preceded a slight jump at the crease, before he brought his arm in a free swing from behind the body to a high delivery action. This easy, rhythmic action allowed him to bowl almost all day, as he often did, sometimes opening with the new ball, bowling his fast medium inswingers, and then changing to spin. He was a quicker bowler than Rhodes or Dennett, and did not rely on variations on flight so much as variations of pace and spin. His style was therefore nearer to Verity or Underwood than a classical spinner and, like Underwood, was not always as effective against a left-handed batsman. *The Cricketer* commented that "it did not seem to matter what wicket he had to bowl upon, he was always getting people out. He seems to have that rare gift of adapting his pace to the actual wicket he is bowling on. At times he is almost a slow bowler, and again, when the wicket helps him, his pace increases according to the amount of spin he is able to get out of the pitch." He bowled with his shirt sleeves flapping in the wind and his cap on at an angle. He liked to decide upon the length of his own bowling spells and wanted fielders to the exact inch: "Make a mark and stay there – there's a catch coming."

Though some of the Gloucestershire fielders lacked ability and mobility, of which Parker himself was a prime example – "I'm a bowler not a bleeding fielder" – Parker had that prince of slip fieldsman Wally Hammond to snaffle many of the edges. It was off Parker's bowling that Hammond caught eight of the ten catches he took in the match against Surrey in 1928. One famous story, whose fame does not necessarily guarantee truth, concerns a Cheltenham festival game. An oversight on the captains's part left the leg side field in the sole care of three of the older members of the team, Alf Dipper, Percy Mills and George Dennett. A ball was eventually hit towards the leg side boundary. The fielders left the ball to its own devices in the fond hope that it would roll over the boundary. The batsmen were running. The ball stopped a few feet short of the boundary and as yet no fielder had moved: all clinging to the optimistic belief that it must be nearer one of the others. Parker was blowing a gasket when a plaintive cry from the captain at mid off set off all three fieldsman on a brisk walk after the ball. "There go my greyhounds," groaned Parker. The fieldsmen eventually conspired to prevent the batsman running a sixth.

In 1921, a very dry year, Parker took 164 wickets and was selected for the fourth test at Old Trafford. There was no play on the first of the three days and on the second Lionel Tennyson declared at 5.50pm on 241-4. The Australian captain argued that Tennyson was not entitled to declare as the match was now being played under two-day rules and by these Australia must be entitled to 100 minutes' batting, so England had to resume their innings. Armstrong bowled the last over before the failed declaration and the first after it. England declared overnight at 362-4. Rain fell during the night but the pitch did not become the threatened sticky, for the sun never came out. Australia, strong in batting, were bowled out for 175, Parker bowling Macartney for 13 with an unplayable delivery as one of his two wickets. With only half an hour remaining

Tennyson did not enforce the follow on and Parker was able to bat at three in the second innings, as those who had not batted in the first innings were given a chance. He made 3 not out.

This batting position and the fact that he was never dismissed in a test, was a source of pride to him. He fancied his batting and every year would swing two new bats around the dressing-room and announce that nothing would stop him making a thousand runs that season. Once, he managed to reach 500. His batting was orthodox and relatively correct for he did not believe in tail-enders slogging: he had a mastery of batting theory which enabled him to become a successful coach when he retired. This did not prevent Parker's opinion of himself as a batsman to be a source of quiet amusement to his fellow pros. At an away match at Kent he gave the side a lecture on how to play Freeman: "It's the same every season – he goes through you like a dose of salts." Rejoinders that Freeman was a good bowler he ignored. "Ah well, I suppose I'll have to show you," he announced finally. When his turn to bat came he crouched to smother the spin, as Freeman normally did not get a lot of bounce, and a googly hit him between the eyes. Shortly afterwards he was out, returning to the pavilion having acquired two black eyes and a foul temper. A young, innocent pro asked what was that he was saying about playing Freeman? Parker's bat was hurled through the dressing-room window.

In 1926 the selectors were Arthur Gilligan, Percy Perrin and Plum Warner. After the first two tests, at Trent Bridge and Lord's, had been drawn, Parker was selected in the party for Headingley. All indications were that it was going to be a wet wicket – the type on which Parker excelled. But he was left out. Parker was in no doubt that it was Warner who left him out. R.E.S. Wyatt called it "the most extraordinary mistake in test history". In his book, *Three Straight Sticks*, he wrote "if the pitch justified sending Australia in to bat, it certainly justified including Parker." *The Times*, writing of Carr's decision to insert the opposition on a damp pitch wrote: "If ever in the last twenty-nine years appearances have justified that policy, this was the occasion. The sun was shining fiercely on a damp marled wicket and the weather seemed to be set fair. But there would seem to have been some lack of co-ordination between the captain and his colleagues of the selection committee, for it was illogical to omit Parker and subsequently put the other side in." Wally Hammond in *Cricket My Destiny* opined, "His presence [...] would have won us the match."

Warner in *The Fight for the Ashes* wrote of Parker's omission, "I need only say with regard to this that Carr had exactly the side he wanted, and preferred Macaulay to Parker. It was thought that the Yorkshire-man, on his own ground and before his own people, would be inspired to great bowling achievement. The anticipation was not justified in the result. But if he failed completely as a bowler, Macaulay proved himself a great-hearted and skilful batsman at a time when every run was of untold value to England." Macaulay took 1-123 off 32 overs, and scored

76, batting at number ten. This though was an unlikely bonus as his highest score in his previous eight test innings was 19, and he had not reached double figures in any of the others, and his batting ability can hardly have been part of the original cause of his selection. Warner has never gone on record admitting to any part in the controversial selections of his career.

Parker was again in the party for the fourth test for which Macaulay was dropped, but this vacancy went to G.T.S. Stevens.

In 1930, with the Ashes series standing at one-all, Parker was called up for the last test at the Oval. Parker was 46 and that season was engaged in taking 179 wickets at 12.84. *Wisden* commented on his omission, "Even at the risk of weakening the batting, Parker, who had been asked to be present, should have been included, for there was nobody in the side able to bowl the ball going away from the batsman which, as was shown time after time during the tour, was the one best calculated to cause trouble to Bradman. [...] The bowling, too, apart from that of Peebles, never looked really good enough to get Australia out at reasonable cost." Wyatt, making his debut as captain, believed that if a batsman got after him, Parker lost control. Australia made 695 and won by an innings.

Bev Lyon, captain of Gloucestershire from 1929 to 1934, had, unknown to Parker, made arrangements for the Anglo Oil Company to place their private aircraft at the county's disposal, and to rush Parker from Croydon aerodrome to Cheltenham, if he was left out of the test side so he could play against Leicestershire. Lyon was at wicket when the plane circled the College ground and dropped a message on a nearby road. Amid much excitement, play was held up as the message was taken to Lyon. Parker had declined the offer as he hadn't flown before and had only learnt of his omission just before eleven o'clock that morning. Lyon, who would have savoured the publicity from such a venture, was disappointed and publicly criticized Parker. "I cannot understand Charlie's action – I thought his enthusiasm would have been sufficient for him to take advantage of any means of coming to Cheltenham. We are in the running for the championship and could have done with him." This incident caused a fracture in the friendship between Parker and Lyon, but it was swiftly healed, and Lyon was criticized in the press.

Though Parker's relationships with amateurs and amateur captains were frequently prickly, he got on famously with Bev Lyon. They played golf together and drank together. Lyon shared many of Parker's negative views of the cricketing establishment and he too had no fear of controversy. Like Parker, he had little time for the division of cricketers into professionals and amateurs, and after a day's play would charge into the professionals' dressing-room and announce that the drinks were on him and everyone was coming. In a speech in 1930 he advocated Sunday play. In 1932 at the club's annual dinner he advanced the idea of a knockout cricket competition with a final to be played at Lord's or the Oval. A good psychologist, he treated Parker as the star, told him that he was the only one who could bowl and if he didn't bowl they might as well pack up and go home. A Gloucestershire pro said, "Bev treated Charlie as a prima donna and a genius because that was exactly what he was." But most importantly he treated him as an equal, and Parker could respond to that.

Starved of international recognition, Parker was left to rewrite the Gloucestershire record book. He holds the Gloucestershire records for most appearances (602), most instances of 100 wickets in a season (16), most wickets (3,170) most hat tricks (6), best match bowling (17-56 v. Essex in 1925), most overs, and even most innings. He holds the world record for most wickets in three consecutive innings, taking 9, 8 and 9 wickets in 1925. Less welcome records are those for the most runs conceded in a county championship innings: 6 for 231 off 61 overs in 1923, and that for the most number of first-class innings without registering a century.

Five times Parker took 200 wickets in a season: 206 wickets at 13.16 in 1922; 204 at 14.27 in 1924; 222 at 14.91 in 1925; 213 at 18.40 in 1926 and 219 at 14.26 in 1931, when aged 48.

In his benefit match in 1922 against Yorkshire, which raised £1,075, he hit the stumps with five successive deliveries – a unique first-class feat – which included a no-ball. By his seventh over Parker had taken four wickets. The last ball of the over bowled Kilner; the first ball of the next over was a no-ball which bowled Macaulay and the next legal ball also bowled him. Then he took the wickets of Dolphin and Waddington, to claim his first hat trick. He took 9-36 in just over 10 overs – one of nine occasions when he took 9 or more wickets in an innings, including 10-79 against Somerset at Bristol in 1929.

In 1930 Gloucestershire played their famous tied match with the Australians. The Australians had come from the final test at the Oval, for which Parker had been in the party but omitted from the final eleven, and which Australia had won by an innings. After Gloucestershire had batted first and made 72 and 202 in their two innings and the Australians had replied with 157 in their first innings, Australia were set 118 to win. The Australians were bowled out for 117 with Parker, giving a tantalising glimpse of how effective he might have been as an international performer, taking 7-54, in the process bowling Bradman, who was to finish the tour with an average of 98.96.

When Bev Lyon was asked for his view of the match he replied; "Any captain can win or lose a game against the Australians, but there are bloody few who can tie one." Of the completed matches on this tour, this, apart from the first test, was the only one that the Australians did not win.

By 1931 Parker's joints were getting stiffer and his mobility in the field suffered. His deliveries became slightly slower and flight was reduced in favour of length. He started that season with, in consecutive matches, 11-153 v. Surrey at the Oval, 14-91 at Cheltenham v. Derbyshire and 15-113 v. Nottinghamshire at Bristol. He reached a hundred wickets by

12 June, thereby joining J.T. Hearne as holder of the earliest date for a hundred wickets in a season. He took 219 wickets that season. This was the fifth time he took 200 wickets, thereby creating a world record. In 1932 he took 134 wickets at 20

1933, now aged 51, at pre-season nets he went without lunch and bowled for three hours as he feared he was losing his 'flighty one'. Reg Sinfield noticed that he was bringing his arm too far over. He returned in the afternoon, and his flighty one was back. When Somerset came to Bristol in 1933 they took 20 from his first four overs. In his next 45 balls Parker took 6-2. That season he took 119 wickets at an average of 27.

In 1934 he took 117 wickets and in 1935 he took 108 and played his last first-class match, against Middlesex. He bowled 54 overs and took 3-166. Five years before, against these opponents, he had taken 16-109 which are still the best bowling figures by any opponent of this county. He left to join the first-class umpires' list. After World War II he continued his connection with Gloucestershire CCC, becoming their coach before moving on to coach at Cranleigh School in Surrey.

First-Class:

| Matches | Inns | NO | Runs | HS | Aver |
|---|---|---|---|---|---|
| 635 | 954 | 195 | 7951 | 82 | 10.47 |

| Wkts | Average | SR | Best | 10wm | 5wi | ct |
|---|---|---|---|---|---|---|
| 3278 | 19.46 | 48 | 10-79 | 91 | 227 | 248 |

Players: 3 appearances

| Inns | NO | Runs | HS | Aver | O | M | R | W | Aver | BB | 5wi |
|---|---|---|---|---|---|---|---|---|---|---|---|
| 3 | 0 | 52 | 36 | 17.33 | 85.5 | 23 | 191 | 11 | 17.36 | 5-42 | 1 |

# 17   G.B. Street (Sussex)

Born: 6 December 1889, Charlwood, Surrey. Died: 24 April 1924
3rd Test, 1922–23 v. South Africa
Batting:   1st Inns: (No.10)   4   2nd Inns: (No.1)   7 no
Fielding:  1st Inns: 1st          2nd Inns: –

George Street was born in Surrey, but went to live in Warnham when he was six. Playing for Sir Henry Arben's XI against the Old Malvernians, he was spotted by one of the Sussex committee, and joined the ground-staff at Hove in 1909. In June that season he played his first match for Sussex but had to wait until 1912, and the retirement of Butt, to become a regular member of the side.

That season he played 23 matches, made 23 catches and completed 16 stumpings. The same number of games in the following year brought three more dismissals, and in the final season before the war he dismissed 73 batsmen, including 15 stumpings.

During the war he enlisted in the 2nd/6th Sussex Cyclist Battalion, and served in India where he gained experience of playing on matting wickets, which was to prove useful a few years later when he was called up to join the tour of South Africa. He missed the 1919 cricket season due to a late discharge from the army.

In 1922 he bettered his previous seasons, dismissing more batsmen than any other wicket-keeper, and came close to selection for that winter's tour to South Africa. *The Cricketer* commented that "on last season's form, Street was as fine a wicket-keeper as any in England; many good judges, indeed, considered him actually the best."

The tour was anticipated with confidence, despite Hobbs and Hearne declining invitations. The two wicket-keepers in the fourteen-man party were Livsey and Brown. On 30 November Livsey broke a finger on his left hand and, with Brown suffering from an illness, Street was sent a cabled invitation. He sailed on 8 December.

It was a shock to English cricket followers when England lost the first test, begun on 23 December, by 168 wickets. England scraped home in the second test by only a wicket.

Street played the next game after this test versus the Northern Orange Free State XV and *The Cricketer* remarked that he "kept wicket very finely". In the first innings he made two stumpings and took a catch; in the second he stumped one and caught three. He opened the MCC innings and made 23 out of 325 as MCC won by an innings and 35 runs. This was the thirteenth match of the tour. Street played in the next match too, which was against Natal, not dismissing anyone and scoring 8 not out.

The fifteenth match was the third test, played over four days. England won the toss and batted. Brooke bowled the first ball of the match to Russell who was then missed in slips. Following a single, Sandham fell to a 'wonderful' catch in the slips by Nouse, who shortly brought off another fine slip catch to dismiss Woolley, leaving England at 2-2. Russell and Mead put on 61 and Mead went on to bat for eight hours and twenty minutes for 181. This had been the first international played at the ground and, later, at the request of the Durban Cricket Authorities, Mead planted a tree in commemoration of this, the ground's first international century. England made 428. At the close of the second day South Africa had reached 70 without loss; the third day was rained out.

As the test was played on a matting wicket which, unlike grass, does not become difficult after rain, South Africa were able to progress to 368 and a comfortable draw on the fourth day. Street opened England's second innings, which lasted four overs, in company with Macaulay, who had batted number eleven in the first innings. The fourth test was drawn, and England won the fifth by 109 runs.

Street came fourth in the tour averages for all matches, nine innings, three of which were uncompleted, bringing 206 runs at 34.33. His highest score was an innings of 88 out of 282 against Orange Free State. He finished ahead of the fifth-placed Frank Woolley, who averaged 29, and who had made 115 not out in the fourth test after the first ball he received had hit the wicket without dislodging a bail.

In the following season England did not play any tests, but Street was at the peak of his form, making 97 dismissals; 95 of these – 69 caught, 26 stumped – achieved in Sussex colours, remains a county record.

On 24 April 1924, Street proudly showed off his new motorcycle to his team-mates at pre-season nets. Alan Saunders, captain of the Nursery side came over to the group and warned him, "If you cut corners like you did just now you won't ride that bicycle very long."

Later that morning Street had a long chat with his captain, A.E.R. Gilligan, telling him how much he wanted to make the MCC party for the forthcoming tour to Australia.

That evening, on his way back from watching Brighton and Hove Albion, he swerved to avoid a lorry and accidentally put his hand on the accelerator rather than the brake and crashed into a wall. He was killed instantly.

A.E.R. Gilligan wrote, "It was a terrible shock for everyone, and I felt as if I never wanted to play cricket again. I felt George Street's loss very keenly; he was a sterling fellow and always full of fun, but a tremendous fighter, especially when things really looked black for his side. He had improved very much behind the stumps during the previous season, and he was very nearly international class."

"One of the best of wicket-keepers", was mourned by *The Cricketer.* "It is no exaggeration to say that English cricket, as well as the game in Sussex, has sustained a great loss in consequence. It seemed likely that, provided he retained his form, he would have been chosen for this year's test matches against South Africa for he was so well acquainted with the bowling of A.E.R. Gilligan and Maurice Tate."

First-Class:

| Matches | Inns | NO | Runs | HS | Aver | 100 |
|---|---|---|---|---|---|---|
| 197 | 304 | 73 | 3984 | 109 | 17.24 | 1 |

| Wkts | Average | SR | Best | 10wm | 5wi | ct | st |
|---|---|---|---|---|---|---|---|
| 3 | 22.00 | 35 | 3-26 | – | – | 308 | 121 |

Players: dnp

# 18   J.C.W. MacBryan (Somerset)

Born: 22 July 1892, Box, Wiltshire. Died 14 July 1983
4th Test, 1924 v. South Africa
Batting: dnb

A one test wonder at cricket gets at least up to five days to represent his country, even if not actively involved in the play. Footballers, for instance, can have an international career lasting, almost literally, seconds: the West Ham footballer, Jimmy Barrett, and the Brighton striker, Peter Ward, are credited with the shortest international careers for England; Barrett played for eight minutes against Northern Ireland in 1928 before going off injured and Ward came in as a substitute for the final eight minutes against Australia in 1980. Kevin Hector of Derby gained two international caps, but they involved only seventeen minutes of football. Even in days before substitutions, goalkeeper W.H. Carr managed to play less than a full football international. He missed his train from Sheffield for the match in London and still had not arrived by kick-off; the Scottish captain suggested delaying the start, but the English captain, Charles Alcock, declined the offer. He put a forward, A.G. Bonsor, in goal, and Bonsor kept the Scots forwards out for a quarter of an hour, before Carr arrived and took over. Carr then let in two goals. England drew 2-2 and Carr did not play again.

But Jack MacBryan did not get five days of international play. Picked to play in the fourth test in 1924, the match was ruined by rain: just two and three-quarter hours' play was possible. He took his place in the slips and hardly touched the ball: the only test cricketer not to have either bowled, batted or dismissed anyone.

Only three other men have played for England without batting: fellow one test wonders Clay and Read, and Fred Root, who played three times. Root, a good enough bat to do the double in 1928, was listed at number ten in his three matches, all against Australia in 1926. In his debut match only an hour's cricket was played. In his second match England declared at 475-3 in their only innings, and in the rain-affected third test at Old Trafford, England reached 305-5 in response to Australia's 335 as the game ended in a third consecutive draw.

MacBryan did not have much luck with showpiece events. Twelfth man for Cambridge University the year before, he was selected to play against Oxford in the Varsity match of 1920, in a side which included F.W. Gilligan and Percy Chapman. Douglas Jardine, G.T.S. Stevens and R.C. Robertson-Glasgow were all on the Oxford side. There was no play on the first two days, and only two hours on the third. The game was to have lasted only three days and should have ended there, but was extended to a fourth, which didn't allow for a result but at least let some of the blues get involved. Oxford's innings ended at 193 and in reply Cambridge made 161-9, MacBryan stumped for five. He told his biographer, David Foot, "I wasn't only stumped. I was bowled and caught as well. I got a touch to a very good ball from Reg Bettington as I played forward. It hit the wicket and went into the wicket-keeper's hands. Then with my foot still raised the Oxford skipper also took the remaining bail off."

There was an old don at Jesus, MacBryan's college, who watched all the matches at Fenners, and he said that of the 1920 side only Chapman and Gilligan lacked leadership qualities. Both went on to captain England, which perhaps says something about dons or selectors.

MacBryan was coached in batting at his prep school, St Christopher's, in Bath, when he was about seven. The Headmaster would line up about a dozen boys in the dining-room, give them a bat and, from the other end of the room, would mime the delivery of a ball. When the imaginary ball left his hand he would shout 'play' and expect the boys to go through the motions of playing a forward defensive. He would then go along the line carrying out an inspection of the boys' positions. MacBryan grew up to be a batting purist, which he attributed to this early tuition.

Aged fifteen, MacBryan played for the Wiltshire Boys in a match against the Somerset Boys. He batted well, watched by many of the Somerset committee, some of whom knew MacBryan's father – one presumes as a spectator of Somerset's matches at Bath, rather than in his capacity as the doctor in charge of the mental home there. The President of Somerset, watching MacBryan's innings, remarked that it was a shame the doctor lived in Wiltshire, before enquiring whether he owned any property in Bath. The doctor did, and thus MacBryan qualified for Somerset.

MacBryan later regretted his innings that day. He always hankered after playing for one of the London clubs. His character was out of kilter with that of Somerset's cricket. A serious man, he did not fit into a county where the captain, one day when bowling to his brother after tea, bowled him a doughnut. One of his proudest moments came when he was playing for the MCC against Yorkshire at Scarborough and he heard Wilfred Rhodes remark to the umpire, George Hirst, "That one looks more like a Yorkshire professional than a Somerset amateur."

MacBryan was not good at winning friends. His relationship with his father was a rocky one. His mother had died when he was ten; MacBryan wanted to follow his father into the medical world but his father disagreed and directed him towards the army. MacBryan joined the 13th, The Prince Albert Light Infantry, but, on reaching his twenty-first birthday he made his father send him to Barts to study medicine. He passed the first Medical Board a month before war broke out, when he joined his regiment for the special reserve.

Because of his medical studies MacBryan was entitled to opt out of military service but did not and two years later, after he had been captured, he became friendly with a German camp officer who told him to write home and obtain influence for an exchange. His father did nothing, despite having useful connections.

MacBryan had been wounded at the Battle of Mons, and had been taken prisoner on the retreat. During his three and a half years as a POW he taught Russian officers arithmetic in French. One day he found himself one of fifteen prisoners idly throwing a piece of German war bread around in rugby style, when one of them dropped it and kicked it on to another. They were promptly arrested by the guards. The fifteen of them ended up on trial in Berlin for "insulting the German nation by kicking their war bread about." The senior British officer present was sentenced to ten days' solitary confinement; the remainder got seven.

MacBryan missed a blue in 1919. The Cambridge captain had an ostentatious habit of drinking sherry from a beer mug. MacBryan, seeing him doing this at Fenners, remarked loudly that he didn't think much of someone who did that. The captain's mother, hearing and approving of the remark, invited MacBryan to tea. But selection depended upon the captain, not his mother, and he was not so popular in this quarter.

At Somerset he would publicly air his criticism of the set-up and the other players. In his opinion there were too many bad players – in particular, too many bad amateurs. MacBryan disliked many of those he played amongst, and the feeling was often mutual, others finding him cantankerous and stuck up. He criticized the Somerset captain John Daniell as being too old and for having favourites. John Daniell was a test selector. MacBryan's father was once described as jealous and vain, and perhaps some of these characteristics were found in his son. MacBryan seems to have been overly conscious of status. According to David Foot, friends of MacBryan joked that he had wanted to go to Eton, but his father sent him to Exeter College instead. As well as yearning to play for one of the fashionable London clubs, he disliked Peter Johnson, a team-mate and successful stock-broker. MacBryan had become a stock-broker with less success.

Although he had made his debut for Somerset at Bath in 1911 when on leave from Sandhurst, he rarely played before the war. However, in 1920 he made his first century for the county, and rapidly established himself as Somerset's best bat. He was one of the most correct and attractive batsmen on the county circuit. He found an intellectual challenge in batting: he studied the bowlers he would have to face and he concentrated fiercely throughout an innings. *The Cricketer* had this to say: "MacBryan is essentially a steady batsman. He is neat and finished in style without being in any way spectacular, and far from being obsessed, like so many of the moderns, by on side play he gets a good proportion of his runs by cutting, this alone making him good to look at."

By 1923 he had risen to national recognition. Chosen in the second of the test trials, he made 80 in the first innings in three and a half hours. *The Cricketer* described his as the best amateur opening bat. Some argued that MacBryan's fielding would be a hindrance to the side but *The Cricketer* disagreed: "Some lunatic theorists imagine that MacBryan can't field – as a matter of fact in any of those horrible leg side cribs he is just about the best in England. He doesn't profess to be a country fielder, but we have seen several fielding in the country in test matches, and in Gents and Players matches at Lord's, who would be as slow movers as mutes at a funeral." A wartime injury to his right arm prevented him from throwing long distances successfully and seems to have acted as a disincentive to chase balls into the outfield.

There were no tests in the 1923 season and MacBryan failed to be selected for the Gentlemen at Lord's, although he played for the Gentlemen in the festival game at Scarborough where he made a half-century. He was selected for the Gentlemen at Lord's the following season, and also for a test trial where, in the second innings, he made 59. He was missed twice during this innings. On the first occasion Tate dived forward at short mid on, and held onto the ball before it slipped from his grasp, but the umpire decreed he had not held the ball long enough for it to be a catch.

Through winning the first three tests of 1924 against the South Africans, twice by an innings, once by nine wickets, and thereby the series, the English selectors felt able to field an experimental team for the penultimate test, with the forthcoming Ashes series in mind. To this end they gave debuts to Duckworth, Geary and MacBryan. Hobbs and Hearne were left out to accommodate the newcomers. Because Gilligan was suffering from a blow received playing for the Gentlemen, Douglas was recalled to captain England.

On the first day there were only two and a half hours' play. It was a day more notable for when there wasn't play than when there was. "The cricket, so far as it went, was by no means stimulating," reported *Wisden*. Heavy rain after four o'clock soaked the pitch and, after repeated inspections, the umpires declared that play was not possible. A section of the crowd, not huge at seven thousand, disapproved and a few hundred demonstrated noisily in front of the pavilion. Walter Brearley, no stranger to noisy demonstration at Lord's, spoke to the demonstrators and managed to quieten the crowd.

Hearne and Hobbs, on his home ground, were restored for the Oval test. England's batting order read: Hobbs, Sutcliffe, Hearne, Woolley, Sandham and Hendren, and it is hard to see how, on ability, MacBryan would have deserved a place in front of any of that able sextet.

MacBryan averaged 43 in 1924, and privately had been led to believe that he would be in the touring party for that winter's Ashes series. In the end he was not; none of the debutants of the fourth test had been included. MacBryan told David Foot, "The chairman of selectors told me that Peter Johnson said I didn't have the right temperament. What he should have said was that I was utterly disgruntled with the Somerset set-up." *The Cricketer* wrote that MacBryan "made a great advance in reputation and, according to general report, would probably have been in the MCC's team for Australia if the doctor had not approved of J.W. Hearne going out."

He went instead to South Africa with Joel's side, where he was not a success, playing in four of the five unofficial tests but scoring only 44 runs.

Two more seasons with Somerset constituted virtually the remainder of his career, although he continued to play intermittently for them until 1931. There were rumours that he had fallen out with too many people too often, but in fact he was not a wealthy amateur and could ill afford the time to play cricket. In 1932, with only three first-class counties fixtureless and so able to provide individuals for the Gents versus Players game at the Oval, MacBryan played for the Gents, making 3 and 1.

For someone who so disliked the county for which he played cricket, it is ironic that he is one of Somerset's more notable sportsmen, having also played golf and rugby for the county. He also represented Britain in the Olympics at Hockey.

First-Class:

| Matches | Inns | NO | Runs | HS | Aver | 100 |
|---|---|---|---|---|---|---|
| 206 | 362 | 12 | 10322 | 164 | 29.49 | 18 |

| Wkts | Average | SR | Best | 10wm | 5wi | ct |
|---|---|---|---|---|---|---|
| 0 | – | – | – | – | – | 128 |

Gents: 4 appearances

| Inns | NO | Runs | HS | Aver |
|---|---|---|---|---|
| 7 | 0 | 128 | 53 | 30.20 |

# 19  H. Smith (Gloucestershire)

Born: 21 May 1891, Gloucester. Died: 12 November 1937
1st Test, 1928 v. West Indies
Batting: 1st Inns: (No.9)   7
Fielding: 1st Inns: 1 ct          2nd Inns: –

Contemporary commentaries about Harry Smith tend to make two main points. The first is that had he played for a more fashionable county he would have received more recognition. *The Cricketer* mentions this twice in the same issue in 1928: "It is safe to say if he had been identified with one of the more prominent counties his worth, both as wicket-keeper and batsman, would long ere this have been recognized more generally." Later, in a different piece it says, "He is one of those cricketers of whom it can be said with truth that, had he been associated with one of the leading sides, his merits would have been recognized more generally."

An analysis of where players get selected from is somewhat problematic. Once on the side it is normally the performance in the test match, rather than county form, which ensures future selection. Therefore a true analysis would have to look at debutants, to eliminate this factor. But even here there are problems with players who have played for more than one county, and in particular those who played in the same season for a university and a county side. Nick Knight was first selected for England's test side whilst a Warwickshire player, but had been selected for the previous winter's A team tour while playing for Essex. It was as an Essex player that he received selectorial attention, though it was in Warwickshire colours that he was first capped. Indeed, an opening batsman, he had not scored a century for his current county when he first played test cricket. Particularly in the earlier days of test cricket, when some amateurs played only a fraction of their county's pro-grammes, it might have been their performances for a select side, such as the MCC or Gentlemen which drew attention to their ability. For instance A.J. Evans owed his selection more to an innings for the MCC than through his very limited county appearances.

That said, an examination, albeit slightly approximate, can be made of players' backgrounds. Figures – which have to be considered approxi-mate as they are open to interpretation – show that some counties provide significantly more test players than others. To the end of the 1998–99 season Yorkshire, the greatest provider, with 70 cricketers, has supplied over five times that of Hampshire, and if one excludes late entrants to the championship Glamorgan and Durham the least. But then Yorkshire have won the county championship more often than anyone else: twenty-nine times outright, with one shared championship; Hampshire have won it only twice.

After Yorkshire, the counties providing most debutants are Surrey, with 62, Middlesex 58, and Lancashire 57. After Yorkshire, they are also the most successful counties, with fifteen, ten and seven outright wins respectively. Next in the list is Kent, for championship victories, six, and test recognition. This makes sense. To win the championship one presumes you must have good players and good players get selected for England. Around half of England's test players have come from the five most successful counties.

The correlation between county success and test recognition is not so exact at the other end of the scale. But then one should not expect it to be. That Yorkshire have won almost a quarter of modern county championships suggests a regular depth of talent. It does not suggest that Yorkshire's best player in any one season is necessarily better than the best player of any other county. Bobby Moore never won anything with West Ham. The only winners' medal he received was for the World Cup.

But there is some correlation. Excluding later entrants to the championship, Glamorgan and Durham, just above Hampshire at the bottom of that table of test recognition are Somerset, and Northamptonshire with eighteen cricketers each. Neither Somerset nor Northamptonshire have won the championship. Therefore, two of the four long established counties who have never won the championship appear amongst the three least successful at having their players selected for England.

However, one of the counties which has not yet won the championship, with 26 cricketers attaining selection, is clearly more successful than not only Leicestershire (three championships), Derbyshire (one championship), and Warwickshire (five championships). This county is Gloucestershire. This means that Gloucestershire players receive recognition out of proportion to the county's success. Does this in fact make Gloucestershire, the county of the Graces, Hammond and Jessop, a fashionable county? Sussex, the fourth county never to have won the championship, has the sixth-highest number of representatives in England teams.

After the 1983 season Chris Broad left Gloucestershire in the belief that he needed to play elsewhere if he was to be selected for England. At the same time Bill Athey joined Gloucestershire, with the aim of resurrecting an England career. Both succeeded in their aims.

Geography may well have an influence on selection in that a good performance in London, especially at Lord's is often considered to attract greater attention than in other venues. This could be explained partly through the national press outlets tending to be London-based, and that, with selectors normally having day jobs, also often London-based, then Lord's and the Oval provide the easiest grounds for them to get to. In an interview in *The Cricketer* after his retirement in 1988 from a seven-year stint as Chairman of Selectors, Peter May said: "My own approach to seeing players was to travel up to Lord's or the Oval for a couple of hours to have a look at someone. Of course very often he'd be out for nought or taken off as soon as I arrived. [...] Half of any county's matches are away so I got quite a wide spread by staying most of the time in London." In 1981, against Essex, Middlesex became the first county to send out an eleven comprised entirely of test players when the West Indian Wayne Daniel and the Australian Jeff Thomson joined the English test players Brearley, Downton, Radley, Gatting, Butcher, Barlow, Emburey, Edmonds and Selvey.

Where the players of one county might have an advantage concerns the England captaincy. Les Taylor received England recognition when his team-mate David Gower was England captain; Brian Rose was recalled when his team-mate Botham was captain; when Gooch was captain and Keith Fletcher was England coach Essex players were well represented in England and England A touring parties. This is not to allege wrongful bias: it is surely a natural bias. Obviously selectors, of whom the captain is one, will go for players about whose ability they feel confident. Logically they will feel more confident in their judgement of a player they see regularly, and whose character they know, than one of whom they have little knowledge. This might work both ways: Phil Edmonds feels his selection was hindered by his rocky relationship with his county captain, who was also the England captain.

Fashion does not have to relate solely to counties. Types of players can be in fashion. Fast bowlers are almost perennially in fashion. Recent years have seen the leg spinner grow in popularity through the success of overseas leg spinners at test level. This prompted one selector to declare that the only type of spinner who wins test matches is the wrist spinner – a contentious view in light of the fact that only five times has a leg spinner taken ten wickets in a match for England, whereas, between them the off-spinner, Jim Laker, and slow left-armer Tony Lock have done so six times. Leg spin being in fashion clearly helped Ian Salisbury to be selected for England, despite at the time of his debut having a first-class career average in the 40s, which would normally preclude a regular county place, and despite returning mediocre figures for England.

The other point often made in contemporary comments about Harry Smith relates to a lack of faith in his ability. "Good but not quite good, or consistent, enough", is a recurring theme. *The Cricketer* writes in 1923, for instance, that Smith was "rather uncertain, but on his day is excellent." Three years later they were writing, "He can only be termed a fair wicket-keeper, for he misses a good many catches. On his day he is brilliant."

Bert Strudwick 'kept for England in the 1924–25 and 1926 series. He retired in 1927. The wicket-keeper for that winter's tour was Stanyforth, who also captained the team, with Harry Elliott – who played in the final test because of an injury to Stanyforth – as his deputy. Stanyforth, however, was not a regular county player, so another wicket-keeper was required for the 1928 series. Smith was chosen in the 'England' side for the test trial, with Ames behind the stumps for the Rest. *The Cricketer* report of the match stated that both were "excellent".

Smith was picked for the first test, but *The Cricketer* commented that "the wicket-keeper was not up to the old standard of Lilley, Strudwick etc. He was not too clean in his taking of the ball." Elliott came back into the side for the next test.

Harry Smith came to Gloucestershire from Frenchay CC, where he was a leg spinner and batsman. Playing for Bristol Colts against

Gloucestershire in 1911 he was asked to keep wicket in an emergency, and so impressed the county that he was offered a trial and taken on as deputy wicket-keeper. In 1914 he succeeded Jack Board becoming the second in a succession of long-serving Gloucestershire wicket-keepers. Board played from 1891 to 1914; with 1,016 dismissals he was easily the county's most successful 'keeper. After Smith, A.E. Wilson 'kept wicket from 1936 to 1955 and B.J. Meyer from 1957 to 1971. Jack Russell has 'kept wicket since 1981.

After the First World War, Smith played three seasons as a batsman, before resuming wicket-keeping duties. He possessed a sound defence and a straight bat and was a good judge of a run. He made his maiden century in 1919 against Hampshire at Southampton, making 120 in the first innings. In the second he made 102 not out. This was an eventful match for Smith as Pothecary, the last Hampshire batsman, played a ball from Parker into the top of his pad, shook it into Smith's hands, and was given out, caught – contrary to law 33B which states that in such circumstances the ball becomes dead.

In 1922 against Surrey he made 77 and 109, Dipper made 92 and 62 and no one else reached 20 in either innings. They scored 340 of the 465 runs obtained from the bat for Gloucestershire. In 1923 he made his record score of 149 versus Essex at Cheltenham, with twenty-four fours in three and a half hours.

That season he played for the Rest in the test trial, coming into the side because M.D. Lyon had dislocated a finger. *The Cricketer* reported that Smith "is not yet an England wicket-keeper." That season he also played for the Players at the Oval and Lord's. At the Oval he took four catches in the first innings. At Lord's he made 28, batting for an hour and a half before getting off the mark. Of his Lord's performance *The Cricketer* commented, "Smith, although he did some very smart things behind the wicket, is not yet up to England form."

In 1924 he began a run of matches at the Oval which saw him concede five byes in four matches at the Oval. In 1924 he conceded three byes whilst Surrey scored 558 runs. He did not play at the Oval in 1925, but in 1926 he conceded two byes out of 426 runs and in 1927 none in a combined total of 588 and none again in 1928 while 722 runs were scored by the host. At the beginning of the 1927 season in four innings and three matches 1,374 runs were conceded against Gloucestershire, but Smith let through only one bye. *The Cricketer* said, "He deserves such success, for he is a very keen, hardworking cricketer."

Illness caused him to give up county cricket in 1932, but he was able to make a return to the Gloucestershire side in 1935, playing fifteen matches, batting well down the order. He retired for good after this season and was for a time coach to the county colts. In retirement he ran a pub.

First-Class:

| Matches | Inns | NO | Runs | HS | Aver | 100 |
|---------|------|-----|-------|-----|-------|-----|
| 402 | 656 | 56 | 13413 | 149 | 22.35 | 10 |

| Wkts | Average | SR | Best | 10wm | 5wi | ct | st |
|------|---------|-----|------|------|-----|-----|-----|
| 0 | – | – | – | – | – | 457 | 266 |

Players: 2 appearances

| Inns | NO | Runs | HS | Aver | ct |
|------|-----|------|-----|-------|-----|
| 3 | 0 | 53 | 28 | 17.56 | 7 |

# 20   H.W. Lee (Middlesex)

Born: 26 October 1890, Marylebone, London. Died: 21 April 1981
4th Test, 1930–31 v. South Africa
Batting: 1st Inns: (No.2)   18   2nd Inns: (No.2)   1

Three English one test wonders have owed their test appearances entirely to being in the right place at the right time. Most recently, Tony Pigott was called into the team in New Zealand in 1983–84 because Dilley and Foster were injured and the team wanted a replacement pace bowler. They had no opportunity to fly someone in from England, so they went with the local talent: Pigott, who was playing for Wellington. An alternative would have been to pick one of the spinners from the party, Nick Cook and Vic Marks. For only the third time England went into a test without a recognized spin-bowler. As was the case in the previous two instances, England lost, doing so by an innings. *Wisden* reported, "Abysmal bowling, branded by Willis as among the worst he had seen in more than eighty tests, enabled New Zealand to reach 307 in conditions in which 180 to 200 should have been the upper limit." Pigott had postponed his wedding, due to take place on the fourth day, to play in the test. This turned out not to have been necessary as England lost in three days and 12 hours' playing time. Pigott took 2-75 in 17 overs.

In 1964–65 England urgently needed a new-ball bowler for the final test, and Ken Palmer, coaching in South Africa, was on hand. The third was Harry Lee.

Harry Lee was born in Marylebone and learnt his cricket in the streets there, principally Barrett Street. In 1919 when Lee first played for Middlesex at the Oval he was greeted by the dressing-room attendant: "You don't know me, but I've been expecting you along here for a good many years." The attendant's son was a policeman who used to watch the boys playing in the street, and the attendant explained that "He often used to wonder whether he oughtn't to step along and send you packing.

But he liked your style of play, so he'd wait until he thought you'd been in long enough, and then stroll down to break up the game. But he spotted you all right, and told me about you, and I've been expecting you along these many years."

After a few terms at Barrett Street School, where the Headmaster, a Mr Pearson, was a keen sportsman who had played for Blackburn Rovers, Lee moved to St Thomas's School in Portman Square. There the Headmaster, Mr Despicht, used to chalk a wicket in the playground and offer a penny to any boy who could bowl him out. "He used to keep me in extra cakes," Lee recalled. At school Lee was a bowler and it was as a bowler that he attended a trial at Lord's in 1906. His first ball was a wide into the far corner of the net; his next delivery was a long hop. Despite this beginning he was taken onto the groundstaff.

Lee bowled medium pace, often taking the new ball, and was able both to spin the ball and float the ball away from the batsman. He was a patient opening bat, with a cramped style.

He first appeared for Middlesex in 1911. Limited opportunities over the next two seasons led to him asking the Middlesex Secretary, A.J. Webbe, if he could play in some MCC matches to gain experience. Webbe suggested that he joined the Lord's bowling staff, which led to him playing for the MCC in country house cricket, which Lee described as "cricket at its most perfect".

In one match, at Moreton Morrall in Warwickshire, Lee had moved to a half-century by lunch. It was a hot day and the Essex cricketer Bill Reeves encouraged Lee to try some iced hock. Lee had never come across it before. He found it most refreshing and, urged on by Reeves, he drank plenty more. Lee, in his own words, "floated out to bat and floated back again." Reeves found this hilarious, declaring that he could drink all the iced Hock he wanted and still knock the bowling all round the ground. Endeavouring to prove this, he was out first ball.

In 1913 Lee went in at number ten to join J.T. Hearne with 60 still required to avoid the follow-on. This they did, Lee making an undefeated 35 and the captain, Plum Warner, promoted Lee to number five for the second innings.

Lee made a name for himself at the end of the 1914 season. War had been declared and several of the amateurs had joined up. For the Northern tour to the Roses counties, originally called off because of Middlesex's selection problems, Lee was promoted to opening bat. He batted for an hour and a quarter against Rhodes and Hirst on a sticky wicket. Against Lancashire he and the Australian Frank Tarrant took Middlesex to a ten-wicket victory after they had been set 145 to win in just under two hours, Lee contributing 44 and Tarrant making 101. Against Nottinghamshire Lee made his maiden first-class century. He had reached 97 and Wass was bowling to him, 'Old' Joe Hardstaff at mid on called out to the bowler, "The lad's never made a century – give him one." Wass, one of the worst bats in county cricket replied, "No one's ever given me one for my century." The next delivery Lee pushed out between the bowler and Hardstaff who, as the batsman recalled later, set off after it "as eagerly as if he was off to the dentist".

At the end of the season Lee joined up, going into the County Of London Regiment. In March 1915 he was shot in the leg, which left his thigh badly broken, at the Battle of Neuve Chappelle. He lay between the lines for three days before being picked up by the Germans. He was reported Killed in Action and a memorial service was held for him in England.

Meanwhile Lee was in a POW hospital, his leg healing rapidly. A fellow POW warned him not to heal too quickly. Lee did not at first understand, but a few days later, now aware that bad hospital cases got repatriated he "suffered a relapse" and in a week "was the sickest man in the ward". When the examining officers came round it seemed he could barely walk. Although apparently hardly able to walk, he gave a helping hand to a blind sergeant who was having difficulty boarding the boat that was to repatriate the severely wounded to England. The next day Lee was walking freely along the deck, when he met the sergeant coming in the opposite direction. "Isn't it a lovely morning?" the sergeant remarked. "Have you ever seen such a blue sky?"

The injury however had left Lee with one leg much shorter than the other, and he was told that he would never be able to play cricket again. He went to work in the War Office. But Middlesex paid for him to receive specialist medical treatment and early in 1916 he was asked if he would play for the MCC against Lancing. He accepted and scored a century. *Wisden* reported, "No one watching Lee bat, bowl, or even more, chase the ball in the field would have known he had been injured."

In the autumn of 1916 he met Mrs Tarrant by chance. She was about to go to India, where Frank was. She asked Lee if he would like to go and he said he would. He thought no more about it until a few weeks later a cable arrived: 'Proceed at once to Bombay. See you on arrival – Frank.' But in the meantime Lee's mother had died, and he had promised her that he would look after his younger brothers, aged 11 and 14, and so declined the offer, saying that if the offer was still open in a year's time he would gladly reconsider. A year later he received another cable inviting him. This time he accepted.

He had wanted to go to Bombay, but the only berth available was on the *Nyanza*, sailing to Calcutta. Then, at the last moment he was told he had been transferred to the *Nagoya*, sailing the same day for Bombay. Just out of Portsmouth the *Nyanza* was torpedoed.

He became the cricket and football coach to the Maharajah of Cooch Behar. This Middlesex professional found himself with his own servant and a room in a palace. His first duty was to attend a tiger shoot, which, he wrote later, he found "rather more terrifying than the Battle of Neuve

Chappelle." He played plenty of cricket in his year and a half there, but when he learnt that the county championship was to be held again in 1919, he returned to England.

The years immediately after the war were his best as a cricketer. In 1919 he made two centuries in the three-day, non-championship match against Surrey. In the first innings he made 163, putting on 104 for the first wicket with W.P. Robertson and 226 for the second with J.W. Hearne. In the second innings he made 126.

The next season he took 5-21 in Sussex's first innings at Lord's, including a spell of three wickets in four balls. He opened with Warner and in three and a half hours they put on 241, both scoring centuries as did the next two batsmen, Nigel Haig and J.W. Hearne. In Sussex's innings he took 6-47. In 1923 the first four Middlesex batsmen again made centuries, including Lee with 107, and J.W. Hearne with 232.

In 1920 he scored 1,473 runs at 44, and took 40 wickets at 24 to help Middlesex to the championship, and was seriously considered by the selectors for the tour to Australia. He did not make the tour, and in the following season he was less successful as a batsman, despite playing the highest innings of his career, 243 not out against Nottinghamshire at Lord's. However he had his best season with the ball, taking 61 wickets at 21, and he was again mentioned as a possible test player, but scores of 21, 0, 9, 5, 9 and 64 in matches against the Australians did not advance his cause.

He never again reached his peak of performance, though remaining a reliable player for Middlesex. In 1928 he again scored two centuries in a match for Lancashire, against the bowling of Ted MacDonald. The previous winter Lee had coached with MacDonald in South Africa, who had commented to him that all southerners were yellow when it came to playing fast bowling.

During the summer of 1920 Lee had been invited by the Wanderers Club to spend the forthcoming winter as their professional. He also went out to South Africa to coach in the winters from 1926 to 1928. In 1930–31 he went to Grahamstown as coach at St Andrew's College and Rhodes University. The MCC toured South Africa that winter under the captaincy of Percy Chapman. Sandham was injured in a motor accident, and at various other times Chapman, Allom, Hammond, Hendren, Duckworth and Tate were all injured. Chapman asked Lee if it would be possible for him to gain leave from his coaching duties to join the touring party as cover. Lee made the request, and believed he had the assent of his employers. He played in three matches for the MCC and also played in the fourth test.

While he was playing for the MCC, however, Grahamstown wrote to the MCC complaining that Lee had not sought permission from them; upon return from South Africa he was summoned to Lord's and accused of breaking his contract with Grahamstown. Lee explained that the sportsmaster at Grahamstown had told J.C. White, vice-captain of the touring party, that he had full permission to join the MCC tour. Lee was told that he would have to write an apology to Grahamstown. Lee replied that he had nothing to apologise for. He was informed that he would not be given his England cap or blazer until he had apologised. Lee never did, and wrote of his missing clothing, "I didn't deserve them, but they would have been nice souvenirs." It is an odd quirk of England's test history that Alan Jones, who did not play test cricket, was given a test cap and blazer, whereas Lee, who did play, was not.

It was not the first time Lee had been summoned to a committee meeting at Lord's. In 1923 in the match against Kent, a ball from Collins had clipped the edge of Lee's stumps, dislodging a bail from its groove. As the bail had not fallen Lee was given not out. That winter he was called before a meeting at Lord's with Lord Harris in the chair. Lee describes the experience in his autobiography. Having just explained to his Lordship what had happened, he was then asked what he thought of it:

"'Well sir, as a batsman, I was glad I wasn't out. But as a bowler, I think I should have been out.'

'You seem to want to have it both ways,' said Lord Harris in a dis-satisfied voice.

I was by this time feeling as if the prison gates yawned. But Mr Webbe came gallantly to my rescue.

'That's a very good answer,' he said. 'I see exactly what you mean Harry.'

Lord Harris's eyebrows rose as dangerously as a short bumper on a fast wicket.

'Harry?' he said. '*Harry?*'

'Why yes,' said Mr Webbe. 'Harry's one of our men.'

'Very well,' said Lord Harris, who seemed to feel that discipline had been strained to its limits. 'Very well, *Lee,* that will do.'

I went thankfully. I neither knew why I had been sent for, nor what would be the result of the interview. But the next season a note was added to law 21 which said, 'the striker would be out under this law if any part of either bail is "struck off" the top of the wicket.'"

First-Class:

| Matches | Inns | NO | Runs | HS | Aver | 100 |
|---|---|---|---|---|---|---|
| 435 | 720 | 49 | 20007 | 2438 | 29.81 | 37 |

| Wkts | Average | SR | Best | 10wm | 5wi | ct |
|---|---|---|---|---|---|---|
| 390 | 31.02 | 68 | 8-39 | 3 | 12 | 179 |

Players: 1 appearance

| Inns | NO | Runs | HS | Aver | O | M | R | W | Aver | BB |
|---|---|---|---|---|---|---|---|---|---|---|
| 1 | 0 | 56 | 56 | 56.00 | 3 | 0 | 25 | 1 | 25.00 | 1-25 |

# 21   J. Arnold (Hampshire)

Born: 30 November 1907, Cowley, Oxfordshire. Died: 4 April, 1984
1st Test, 1931 v New Zealand
Batting: 1st Inns: (No 2)   0   2nd Inns: (No 2)   34

In 1929 Johnny Arnold scored 650 runs at an average of 53 for Oxfordshire. His 62 not out, in the Minor Counties Challenge match, described
by *Wisden* as a "splendid innings", helped to secure the minor counties
championship for Oxfordshire. Though not yet qualified for county
championship matches, he played that season for Hampshire against the
South Africans. In 1930 he became a regular member of the side once
his qualification period had been served, which had prevented him from
appearing in the first five matches. Despite missing these games, he
completed a thousand runs in the season, ending with 1,186 runs at 32.
In their review of the season *The Cricketer* said, "Hampshire cricket had
no more hopeful feature than the pronounced success of Arnold [...] a
really fine batsman with plenty of strokes. Sending him in regularly to
open the innings in company with Brown might have had the result of
cramping his naturally free style but, happily, he possesses an excellent
temperament for a batsman and when necessary can graft for his runs."
   The balance between attack and defence was always an intriguing one
with Arnold. A natural attacking batsman, he would often fall back on
defence if feeling unsure or out of touch. Perhaps his style was not helped
by the fact that he had been converted from a middle-order batsman to
an opener early in his career. As a guide, it is possible to divide Arnold's
batting style into three general periods – as outlined in *Hampshire County
Cricket: the Official History* by Altham *et al*: "At first he was a fine
punishing player, outstanding for his hooking, but good all round the
wicket; he then fell onto defence, partly in response to the team's
needs and then finally, he returned to some brilliant and militant stroke
play."
   At his best Arnold was a fine attacking player, always a good hooker
and, increasingly, a fine driver of the ball through cover. He was confident against quick bowlers, being particularly partial to inswing bowling,
but he was at his best against the spinners, quick on his feet and eager
to attack them and merciless on anything short. He possessed the full
range of attacking strokes and for this reason he was sometimes criticized
for seeming too eager to fall back upon what was admittedly a sound
defence. Considering this matter, *The Cricketer* commented, "Under
average height and of sturdy physique, he is not unlike Bradman in
technique, and nature undoubtedly intended him to be an aggressive
batsman. Therefore, if his play is open to any criticism it is, perhaps, that

he occasionally falls back unnecessarily on defensive methods when his ability to attack would stand his side in better stead."

He was a first-rate outfielder, quick to the ball with a safe pair of hands and with a good throwing-arm. Such quickness could be expected in someone who made a professional football career as a winger.

For many years England's opening batsmen had been Hobbs and Sutcliffe. Thirty-eight times they had opened England's innings together, fifteen times hoisting a century partnership and averaging 88 for their partnership. But Hobbs retired from test cricket at the end of the 1930 season. So the English selectors were looking for at least one new opening bat. The tourists in 1931 were New Zealand, who were scheduled to play a test match against England at Lord's at the end of June. Had the opponents been Australia the experience of Holmes or Sandham might have been called upon, or Douglas Jardine could have been moved up the order. But test matches against the lesser sides were often used to try out players who might serve England well in Ashes matches.

In striving for new, young, opening batsmen the selectors were not presented with a wealth of options. Indeed there were almost as many of the regular county openers in that early part of the season in their forties as were in their twenties. There were only seven of the latter.

Arnold's twenty-three year-old opening partner, Jim Bailey, was to play 48 completed innings that season yet fail to make a thousand runs, averaging less than twenty. A.H. Dyson of Glamorgan, two years older, did manage a thousand runs in the season, but with a top score of 77 and an average of 21. Worcestershire's Wright was twenty-eight and so not really qualifying as new young blood. He had made two centuries the previous season – although averaging only 23 – but in 1931 was so lacking in form that he failed even to make the season's averages published by *Wisden*. That required an average of 10, which was managed by 226 cricketers. His county championship average was 9.77 from 14 matches. At Sussex, John Langridge, twenty-one, was to score 874 runs at 22.

Opening for Essex was the twenty year-old Dudley Pope. Having played for Gloucestershire from 1925 to 1927, he appeared for Essex in 1930. That season he made a thousand runs with figures similar to Arnold's – he had one more completed innings, and 47 more runs. In 1931 his form fell away as he failed to reach a thousand runs, averaging under 22 from his 45 completed innings. He died in a car crash in the autumn of 1934, aged twenty-five. That season he had scored 1,640 runs at 34, with four centuries.

At Derbyshire the twenty-four year old Denis Smith was opening the innings. A tall and elegant left hander, he had made his debut four years before, and in the previous season had made 83 and 107 against Nottinghamshire at Trent Bridge, and in the next match made 107 at the Oval in Derbyshire's first victory over Surrey for twenty-six years. That season he narrowly missed a thousand runs, making 975 at 29.54, whereas Bakewell made 1,701 at 35.43 and Arnold 1,186 at 32. At the beginning of the season he must have been considered a strong contender for the place Arnold eventually gained, but his start to the season was erratic. Of the seventeen innings he played before the test, in eight of them he was dismissed for less than 14 yet twice he scored centuries. His record, 584 runs at 39, though good, could not match Arnold's 833 runs at 49. He was to receive test recognition in 1935 when he played two tests against South Africa, one of thirteen Smiths to play for England.

The other young opener selected in the party was Northamptonshire's Fred Bakewell, an attacking bat who had made a thousand runs in each of his full seasons to date. He had begun 1931 well, scoring 109 in the first innings of Northamptonshire's match against the New Zealanders and carrying his bat for 83 in the second. He entered the test averaging 52 for the season.

Sutcliffe was also selected, subject to his fitness, for he was troubled by a leg strain. If Sutcliffe had not been sufficiently fit Frank Woolley was to have taken his place. It was in this respect that probably the most significant decision regarding Arnold's test future was made, and it was made not by the England selectors but by the Yorkshire captain.

In the match immediately prior to the test Yorkshire played Hampshire at Portsmouth, in which Sutcliffe scored his fifth century of the season. His innings included eleven fours and a six and his century, out of 166, came up in less than three hours. Immediately after this innings Frank Greenwood, the Yorkshire captain, sent a telegram to Lord's saying: "Sutcliffe's leg definitely not fit; although played brilliantly was conscious of strain. I suggest leave definite decision until later after fielding." Later that day the selectors sent Sutcliffe a telegram saying "Most sincerely regret, but as your strain is not quite recovered, the committee is unable to play you on Saturday." Sutcliffe was disappointed at the selectors' decision and wrote to Plum Warner, chairman of selectors, expressing his regret that more time had not been allowed him before the decision was made.

Woolley played and, coming in at 62-4, scored 80 to help put the English innings back on track. Centuries by numbers seven and nine, Les Ames and Gubby Allen, who put on 246 for the eighth wicket, took England to 454 and a lead of 230. But New Zealand made 469-9 in their second innings and that allowed them to make a token declaration, setting England 240 in 140 minutes. Sutcliffe, meanwhile, was playing for Yorkshire against a Woolley-less Kent, where he scored a double-century in five hours.

It had originally been arranged that the Lord's match should be the sole test on the tour, but the New Zealanders' form, and their performance at Lord's, caused a change in the itinerary. Two more test matches were scheduled for the Oval and Old Trafford in place of their matches with Surrey and their second match with Lancashire.

After his first innings' performance Woolley had to be retained for the second test, and Sutcliffe, who was the established opener, and was fit and in form, was recalled. This left only one vacancy for an opener. Neither Arnold nor Bakewell had had a successful test, although in the second innings they had put on 62. Arnold, who had not played at Lord's before, had been well caught at short leg to record a duck in his first innings, and in the second had made 34. Bakewell made 9 and 27 and it was he who was retained for the next test. Batting well, he was on 40 when he allowed himself to be run out in favour of Sutcliffe. He was dropped for the next test, Eddie Paynter receiving his debut. After the test match Arnold's form for the remainder of the season tailed off, and he became overly defensive.

Over the next twenty years he became a most dependable county batsman, heading Hampshire's averages in 1930, 1932, 1937, 1939, 1946, 1947 and 1950. In the seasons from 1930 to 1937 he reached a thousand runs, scoring seven centuries in 1934, reaching 2,261 runs at an average of 48.

In 1938, although winning nine matches, their best record since 1926, Hampshire lost more matches than any county bar Northamptonshire, and for the second year in succession finished 14th. They fell away in August. In their last seven matches they were dismissed four times for double figures; of the final nine games, seven were lost. *The Cricketer* reported, "Hampshire suffered to an extent almost impossible to calculate by the astonishing decline of Arnold. A few seasons previously, Arnold opened the England innings in a test match; last summer he could not hold a regular place in the county side. In his most successful years, Arnold concentrated mainly on driving, but in 1938 he appeared to rely chiefly on deflections to leg and through the slips. Against a swinging or turning ball, the slightest error in this type of play generally brought disaster."

Arnold managed only three half-centuries and no full centuries in 41 innings, and his average dropped to 21 as, for the first time in a full season, he failed to reach a thousand runs. The county caused a big stir when, early in September, they announced that he would not be re-engaged. Soon afterwards Herman, the fast bowler, signed a contract to play for a league club for the next two years and Hampshire, on reviewing their financial position, found it possible to retain Arnold's services.

It seems daft that county committees are so keen to sack players after one poor season. Good players rarely become bad ones overnight and, as no one bar the mediocre can play to the top of their game every season, there is even a case after an atypical poor season for keeping players on, since they will have got the bad season out of their system.

Such proved to be the case with Arnold. In 1939 he continued where he left off in 1937, scoring 1,467 runs at 34, including three centuries. When play resumed after the war he again picked up where he left off, scoring a thousand runs in each of the seasons until his retirement in 1950. In 1961 he was appointed a first-class umpire.

Arnold had the distinction of being a one-cap wonder in two sports. After performing well in an England soccer trial he was selected to play against Scotland at Hampden Park in 1933. England lost 2-1. He was a mobile and assertive outside right. His football career had begun at non-league Oxford City before joining Southampton in 1928 for whom he played 120 games in five years, scoring 47 goals. In 1933 he joined Fulham, along with Mike Keeping, for a club record fee of £5,110. He helped Fulham to the FA Cup Final in 1936 and made his last appearance for them in 1945.

Altham *et al*, in *Hampshire County Cricket: the Official History,* argued that perhaps Arnold was chosen for England too soon. *Wisden,* however, wrote of Arnold's "ill luck to be chosen by the selectors, faced with a difficult situation, for a task for which neither then nor later was he really suited."

Clearly timing is the determining factor in some players becoming test players; for others it dictates the length of their career.

For some, early selection may be a hindrance to establishing a test career. Picked before they have reached their full potential, these players are often labelled as not being test class – they've been tried and found wanting – and are later ignored, despite their potential ability, at this stage, to justify a test place. This is particularly so with batsmen, picked in their mid-twenties, and ignored by the time they reach their peak, often reached by batsmen in their early thirties. Such an instance is perhaps another Hampshire opener, Chris Smith. Picked when 24, he played in seven of the next eight tests, averaging 32.54, a steady rather than a compelling average. Two years later, in 1986, he was a late call-up to a team riddled with injuries, and that was the end of his test career. Yet, later, he was batting better than he had ever before; in the next five seasons he scored nineteen centuries and averaged 49 over this period. He was hardly even mentioned as a possible inclusion in the test side – after all, he'd already had his chance and proved to be not quite good enough, hadn't he?

However, some players have to be picked early if they are to be selected at all. In a career so short it is hard to pack in both success and failure in any great amount, so one aspect can predominate purely as a reflection of the limited sample of the individual's performance. At such an early stage a few good performances will not have been outweighed by a few poor ones, and vice versa. This perhaps explains why some great white hopes fall by the wayside, with people muttering about 'failure to fulfil their promise'. Perhaps this promise, all along, was merely illusory.

Arnold's career shows that he was likely to be selected earlier rather than later in his career; and that whenever he was selected, although not blatantly out of his depth, he would never have achieved much of a run in the team. As such he may feel grateful that selection came when it did; it probably would not have come otherwise.

First-Class:

| Matches | Inns | NO | Runs | HS | Aver | 100 |
|---|---|---|---|---|---|---|
| 402 | 710 | 45 | 21831 | 227 | 32.82 | 37 |

| Wkts | Average | SR | Best | 10wm | 5wi | ct |
|---|---|---|---|---|---|---|
| 17 | 69.52 | 90 | 3-34 | – | – | 184 |

Gents: 5 appearances

| Inns | NO | Runs | HS | Aver | 100 |
|---|---|---|---|---|---|
| 7 | 0 | 201 | 125 | 28.7 | 1 |

# 22   C.S. Marriott (Kent)

Born: 14 September,1895, Heaton Moor, Lancashire. Died: 13 October, 1966
3rd Test, 1933 v. West Indies
Batting:   1st Inns: (No.11)   0
Bowling: 1st Inns: 11.5-2-37-5    2nd Inns: 29.2-6-59-6

'Father' Marriott was a leg break bowler who bowled at almost medium pace. Only for a brief period in his career did he employ the googly: normally he relied for variation on a top spinner and off break. He would run in at an angle and bowl with a high action, bringing his long arms from behind his back; his loose arm would swing behind his back hitting it so that the batsman heard the slap, and the spin was imparted by his long fingers. He maintained a tight accuracy through many variations of pace and flight.

In the words of a *Cricketer* portrait: "Marriott's cricket ends with his bowling, for he is a most indifferent fieldsman and an exceedingly poor batsman. He does not seem to know the first principles of fielding, but snatches and 'jabs' at the ball." His team-mate 'Hopper' Levett recalled that "he added a lot of fun to the proceedings because he was a terrible fielder and if the ball was hit in the air Percy Chapman would shout 'Get out of the way Father,' and name one of us to take the catch."

Cricket possesses the rare quality that its practitioners – often its most successful ones – can be highly skilled in one area and inept in many others, and will demonstrate this regularly. It is impossible to imagine a Ryder Cup golfer being a good driver but absolutely hopeless at putting; other sports allow for players who don't possess all the skills of the game – few in a rugby fifteen are capable of converting a try from over towards the touchline, and a prop forward would almost certainly be incapable of outpacing his opponents in a seventy-yard sprint to the touchline. Such is the pattern of play that they are not required to. Cricket, however, requires all of its participants both to bat and to field.

Marriott was second in a line of Kent bowlers notable for their lack of success with the bat. In 1879 James Bray made his debut for the county. In his 37 innings for them he never made it into double figures, ending with an average of 2.74. After Marriott – 105 innings, highest 21, average 5.24 – there was a hiatus until 1962. That was the year John Dye made his debut. His Kent career was to give him the same average as Marriott, although his top score was a full six runs higher, and was unbeaten. John Graham made his debut two years later, and gave the Kent team a bit of a tail as his average from his 175 innings was 3.88, with a highest innings of 23. Overlapping with John Graham's career was that of Kevin Jarvis who, in 105 innings, garnered 356 runs for the county at 4.81.

But Marriott's batting could have its moments, successful as well as farcical. The writer, and Somerset opening bowler, Robertson-Glasgow recalled that "once but overwhelming, I said to him down the pitch. 'Father, I am going to bowl down your stumps.' He hit the next ball clean out of the ground."

Though born in Lancashire, Marriott was brought up in Ireland and the first county game he saw was when he made his debut for Lancashire in 1919 against Essex. That season he took 26 wickets at an average of 26. The following year he went up to Cambridge and headed the university's bowling averages with 50 wickets at 13.58. The year following, he also topped the university bowling averages, with 57 wickets at 18, and his 5-44 and 2-67 in the Varsity match contributed towards Cambridge's innings victory. He also took 5-38 and 3-57 when the university beat Yorkshire by 123 runs, and he was selected for the Gentlemen at Lord's, taking 5-76. He was picked in the party for the Old Trafford test, but did not make the final eleven.

After graduation he went to Dulwich College as master in charge of cricket and qualified for Kent through residence. He was to play for them in the school holidays. In 1924 he headed Kent's averages with 43 wickets at 14. His best performance was against the county of his birth when he took 5-31 and 6-48. In 1924–25, he toured South Africa with Joel's team but only played one representative match, taking 2-76, although in all matches his figures were 43 wickets at 18.65. And in 1925, for Kent, he took 43 wickets at 18.65, with a best of 11-116 against Hampshire at Canterbury.

There then followed several seasons of consistent accomplishment. In 1926 he took 30 wickets at 29; in 1927, 16 at 24; in 1928, 53 at 20. A hiccup followed in 1929, when he took 20 wickets at 41.70, and he did not play at all the following year. But then, in 1931, he bounced back with 76 wickets at 14.61, and was selected for the Gents at Lord's. On the soft pitches that predominated that summer he dominated the batsmen, never once failing to take at least two wickets in an innings. In nine championship games he took 61 wickets at 15, with a best match return of 10-115 against Nottinghamshire, including a second innings haul of 7-67.

In 1932 he captured 63 wickets at 17.19 and in 1933 he had another prosperous late summer taking 4-87 in the Players' first innings at Lord's. He was selected for the final test of the summer.

For the first time in an Oval test there was no one from Surrey representing England, but the crowd found a new hero in Marriott. He bowled England to victory, with the West Indian batsmen showing an inability to deal with leg spin, a recurring aspect of their test history. Marriott's first innings capture of 5-37 was attributed by *Wisden* to "clever flighting of the ball, perfect length and spin." Of his second innings return of 6-59 *Wisden* wrote that "Marriott disguised his spin very well and never made the ball break too much." England won probably just in time, as heavy rain began to fall five minutes after the match ended, ten minutes into the final day.

Marriott's test return is by far the best by a one test wonder from any country. Indeed, only four bowlers have been more successful on debut. In 1924–25 the Australian Clarrie Grimett took 11-82 against England at Sydney. At Lord's in 1972 the Australian Bob Massie took 16-137 with his swing and, at Madras, on a pitch prepared in favour of spin, the Indian leg spinner Hirwani returned figures of 16-136 in 1987–88. Although Grimett went on to a long and successful test career, Massie managed only another five tests and by the end of the 1998–99 season Hirwani had gained only another 16 caps.

The most successful English bowler on his test debut was Frederick Martin. Like Marriott, he played for Kent and bowled spin at almost medium pace, although in his case left-handed. He was selected for the second and final test of 1890. He was not the first choice, but Yorkshire would not release their left-arm spinner, Peel, for the match and Briggs, the Lancashire left-arm spinner, was unavailable through illness. On a rain-affected pitch Martin took 6-50 and 6-52, as England won by two wickets. That winter England sent two touring teams abroad, to Australia and South Africa, and contested two series simultaneously. Martin went to South Africa, and played in the only test of the tour. South Africa were bowled out for 97 and 83. Martin did not bowl in the first innings and took 2-39 in the second. He never played test cricket again. J.J. Ferris took 6-54 and 7-37 on his English test debut against South Africa in 1891–92, but he had already played in eight tests for Australia.

Of one test wonders, only five have taken as many as six wickets in their test. In addition to Englishmen, Carr and Warren, there are the

Australians Callen and L.J. Johnson, and the South African, Ashley.

Ashley played in the second test of South Africa's first, two test, series. He took 7-95 with his left armers, bowling 43.1 of the 123.1 overs, to dismiss England for 292; South Africa in reply made 47 and 43. The next time South Africa played a test match was seven years later. Leonard Johnson played against India at Melbourne in 1947–48, taking 3-66 and 3-8, but found that the strength of Australian bowling at the time – Bill Johnston, Lindwall and Miller – hindered any further test appearances. Ian Callen, a right arm fast medium bowler, played for Australia against India in the 5th Test in 1977–78, taking 3-83 and 3-108. He went to the West Indies on the tour beginning later that month, where back injuries limited him to eleven wickets at over 50 each, and Pakistan in 1982-83 when he played in only two of the nine games.

After his successful test debut, Marriott was picked for that winter's tour to India. Also in the party, in addition to Hedley Verity, were two spinning all-rounders, Townsend and Langridge. Marriott played in only three of the seven matches leading up to the first test. In the opening match of the tour he took 1-44 and 1-52; in the third he took 0-86 and in the seventh 1-19 and 1-44. The English spin attack for the first test, won by nine wickets, was Verity, Langridge and Townsend. England's opening bowlers were Clark and Nichols and this attack remained in place for all three tests. Townsend took only two wickets in the tests, although he topped the first-class bowling averages with 43 wickets at 14.13, and did not play test cricket again after this tour. Marriott only really found form after the second test when, in the two first-class games he played between the second and third tests, he took 6-35 and 1-50 against Central Province and Barar and 3-35 and 5-43 against Madras, including a hat trick, and he came in last in the tour averages amongst the regular bowlers.

Marriott played his last first-class game in 1937, and *The Cricketer* mourned his retirement saying it would "bring a pang because the eccentricity of his batting and the superb skill of his curiously distinctive bowling will provide happy memories."

First-Class:

| Matches | Inns | NO | Runs | HS | Aver |
|---------|------|-----|------|-----|------|
| 159 | 178 | 48 | 574 | 21 | 8.72 |

| Wkts | Average | SR | Best | 10wm | 5wi | ct |
|------|---------|-----|------|------|-----|-----|
| 711 | 20.11 | 52 | 8-98 | 10 | 48 | 47 |

Gentlemen: 4 appearances

| Inns | NO | Runs | HS | Aver | O | M | R | W | Aver | BB |
|------|-----|------|------|------|-------|-----|-----|-----|-------|------|
| 7 | 4 | 15 | 7no | 5.00 | 107.4 | 28 | 240 | 14 | 17.14 | 4-55 |

# 23  W.H.V. Levett (Kent)

Born: 25 January 1908, Goudhurst, Kent. Died: 30 November 1996
2nd Test, 1933–34 v. India
Batting:   1st Inns: (No.7)   5   2nd Inns: (No.4)   2 no
Fielding:  1st Inns: –         2nd Inns: 3ct

It was at prep school that 'Hopper' Levett became intrigued by the art of wicket-keeping, but it was in the boot-room rather than on the playing-fields that he taught himself to keep wicket. His equipment was an old tip-up desk and the gutta percha inside of a deceased golf ball. He would throw the ball against the wall so that it would bounce back off the lid of the desk, providing catches at various angles. He would practise this for hours. Perhaps we should call it 'playing'.

Later, when he was a county and test player, this same activity could have been called practice. But then, to him, it was probably still only playing. He was still using a wall and a golf ball. If he missed a catch he would add an extra dozen to the demand. To Levett there was "a joy in everything you do as a wicket-keeper. It is lovely being there. I saw the best batsmen in the world from a closer view than anyone else ever had. It was a joy to see them get runs. I had a lot of fun." The fun he found could be heard by any spectator, in the way he would roar with delight and laughter when he took a catch.

His father provided encouragement to his wicket-keeping, albeit unwittingly. At the age of eight, Levett was playing for his prep school, Linden Park, in Tunbridge Wells, against the Fathers. His father came in to bat, and Levett was standing up to the Prep school's fiercest quickie; he would continue to stand up to all bar the quickest bowlers throughout his career. He missed the first ball bowled to his father. The second fizzed off the pitch and beat Levett senior's forward stroke as he lifted his heel. Levett junior whipped off the bails. The pleasure that first stumping gave him remained throughout a career packed with more illustrious achievements.

He enjoyed himself on and off the field. His friendly manner enabled him to get onto good terms with most people quickly. A natural chatter-box, he often embarked upon the next sentence before finishing the previous one, and he was also constantly talking to, and encouraging, his bowlers, as all good 'keepers should. Even when driving his car he would often turn around to talk to the passengers in the back seat; on one occasion this caused him to drive off the road and run aground on a pile of sand. Another time the front passenger jerked the steering wheel away from an oncoming bus – Levett was quite unconcerned, and carried on talking.

"Above all, to be acceptable as an amateur in my day, you had to cope well with the cricket and the social pressure. It was no good if you couldn't play after a night out because we worked hard and we enjoyed our night-life. We had our own Kent festival at Folkestone and I can remember coming down to play there with Wally Hammond for two years in succession after burning the candle at both ends in the Scarborough Festival. We arrived in the middle of the night and, in both years, we lost the toss and I had to keep wicket all day."

One famous story about 'Hopper' Levett suggests that sometimes evenings could encroach on the activities of the day. One morning-after-the-night-before he remained totally motionless as the first ball of the morning whistled past him for four byes. The next ball was deflected by the batsman down the leg side and Levett dived and came up with it victoriously, "Not bad for the first ball of the day, eh?"

Another oft-told story is from the game against the Australians in 1938. With the Australians needing only 7 to win in their second innings, Levett opened the bowling and substituted a bun for the ball.

As a schoolboy he kept wicket for the Public Schools XV against the Australians at Lord's in 1926. His first match for Kent was in 1930, against Worcestershire. He dropped the opening bat, Fox, off Freeman. Fox went forward and edged the ball: it hit Levett's gloves but he dropped it. "I had followed it instead of going with it, and it went down. At the end of the over 'Tich' said to me 'Young man if you do that sort of thing you won't stay long in the game.' But I don't think it does to start too well. You can only get better."

Of his second game for Kent *Wisden* declared that "he acquitted himself brilliantly" in stumping five batsmen and catching three more.

When he first played for Kent, Frank Woolley stood at first slip. Players were given half a crown for each catch, and Woolley had strong words with Levett when, in his enthusiasm, the wicket-keeper dived across and took a catch that Woolley considered his own.

At first Levett took his time to get fully embedded at Kent. Michael Marshall quotes him in *Gentlemen & Players*: "Kent was, and is, a very social county. So when I was first brought into the side, I was quickly made aware that, as a farmer's son, I wasn't regarded in the same light as the Oxbridge Blues. They were all seen as safe to put on the High Sheriff's table whereas, I suppose, they regarded me as a bit rough and ready – amateur though I was. My first captain, Geoffrey Legge, hardly said a word to me and, as for the committee, I knew that several of them would like to get me out of the side and replaced by a certain university blue whose parents were likely to give some stylish entertainment. I told some of those same committee people, years later, that it was precisely because I knew that was how they felt I worked like mad to keep my place in the side whenever Ames was away."

Levett's performances led to him being picked as the Gentlemen's wicket-keeper in 1931, with Ames 'keeping for the Players. He 'kept for them on six occasions. It is a quirk of this period that probably the four best wicket-keepers were spread over two counties. Kent had Ames and Levett, and Lancashire had Duckworth and Farrimond. Of the 61 tests England played from the seasons of 1930–38, there were only four matches in which one of this quartet did not keep wicket.

Two of these tests were in 1938 when Price and Wood 'kept. The other exception is on the tour to India in 1933–34. There had been two previous attempts to stage an Anglo-Indian test series in India. The first in 1930–31 was cancelled because of the civil disobedience campaign and the second, 1931–32, because of threatened boycotts of all matches played in Bombay.

Apart from the captain, Douglas Jardine, only Verity from the previous year's bodyline tour was selected. It was not until 1981–82, for various reasons, that England sent a full strength side to India. Shortly after the party was announced the MCC received a cable from India informing them that "selection of such a team is a disgusting insult to India. Will recommend tour be cancelled unless more stars added." But before another international storm could brew, it was discovered that the cable had been sent by a clerk at the Indian telegraph office.

It was not a happy tour for Levett, who saw Derbyshire's Harry Elliott keep wicket for the first and third tests. Mihir Bose quotes him in his history of Indian cricket: "Jardine didn't make life easy for me. If I had been to a university and got a blue he would probably have treated me differently. I had not been to Eton or Harrow. I rather felt he was a snob, one of those old la-di-dah, aloof men who preferred people who had been to university. [...] After the war at the Oval during test matches on a couple of occasions when I was there he came to me. No one else seemed to want to know much of him; he asked me if I would come and sit at the top of the stands and talk with him. I always thought he had done me wrong in India. It was his way of saying sorry."

Wicket-keepers are obviously the most vulnerable to competition from others' talents when it comes to selection. It is theoretically possible to be the second best cricketer the world has ever seen, but still not be good enough to play for one's country.

When Bob Taylor retired, only a couple of dozen Englishmen had played in more than his 57 tests. But had he retired aged 36, not an absurd age to contemplate retirement, he too would have been a one test wonder, from a cap gained seven years before. A superb wicket-keeper, he was a contemporary of Alan Knott, another excellent wicket-keeper and an impish, highly competent, batsman. Like Levett, Taylor's cap had also come from playing in a deliberately weakened England side. In Taylor's case his cap had been awarded as a reward for being a good tourist, with Alan Knott stepping down for the first test against New Zealand, which formed the second leg of the 1970–71 tour. The first leg had been a victorious six-match Ashes series in Australia.

For Levett, Ames was always there, with Kent and for England. Despite offers from other counties, Levett remained with Kent playing cricket wherever it was available, whether for county, select sides, second XI or club and country house cricket. For him the fun was in the cricket itself not the status of the cricket. Of his 175 matches, 142 were for his county.

In Levett's case competition for the national wicket-keeping berth came not only from the batsman-keeper Ames, but also from the Lancashire pair. Lancashire had provided both the wicket-keepers on the tour to South Africa in 1930–31. When England toured Australia in 1932–33 and 1936–37, Duckworth went as Ames' deputy. In the West Indies in 1934–35 Farrimond toured as the reserve wicket-keeper.

In 1938–39 England sent two batsman wicket-keepers to South Africa, the second of the pair being Paul Gibb, not remotely in Levett's class with the gloves. *The Cricketer* wrote in 1938 of Levett that "though occasionally prone to the dramatic, he showed he had no superior in the country, and may feel justifiably aggrieved at not receiving national recognition when Ames was injured. The selectors were, no doubt, bent on maintaining the batting strength of England, which furnishes the explanation." Levett's batting was based on a sound defence. He was in the ability range of a competent tail-ender, though his facility against fast bowling sometimes lead to him opening the innings. From such a position he made 66 in a Folkestone festival game, only ten short of his best ever score.

Despite Ames' presence, Levett often played for Kent, frequently in the same side as Ames. Normally in these circumstances it was Levett who would 'keep, especially as an injury hindered Ames' 'keeping which resulted in him 'keeping little for Kent at various times. Three times in championship matches in 1939, Levett, Godfrey Evans and Les Ames were all on the same side, with Levett keeping wicket. Evans had joined Kent as a batsman, keen to be a wicket-keeper, and he has said that he owed more to Levett than any other person for the encouragement and advice he gave. When they played together in the second eleven, Levett would give Evans the gloves for one of the innings.

Like his father, Levett was a hop and fruit farmer: hence the nickname. He was President of Kent in 1974–75, and a keen supporter of the county throughout his cricketing retirement.

First-Class:

| Matches | Inns | NO | Runs | HS | Aver |
|---|---|---|---|---|---|
| 175 | 264 | 58 | 2524 | 76 | 12.25 |

| Wkts | Average | SR | Best | 10wm | 5wi | ct | st |
|---|---|---|---|---|---|---|---|
| 0 | – | – | – | – | – | 283 | 195 |

Gents: 6 appearances

| Inns | NO | Runs | HS | Aver | ct | st |
|---|---|---|---|---|---|---|
| 8 | 4 | 63 | 13 | 15.75 | 8 | 6 |

# 24   N.S. Mitchell-Innes (Somerset)

Born: 7 September 1914, Calcutta, India
1st Test, 1935 v. South Africa
Batting: 1st Inns: (No 4)   5

Test cricketers are often flawed physical specimens. Many have poor eyesight, including the man who holds the world and test records for the highest innings – as one opponent once said, "God help us if Brian Lara ever gets to see the ball properly." Don Bradman also suffered at times in his career from eyesight and back problems. These two ailments led to him being discharged from the army as a semi-invalid. Recent England captains have included the epileptic Tony Greig and another who as a teenager was advised to give up sport because of his asthma. He was told, however, that asthma can be cured by avoiding that which sets off the allergy. Tests by a respiratory specialist showed that in this particular case it was grass and exercise. Ian Botham has managed quite well despite this handicap. But for Norman Mitchell-Innes, his allergy – hay fever – was the cause of the end of his test career. No cure for his ailment was ever found despite his county, Somerset, offering a large reward for one.

Norman Mitchell-Innes was a fine all-round sportsman. At Sedburgh, as well as captaining the cricket side, he represented the school at rugby and fives. At Oxford he won his cricket blue whilst a Freshman and secured a blue for golf as well. In the 1935 Varsity match he beat his opponent 12 and 10. In 1931 he captained the Scottish Boys at golf against the English Boys.

He made his debut for Somerset aged sixteen. His batting prowess had probably been drawn to Somerset's atten tion through one of the masters at Sedburgh who was a friend of the Somerset captain. At the end of the school term Mitchell-Innes went on a cricket tour to Durham, and when this had finished he had gone on to play in the Boys Golf Championship in Scotland. This Somerset discovered when they telephoned his father with an invitation for his son to play for them. "Well then, tell us when he has been knocked out." This happened on the Thursday. On Friday he was on the course watching when a telegram delivery-boy appeared on a bike. He was to play against Warwickshire at Taunton the next day. He caught the night train but fortunately did not have to bat until the Monday, when he scored 73.

He made a century on his first appearance for Oxford University, scoring 107 against Gloucestershire. He also scored centuries that season for Oxford against Surrey, 171, and against the Minor Counties, 140, and in 21 innings for the university he scored 998 runs at 55.44 to top their averages.

The next year he made three centuries for the university. One of them, his 168 not out against the touring South Africans, was watched by the Chairman of Selectors, Plum Warner. *The Cricketer* of 25 May, edited by Warner, wrote, "Another young cricketer of promise is Mitchell-Innes of Oxford. His batting is founded on the soundest lines, and already he has made two hundreds for the Varsity, against Lancashire and the South Africans. His innings versus the South Africans was a superb display. He is only in his second year at Oxford, but he bats like a seasoned player."

The impression he had made on Warner led to him being selected for the team for the first test despite not having yet made a century for his county.

Batting at number four he played back to Vincent when he should have been forward and fell lbw for 5 in England's total of 384-7 declared. In South Africa's first innings he dropped Wade off Bowes from a difficult chance which went hard and low to his left. Following on, South Africa were 17-1 at the end of the second day and rain washed out the final day.

But Warner kept his faith in Mitchell-Innes for the next test at Lord's. Mitchell-Innes arranged to stay during the match with his friend Errol Holmes, who in *Flannelled Foolishness* described him as "quiet and on the shy side – rather a theorist and an idealist." Others could find him reticent with the appearance of aloofness, but this seems a product of his shyness.

Before the test he was suffering from hay fever and, fearing that he might be a risk, telephoned the chairman of selectors: "I might be sneezing just as a catch comes in the slips ... I, er, feel you ought to know."

He still went to London to stay with Holmes, however, as he had arranged to play for Oxford University against Holmes' county, Surrey. But they were not able to share a cab to the ground as Holmes was called up to replace Mitchell-Innes in the test team. One day during his stay the morning newspaper arrived with, on the front page, a picture of Holmes being presented to the Queen at the test; inside was a report of the undefeated 132 Mitchell-Innes had made at the Oval.

Despite failing in the Varsity match, making 0 and 1, he again topped the university averages with 774 runs at 39 and that season he made his first century for Somerset, compiling a chanceless 139 against Lancashire at Weston-Super-Mare.

In 1936 he was elected captain of Oxford, and again topped the averages with 917 runs at 44. He also bowled more, and with greater success, taking 22 wickets at 26. In the Varsity match, which Oxford lost by 8 wickets he made 43 and 84. He scored a double-century for the university against Leveson-Gower's XI.

By the end of his university career, which came in 1937, he had scored more runs for Oxford than anyone before or since, making 3,319 runs at an average of 47 with nine centuries – a shared record – in 78 innings. After university he joined the Sudan Political Service. When he came back on leave, he played when he could; this was not often and in thirteen seasons he made only 69 appearances for his county. Years later, Somerset, desperately seeking an amateur captain, made him an offer to return with the promise of the Assistant Secretaryship. But Mitchell-Innes wanted £1,000, which was too much. Various people were sounded out at various times, including Trevor Bailey and Richie Benaud, but the county had to appoint professional captains. When they did, results improved.

Mitchell-Innes was appointed Somerset captain in 1948 in a bizarre arrangement which, in their reluctance to appoint a professional captain, the Somerset committee embarked upon whereby Mitchell-Innes captained the side in May, J.W. Seamer in June and part of July, and G.E.S. Woodhouse for the rest of the season. Somerset earned no points in the five matches Mitchell-Innes captained.

A physical imperfection – in his case poor eyesight – also affected the career of New Zealand's most spectacular one test wonder, Rodney Redmond. Picked for the final test against Pakistan in 1972 he watched Pakistan score 402 before it was his turn to open the innings. From shaky beginnings he built an innings full of shots: in one Majid Khan over he hit five fours, and he went from 44 to 86 by way of ten fours and two singles. On 89 a slash at Intikhab sent the ball lobbing up between the bowler and Mushtaq, who left it to each other, and the chance went to ground. On 97 he hit a ball to leg and Asif chased, pulling the ball up just inside the boundary for two. The crowd, thinking the ball had crossed the boundary, invaded the pitch and mobbed the batsman. Eventually the ground was cleared, leaving a blood-spattered batsman – one of the celebrants had accidentally opened up a graze he had incurred fielding. A further delay was required to replace a bail taken by a souvenir hunter. After all these delays the batsman hit the next ball through cover for his nineteenth four. His century had come up in 130 minutes off 110 balls. When he was dismissed for 107, the runs had come from 38 shots, in particular cuts, pulls and drives through cover and mid on. In the second innings he made 56 as New Zealand batted out time.

He was selected to tour England, but by now was having problems with his eyesight. Problems with a contact lens coupled with difficulties adjusting his flashy style to English pitches lead to him being dropped from the first eleven after the one-day internationals. He continued to play domestic first-class cricket in New Zealand, but, aged 31, only three years after playing test cricket, eyesight trouble hastened his retirement.

First-Class:

| Matches | Inns | NO | Runs | HS | Aver | 100 |
|---|---|---|---|---|---|---|
| 132 | 239 | 18 | 6944 | 207 | 31.42 | 13 |

| Wkts | Average | SR | Best | 10wm | 5wi | ct |
|---|---|---|---|---|---|---|
| 82 | 34.70 | 60 | 4-65 | – | – | 152 |

Gents: 4 appearances

| Inns | NO | Runs | HS | Aver |
|---|---|---|---|---|
| 8 | 0 | 156 | 50 | 19.50 |

# 25　*J.C. Clay (Glamorgan)*

Born: 18 March 1898, Bonvilston, Glamorgan. Died: 11 August 1973
5th Test, 1935 v. Australia
Bowling: 1st Inns: 14-1-30-0　2nd Inns: 18-6-45-0

Johnny Clay came from a keen sporting family. His grandfather was an enthusiastic cricket player and promoter, and his house, Piercefold House, was the venue for a match between the United Eleven of All England and the XXII of Chepstow and District, for whom Johnny's brother, Hastings, played. When Johnny began playing for Chepstow at the age of fifteen his uncle was captain, and his father and two cousins were in the team. In 1915 he played for the first eleven at Winchester College as a fast bowler who would bowl leg breaks later in the innings. In the following season he topped the averages with 40 wickets at 10, including 8-86 in the match with Eton.

He left Winchester in 1916 and served in the Royal Fleet Auxiliary. When the war ended he joined his father's coal-exporting company. He continued to play for Chepstow and in 1919 took 62 wickets at 8.77, and scored 564 runs at 56.4. He made 150 against Cardiff Cliftonians. Against Newbury, Chepstow made 60, of which Clay made half, and then, bowling leg breaks, he took six wickets, including the last four for no runs as Chepstow won by eight runs.

Impressive performances for Monmouthshire the following season lead to a trial at the Arms Park. The upshot of this was that he agreed to play for Glamorgan in 1921 if their application to join the county championship were successful. It was, but he was not selected for their inaugural fixture. Instead he went on a tour of South Devon with the Glamorgan Nomads. On this tour he took 6-48 against Chudleigh and made a chanceless 144 with three sixes and 17 fours against Torquay. As a result he was brought into the Glamorgan side on his return. That season he was Glamorgan's third highest wicket-taker with 41, including returns of 5-37 against Derbyshire at Chesterfield and 6-86 at Leicestershire against the host county. He often bowled with hostility, but, as the youngest and fittest bowler was often called on to do much of the bowling, and this led to him reverting to his Winchester method of bowling leg breaks later in the innings.

In 1922 a series of niggling injuries again caused much of his bowling to be of the leg break variety and in 1923, on the advice of the Glamorgan coach, the ex-Worcestershire player Fred Bowley, he experimented with off-spin. When he was able to bowl at his quickest *The Western Mail* reported that he "often beat the batsman for sheer pace." In J.H. Morgan's history *Glamorgan*, written in 1952, he described Clay as Glamorgan's fastest ever bowler.

Clay first took on the captaincy of the county in 1924, holding it until 1927, a period Clay later referred to as 'the rag-time days'. Stories abound concerning Glamorgan during this period. The captain was never sure who was playing and whether they would number eleven in total. There are tales of Cardiff station being trawled for possible players on the morning of the match and the captain asking the senior pro who that fellow fielding at cover was, and the senior pro replying that he had never seen him before in his life. Tony Lewis, a later Glamorgan captain, recounts the story of the coach leaving one day on his way to Midlands with only ten players on board. The coach stopped at a crossroads in Tredegar, picked up a stranger named Jones who played one match, got no runs and did not bowl and was dropped off on the same corner on the way back without anyone knowing his Christian name.

Clay blooded youngsters including an eighteen year-old Maurice Turnbull, who, alongside Clay was to be a dominant figure in Glamorgan cricket. Another, Cyril Walters, was refused entry to the Oval pavilion by a steward who insisted that he was too young to be a county player.

Because of injury, Clay rarely bowled in that 1924 season, and when he did it was as an off break bowler. In the previous winter he had walked around with a small rubber ball which he used to squeeze in his hands to strengthen his fingers. Clay was well equipped as off-spinner. Tall and thin, he had a good control of pace, which allowed him to bowl both a quicker delivery and a well disguised slower ball. He was a master of flight, with a loop that often fooled the batsmen into playing a good-length ball they had expected to be a half volley.

A thoughtful and astute captain, in his first season he led the county to victory in five of their twenty-four matches, and thirteenth place in the championship. As a result of promotion within his father's company, and his engagement, Clay was unable to devote so much time to cricket and so he relinquished the captaincy at the end of the 1927 season.

A hard-hitting late-order batsman, that season he had made his maiden first-class century against the New Zealanders. Coming in at 34-3, in two and a half hours of counter-attack he hit fifteen boundaries,

making an undefeated 115 out of 199. His other first-class century came
in 1929 against Worcestershire at Swansea. Coming in at number ten with
half an hour of the first day's play to go, he made 22 quick runs as he
and Hill added 53. The Swansea wicket was likely to turn, so Clay opted
to continue batting in the morning. The *Western Mail* takes up the story:
"Clay and Hill not merely forced the pace, they drove, punched and carved
the Worcestershire bowling to all parts of St Helen's in such cavalier
fashion that in 65 minutes 150 runs were added to the overnight score.
The Worcestershire bowlers kept pegging away at a good length and it
was the daring of the two batsmen that resulted in many a good ball
being flogged to the boundary. Clay was more venturesome than Hill
and frequently ran two or three yards down the pitch to drive Root on
the half volley. And what glorious shots he made! One straight drive off
Root cleared the Mumbles Road, and landed in the goods yard of the
Swansea Bay Station from where it bounced through an office window."
Clay's century had come in 95 minutes, with four sixes and nine fours.

In 1929 Clay resumed the captaincy, sharing it with Norman Riches.
But injury and illness had prevented Clay from playing more than
fourteen matches, and Riches' commitment to his dental practice meant
he played only eight matches, so nine different people captained
Glamorgan that season. In 1930 Maurice Turnbull, down from Cambridge University, took over the captaincy.

Glamorgan started the 1932 season £4,000 in debt. This led them to
release four professionals, including the spinner Frank Ryan. Ryan could
well have played for England were it not for erratic performances caused
by a fondness for drink. One night, unable to work out where his hotel
had got to, he went to the cricket ground and slept under the covers. In
1931 he and Clay had bowled Glamorgan to victory against Northamptonshire after imaginative captaincy. With no play on the first day,
captains Turnbull and Jupp got together and agreed to end their first
innings on 50, Northants declaring at 51-1 and Glamorgan at 51-2.
Northants were bowled out for 59 in their second innings, with Clay
taking 5-22.

Turnbull had unwittingly broken law 54 which stated that in a two-
day match declarations by the side batting second must come after at
least a hundred minutes' batting. The umpires and captains were unaware
of the infringement until a newspaperman pointed it out after close of
play. The umpires and captains were summoned to Lord's to explain.
Bill Reeves, the cockney umpire, is reported to have said that the rule
did not apply as the game was in a foreign country. Later that season,
Turnbull and the captain of Surrey, Fender, after two washed-out days,
declared their first innings after one ball. Glamorgan won that one too,
but the MCC was unhappy and it was probably reflected in the fact that
Turnbull, Glamorgan's first test player, was not selected for the MCC's
winter tour.

Glamorgan ended the 1932 season £5,000 in debt and the secretary and treasurer resigned. Clay took over the treasurer's position, and Turnbull acted as secretary. Together they set about relieving Glamorgan's financial plight with the promise that "all donations will be returned if it is found impossible to continue first-class cricket in 1933." An appeal was set up with the aim of raising £5,500 to clear liabilities and provide a small working balance for the 1933 season. It raised £2,677 and the committee agreed unanimously "to take the risk of carrying on."

In 1936 Glamorgan were again in financial difficulties and a sub-committee was set up to raise money. Turnbull, Clay, J.M. Bevan, the club president, and Sir William Reardon-Smith, a close friend of Clay's and an influential figure in the Cardiff docks, all served on the committee, donating £200 each of their own money to the cause. The debt was almost all wiped out and Glamorgan could continue as a first-class county club.

Mindful of the need for Glamorgan to be successful on the field to help their off-field financial problems, Clay arranged to play more regularly than usual for Glamorgan in both the seasons following his winter fundraising activities.

In 1933 he played over half of Glamorgan's games. He frequently played when not fully fit, often bowling leg breaks off one pace in these circumstances, and in a weak attack he was also overbowled: 84 overs in the draw against Nottinghamshire, 49 overs in an innings against Northants. He lost much of his potency as a result, taking 59 wickets at 30.

The following season, 1934, he was fully fit and, once again able to devote plenty of time to playing cricket, he topped a hundred wickets in the season for the first time, finishing the season as the leading amateur bowler. He was selected for the Gentlemen of England against Australia but went wicketless in the match. He was not selected in the party for any of the tests, and finished the season with 103 wickets at 17.76. The extent to which the Glamorgan attack relied on him was shown by the averages. Next in averages was Emrys Davies with 39 wickets at 30.15, next highest wicket-taker was Mercer who, in twenty-one matches – Clay played eighteen – took 41 wickets at 40.

Glamorgan won only three games that season. They recorded their first victory at the Oval with Clay taking 6-33 and 6-51. Maintaining a steady length and varying his pace, Clay bowled without a slip but with three men in close on the leg side. In the first innings he bowled 25.1 overs out of 57.1; in the second he bowled throughout. Against Northamptonshire, a game won by Glamorgan by eight wickets, he bowled 73 of the 178.5 overs, taking 5-39 and 6-76. Against Somerset he opened the bowling in Glamorgan's nine wicket victory, taking 5-44 and 5-73, bowling 67.2 of the 162.2 overs.

His form continued into 1935 when he took 30 wickets in his first three matches, his 15-96 against Northants at Llanelli and 10-89 at Leicester, both bringing victories.

He was included in the party for the third and fourth tests, without making the eleven. He disliked missing out on Glamorgan matches only to miss out on playing for England, and was minded to tell the England selectors not to select him in the party for the final test. His family dissuaded him and he was picked in the eleven for the final test. In the test match he bowled a good length and flighted the ball thoughtfully, but on a good wicket he went wicketless as South Africa made 476 and 287-6.

*The Cricketer* of 13 July 1935 had written that: "If any man is entitled to play for England in the third Test Match, surely it is J.C. Clay – not, as some people may suppose, because he has taken some wickets. Oh dear no. Clay has much better qualifications. How could the selectors possibly ignore a man who wrote an article entitled: 'Cricket Made Easy. Read This and Play For England'?

"However, on reading the article, we really wonder if his advice is quite sound. Practice is essential, we all admit, but Clay says, 'if you cannot get enough at your school – change your school. If business prevents it – change your business; if your wife objects to it – change your wife!'"

John Arlott declared that Clay was his favourite cricket writer. A whimsical humour, which enabled him to bowl a rubber ball against an obdurate, boring batsman, also infused his writing. In 1937 he wrote in *The Western Mail,* "One suggestion for brightening up cricket is that the weaker counties should be given a start, as in billiards so that when Glamorgan play Lancashire for example, the Welsh side should receive 150 runs." Two years later in the Glamorgan Yearbook he offered the advice that "should you ever reach the dizzy heights of county cricket always reserve your best efforts for Saturdays. You will then get your name in the papers twice, on Sunday and Monday."

In 1937 he played in twenty-six out of Glamorgan's thirty fixtures. He turned down the honour of representing the Gentlemen in order to be available for Glamorgan. Increased playing resulted in his breaking county bowling records for match return and seasonal wicket total, taking 176 wickets in the season, with a best return of 17-212 against Worcestershire at Cardiff. In this match he put in a two and a half-hour spell in the first innings for a return of 9-66, and, in a bowling attack hampered by injury, bowled 34 overs in the second innings. In the next game he bowled 62 overs against Somerset to return 12-180. Later in the season he took 5-87 to make Essex follow on, and then continued at the bowling crease for three hours in their second innings, taking 9-59 and moving Glamorgan towards their first-ever victory against Essex. In the return match a week later he took 13-133 as Glamorgan recorded their eighth victory of the season, at that stage their best seasonal return.

Clay began the 1938 season with 9-120 against Warwickshire at Edgbaston and 12-147 against Hampshire at Cardiff. As a result of these performances, following his 1937 triumph, the selectors approached him about playing for England. Clay wrote back that he thought they might like to choose someone younger. Nevertheless he was selected, only for him to withdraw with a mild leg injury. Shortly afterwards he wrote in a South Welsh newspaper that "I do not think it fair either to England or Glamorgan that I should risk playing in an important match over four full days when perhaps it would be too much for me."

Of his performances that year *The Cricketer* wrote, "to praise J.C. Clay is to adorn the lily. His dislike of participating in any but county cricket has not prevented his skill with the ball becoming already legendary. In his forty-first year, he has no superior in his type of bowling. A lad modelled on what he does would soon be a candidate for the test honours which he himself repeatedly hoped to evade."

Clay missed a hundred wickets that season by half a dozen. Had he not strained a muscle in his side as he was about to start bowling against Leicestershire, which meant he was unable to bowl in the match and had to miss the remaining couple of fixtures, he would almost certainly have achieved this landmark.

He recovered from this strain, and was able to pursue his winter pursuits of hunting and riding, when he received an invitation to tour with the MCC on their test tour to South Africa. Clay was inclined to accept. However he injured an ankle jumping over a deckchair in his garden, attempting to show his family how Golden Miller had fallen at the first fence of the Grand National. This, and doubts over his side strain lead him to decline the invitation, officially due to pressure of work.

Niggling injuries and business commitments limited Clay to only eight matches in 1939. During the war, in which Clay served in South Wales with the Royal Artillery, Maurice Turnbull was killed. As a result Clay accepted the captaincy of Glamorgan for the 1946 season. During the war Clay had served on an emergency committee set up to keep the county side ticking over and to raise funds for the war effort. Before the 1946 season Clay told a journalist: "we lost everything during the war. We have no records, but we'll get a few lads together and at least we'll turn up for every match."

Glamorgan came sixth in the championship that season, their highest ranking, and their ten victories included their first-ever triumph over Lancashire. Clay wrote later, "After seeing Lancashire's row of nets, their coaches, their numerous staff (the whole of our surplus staff was acting as 12th man and scorer) and comparing them with our makeshift arrangements, I remarked to Wilf Wooller, 'we've got a bloody nerve to come up here and expect to take them on.'"

As captain Clay sought to entertain and play attractive cricket. For this he was censored by the MCC for not acting in the best interests of the game. This was over a declaration in the game with Somerset, where Branwell had declared the Somerset innings on the final day at their overnight 51-1 and Clay did likewise when Glamorgan reached that total. Glamorgan, with Matthews taking 7-12, won by eight wickets. In the match with the Indians, India had made 376-6 before rain intervened in Glamorgan's reply. When play resumed on the last afternoon Glamorgan were bowled out for 149 and India enforced the follow on. Clay was the undefeated batsman, and after consultation with the Indians and the umpires, he agreed to waive the ten-minute interval between innings, and to continue with the same batsmen. Thus Peter Judge faced the first ball of the second innings, to which he was clean bowled, thereby earning a distinction as probably the only player to be dismissed by successive legal deliveries within a minute. The tourists claimed the extra half hour but Glamorgan, batting in reverse order, held on at 73-7. In the second match against the Indians Clay hit 24 (4, 4, 6, 0, 4, 6) off a Mankad over in a match in which he took 7-72 in the Indians' first knock – one of eleven occasions that season he took five wickets in an innings.

This attitude towards spectators, coupled with Glamorgan's successes on the field, with Clay to the fore with 130 wickets, led to a vast upturn in attendance figures. £4,000 had been collected at the gate in 1939; in 1946 it was almost £15,000. Fund-raising schemes enabled Glamorgan to make necessary repairs and improvements to their war-damaged grounds and Glamorgan finished the season in their healthiest financial state. £4,000 in the black, they were able to set up a second eleven and dismiss forever the spectre that the county club might go under.

Having successfully helped to relaunch Glamorgan cricket, Clay resigned the captaincy, saying, "to be captain of a county side is a full-time job and I have many interests and other things to do. There is less need for me to carry on when we have a fully qualified captain in Mr Wooller ready at hand."

In 1947 Clay played only thirteen matches, but came second in the national averages with 65 wickets at 16.44. That season Glamorgan had acquired the former Middlesex spinner Len Muncer who took 107 wickets. With Muncer established, and with another highly rated spinner in Stan Trick on the staff Clay suggested that the younger men should play. As a result, by the middle of August 1948, he had only played in three championship games, plus fixtures against the Combined Services and the Australians.

With three games to go, Glamorgan were in the hunt for the county championship. The first was against Surrey at Cardiff, starting on 18 August, and Clay joined the side, since Watkins was on test duty and Phil Clift was injured. Glamorgan made 239, leaving the visitors an hour's batting at the end of the day. Wooller soon introduced his spinners and by close Surrey were 47-9, Clay having taken three wickets in one over. The following morning he took the final wicket for figures of 5-15 from 8.2 overs. Surrey followed on and Clay took 5-51 in an innings victory within two days. Had Surrey won this game they would have finished the season as county champions.

The team then travelled to Bournemouth knowing that one more victory would bring them the county championship. Most of the first day's play was washed out and Glamorgan were bowled out for 315 by 5.30pm on the second day. Hampshire collapsed that evening and early on the second day Wooller was able to enforce the follow on. Three of the wickets had fallen to Clay in his eleven overs. Glamorgan now had four hours to bowl out Hampshire. With the score at 116-9, Clay came in to bowl the final ball of his twentieth over, having already taken five wickets for 48. The batsman was hit on the pad and Clay turned and appealed to the umpire Dai Davies who replied "he's out and we've won."

Clay led the side off the field with tears in his eyes. As Wooller had to travel to Lord's for a MCC match, Clay took the side back to Glamorgan. Thousands had travelled to greet the team at Cardiff Central and he made an impromptu speech on the platform, paying warm tributes to the cricketers who had played throughout the season. From there the team went off to a celebration at Cardiff Athletic Club which went on long into the night.

Clay, who had topped the national championship averages with 27 wickets at 13.85, declared that Glamorgan's championship was "the greatest thing that has happened to me in my life." Months later he confessed that "it seems I am still in fairyland."

Two more games for Glamorgan that season against the South of England and All England brought him to retirement; a retirement he came out of for one game in 1949 to have a final tilt at Yorkshire, as he had never won against that county. Yorkshire won to achieve a share of the championship with Middlesex.

After retiring from county cricket – he continued to play club cricket – he joined the boards of Wales Gas, a Cardiff High Street arcade company, and Chepstow Racecourse, where a race was held in his honour each year. He also became Chairman of the Park Hotel in Cardiff.

In 1958 he resigned from the Glamorgan committee in protest at the sacking of Wooller as captain. A series of public meetings were held around Glamorgan, Clay saying at one of them that the sacking was "a tragic blunder, made by a committee out of a combination of ignorance and personal prejudice." At a Extraordinary General Meeting the decision was reversed and eleven committee members resigned. Clay served as President from 1960–1963 and was a trustee of the club from 1953 until his death in 1973.

First-Class:

| Matches | Inns | NO | Runs | HS | Aver |
|---------|------|-----|------|-------|-------|
| 373 | 555 | 90 | 7186 | 115no | 15.45 |

| Wkts | Average | SR | Best | 10wm | 5wi | ct |
|------|---------|----|------|------|-----|-----|
| 1317 | 19.76 | 47 | 9-54 | 28 | 105 | 177 |

Gents: 3 appearances

| Inns | NO | Runs | HS | Aver | O | M | R | W | Av | BB |
|------|-----|------|------|-------|-----|----|-----|-----|-------|------|
| 5 | 1 | 61 | 28no | 15.25 | 85 | 14 | 229 | 5 | 45.80 | 2-63 |

# 26  H.D. Read (Essex)

Born: 28 January 1910, Woodford Green, Essex
5th Test, 1935 v. South Africa
Batting:  dnb
Bowling: 1st Inns: 35-13-136-4   2nd Inns: 10-1-64-2

'Hopper' Read's father, A.H. Read, played for Essex from 1904 to 1910. A keen golfer, he moved the family to Englefield Green in Surrey, so enraptured was he by the nearby Sunningdale Golf Course. This qualified his son for Surrey. In 1933 'Hopper' played two games for them against the universities but, carrying an injury, he did not take a wicket in either game. As a schoolboy Read had been unable to get into the Winchester XI. With this history, it is therefore understandable that the Surrey committee raised no objection to him going to play for Essex, the county he was born in, a month later.

It was in 1934 that Read suddenly burst into the public's consciousness as a result of a dramatic week's cricket at Brentwood. In the first game of this week Essex took on Kent, whom they had beaten in the opening game of the season – their only victory to date in eight matches. At the end of the first day of the match the visitors had scored 623 runs. Ashdown and Woolley had put on 352 in just over three hours for the second wicket. Ashdown ended with 332 and Woolley 172 and Ames, coming in at number four, hit 202 not out as Kent declared next day at 803-4. Ashdown's innings was chanceless during his stay of six and a quarter hours but Woolley was missed when on 2 and Ames when on 30. Not since 1899, when Surrey hit 811 at the Oval against Somerset had a first-class match in England produced such an innings total and they had devastated the previous best Kent total which was 621-6 declared, also made against Essex, at Tonbridge in 1922.

Essex went on to lose by an innings and 192 runs. Changes were made to their bowling attack for the next game. Not for the reason one might suspect when an attack had been hit for over eight hundred runs at little cost, but because two of their bowlers were called up for the test trial. To be fair, one of them, Farnes, had not played against Kent. Read, who had been unavailable earlier in the season because he was taking accountancy exams, was brought into the side. Coming in off his long run and bowling with what was described as a 'tearaway' action, he worked up tremendous pace. His first delivery, pitched in the middle of the pitch, removed Hobbs' cap, cleared the wicket-keeper and bounced twice before hitting the sightscreen. The fourth ball flicked the edge of Hobbs' bat and fizzed through the slips to the boundary. Hobbs got an inside edge to the last ball of the over and his off-stump was knocked out. Read, continuing to bowl at great pace, took 7-35, some of the wickets coming as the batsman played too late, five of his victims being bowled. Walking back to the pavilion he smiled modestly in response to the cheering of the crowd. Keen and aggressive on the pitch, off it he was quiet and slightly shy. Essex went on to win the match by an innings and 192, the exact margin of the previous match. That season Read played in fourteen matches for Essex, taking 55 wickets at 20.69.

*The Cricketer* in 1934 called Read "the find of the season." In 1935 he created the sensation of the season in the match against Yorkshire. The season had started quietly for Read. He had not joined Essex until their tenth game, and in that game bowled three wicketless overs in a curtailed match. He missed the next game against Lancashire and returned to the team against Gloucestershire where he performed the hat trick for the only time in his first-class career and took 6-38 in the second innings. He missed the next game, which was against Yorkshire at Colchester, and then took 4-59 and 4-63 in the three-wicket victory over Northamptonshire. He did not play in the next game against Sussex but then played in Essex's next three games, taking ten wickets for 294 runs during the course of them. Essex's game against Yorkshire at Huddersfield was Read's fourth game on the trot for the county.

Yorkshire had not lost since August 1934, and were in the process of winning the championship for the fourth time in five years. By half-past twelve on the first day they had been dismissed for 31: their lowest total for 26 years. Read took his first wicket when he bowled Leyland first ball – as he was to do in the second innings – and in six overs took 6-11. At one stage Yorkshire were 9-6. The story is told of a Yorkshire committeeman arriving late and asking the gateman the score. "'30-9, Sir,' came the reply. '30-9 – hm, not bad, I suppose. How many has Bowes got?' The gateman replied, 'Not many. He's only just come in.'"

In the second innings Read took 3-51, and Nichols, who had taken 4-17 in ten first-innings overs, took 7-37 as Yorkshire were bowled out for 99 to lose by an innings and 204 runs.

In the next match against Worcestershire few of the batsmen were at ease with his pace as he took 10-109 in the match. But it was his bowling against the might of Yorkshire that ensured his selection for the forth-coming fifth test.

England needed to win the test in order to square the rubber and prevent South Africa winning her first series in England. Wyatt won the toss and gambled by inserting the opposition. Perhaps he was mindful of having batted first in the last two tests and having to declare the second innings in order to try to force victory, or maybe he was hopeful that the bowlers would receive help from any early morning dew. Whatever, the pitch was perfect for batting on, and if there was any moisture in the turf it had completely disappeared after the first quarter of an hour.

Vijoen, who made 60, was not comfortable against Read who had a very confident appeal for lbw against him turned when he had made 3. Read tired later on the first day but *The Cricketer* pronounced him "a distinct success. He is really fast, makes the ball break back, and is a tremendous trier who bowls with fiery zeal and energy. He was not too lucky, often beating the batsman. He is the type of fast bowler England has been looking for. He has stamina, 'the will to conquer', and Tom Richardson's refusal to surrender. We hope much of him." On the second day he was erratic, although he dismissed Vijoen promptly with a ball which rose quickly and hit him on the glove, and his opening spell from the Vauxhall end went for 56 runs. On the third day, after England had declared 60 runs ahead, he took the quick wicket of opener and first innings centurion, Mitchell. Nourse began uncertainly and was eventu-ally bowled by Read for 34 but then Cameron came in to hit him for three fours in an over as South Africa very comfortably batted out the draw.

Read's season tailed off slightly after that but in all that season he had played in sixteen championship matches for Essex, taking 74 wickets at 20, at a rate of a wicket every five overs, and was selected for MCC's 'goodwill' tour to Australia and New Zealand. No official tests were to be played on this tour, the main purpose of which was to restore good relations with the Australians after the bodyline tour. During the tour Read received much ribbing about his inept batting; in the previous season he had scored eight consecutive ducks. Indeed, over his first-class career he comfortably took more wickets than he scored runs.

The tour was captained by Errol Holmes who, in *Flannelled Foolishness* wrote, "if there are nicer people than 'Hopper' Read, they must be very few, for I have not met them." He also described the problems of captaining Read: "I would say that it is not easy for any captain to be one hundred per cent *persona grata* with Hopper Read – mainly for one reason, which was that he disliked, understandably, bowling into the wind. With 'Hopper' this was an obsession. If the slightest zephyr happened to be blowing in any direction, other than directly behind him, he would come up to me, at the end of his first over, with shirt billowing and very much out of breath, and would say, 'Errol, I'm bowling into the teeth of a gale.' As the tour progressed, this sentence was shortened to just one word – 'Teethers,' he would gasp, tucking in his shirt, 'absolute teethers, Errol.'"

During the first unofficial test Holmes dropped Read at first slip, the ball travelling quickly and catching him a painful blow on the thumb. The exact same thing happened next ball, the same spot being hit. In considerable pain, Holmes left the slip cordon and went to mid off, where soon after he shortly dropped a skier. His hand never recovered. Many years later he told Read that he had not been able to write properly since he dropped those three catches. Holmes reports that "Read beamed all over his face, and, in a very gentle and benign manner, he commented 'Well it serves you right.'"

Reports of the tour described Read as failing, which seems harsh when viewed from this distance. One reporter wrote that "his comparative failure was not caused by lack of enthusiastic effort, but he could not reproduce the form that made him so devastating in the English season preceeding the tour." In the first unofficial test he returned figures of 9-1-26-6 coming on as first change to bowl New Zealand out for 81. MCC made 653-5 declared in reply and in the second innings he bowled 27 of the 33 overs from his end to take 5-74, in one four-over spell sending back five men for 10 runs. Human bowled an over of 24 wides and byes in succession to get at the new ball, but bad light stopped play with New Zealand hanging on with seven wickets down. In the second test he returned figures of 11-0-37-0 and 20.1-1-82-1. He did not play in the third match, and in the final game in New Zealand's only innings he took 5-72. He was top of the averages in the representative games, with 17 wickets at 17, and he was also the highest wicket-taker, the next highest being J. Sims with 12. The second bowler in the averages was A.D. Baxter with 11 wickets at 24.18. In all first-class matches on tour Read took 44 wickets at 24.

After tour he was welcomed by a senior partner in the accountancy firm he worked for. "Well bowled Mr Read, now you've got to decide to become a professional cricketer or a professional accountant." Read never played county championship cricket again, although he played league cricket, bowling off a short run, until after the Second World War, and played in a first-class game for the MCC in 1948.

David Lemmon in *For the Love of the Game* quotes Read: "I never had a yearning to go back. I felt I'd done it for a couple of years. I'd played in a test match. [...] I knew pretty well that it was likely to be my last year when I played for England."

First-Class:

| Matches | Inns | NO | Runs | HS | Aver |
|---------|------|-----|------|------|------|
| 54 | 70 | 27 | 158 | 25no | 3.67 |

| Wkts | Average | SR | Best | 10wm | 5wi | ct |
|------|---------|-----|------|------|-----|-----|
| 210 | 22.93 | 38 | 7-35 | 2 | 13 | 21 |

Gents: 2 appearances

| Inns | NO | Runs | HS | Aver | O | M | R | W | Aver | BB |
|------|-----|------|------|------|------|------|------|------|------|------|
| 3 | 0 | 2 | 1 | 0.67 | 55.5 | 4 | 246 | 13 | 18.92 | 5-71 |

# 27   *J.H. Parks (Sussex)*

Born: 12 May 1903, Haywards Heath, Sussex. Died: 21 November 1980
1st Test, 1937 v. New Zealand
Batting:   1st Inns: (No.1)   22   2nd Inns: (No.1)   7
Bowling:  1st Inns: 11-3-26-2   2nd Inns: 10-6-10-1

Sussex cricket has a family tradition. In Parks' time the scorecard often lacked variety, possessing two Parkses, Langridges, Oateses and Cornfields, though the Cornfields were not related. Jim Parks' brother, Henry, first played for Sussex in 1926, making a thousand runs in the 1928 and 1930 seasons and continued to do so each year until his retirement in 1948. Jim's son, James Michael – also known as Jim – played for Sussex from 1949 to 1972 and appeared 46 times for England. Jim's grandson, Bobby, Hampshire's wicket-keeper in the 1980s, made an even briefer appearance in test cricket than his grandfather – at Lord's in 1986. Bruce French, England's wicket-keeper, had been struck on the head when batting in the first innings of the match. He was unable to keep wicket when New Zealand went in to bat so Bill Athey, who was in the eleven, kept wicket for two overs. Then, with the generous consent of the New Zealand captain Jeremy Coney, Bob Taylor, retired for two years, but on the ground, took over in an assortment of borrowed equipment, though he had his own gloves with him. He 'kept until just before lunch on the third day, whereupon Bobby Parks took over for the remainder of the day. On the fourth day French took up the wicket-keeping duties once again.

Jim Parks senior did not play cricket at school, only taking up the game seriously when he was sixteen. His early sporting love was football, playing inside forward for Haywards Heath, for whom two of his brothers also played. His mother would cheer on her sons, urging the rest of the crowd on to support the side; in bad weather she would brandish her umbrella at those not offering encouragement. After the war, encouraged by his father, he answered an advertisement by Haywards Heath cricket club for second-team players. He earned rapid promotion to the first eleven, mainly on the strength of his slip fielding. He twice went to Sussex for trials, but did not impress. However when Sussex Club and Ground came to play his club he top scored with 50 – the next highest was 9 – and took 6-44. In 1923 he joined the Sussex nursery.

He first came to the notice of a wider cricketing public in his third match for Sussex. With Arthur Gilligan and Maurice Tate away with the test side, Parks played and was given the new ball. He took 7-17 in Leicestershire's second innings at Horsham, paving the way for a victory by ten wickets. Meanwhile, Sussex's normal opening bowlers were dismissing South Africa for 30 at Birmingham.

Parks' performance was an exceptional one: the remainder of his wickets that season, 15, came at 55 runs apiece, and he averaged 11 from fifteen completed innings. His fielding ability helped him keep a place in the Sussex side while he worked on his batting. It was not until 1927 that he produced a seasonal return that justified Sussex's perseverance with him. That year he made 1,036 runs at 23.54 and took 44 wickets at 26.93.

In developing his batsmanship he relied heavily upon the coaching of Albert Relf. Bowling came more easily to him, and he was able to swing the ball naturally. Bowling at a slow medium pace, he could also cut the ball. He was a steady, stocky, batsman, strong on the off side and favouring the cut. Sound in defence, he made his runs through careful placement of the ball, but was able to score quickly when required. If Parks left an impression on spectators it would probably have been through his fielding. His Sussex captain Gilligan, in his autobiography *Sussex Cricket*, wrote: "I always likened him to a cat in the field, for he would pounce on hard drives, and return the ball to the wicket with a lightning delivery."

In 1928 he made his maiden first-class century, and in the next season made 110 in a Sussex record first-wicket partnership of 368 with Bowley. In 1935 he was selected for the MCC's non-test tour to Australia, under E.R.T. Holmes. His tour captain wrote of him that he was "very quiet and unassuming, but had a most cheerful disposition, and was always ready to do anything asked of him. A most likeable and charming character, and a wonderful travelling companion." Perhaps part of these characteristics owed themselves to the atmosphere in which he played his county cricket, *The Cricketer* remarking in their review of Sussex's 1926 season that "once again this southern county side played the happiest cricket, defeat or victory being the casual result of cheerful sporting matches."

In 1934 he first completed the double, making 1,633 runs at 33.32, with four centuries, and taking 103 wickets at 19.57.

Parks' wife died in 1936, and Parks' son reckons that in the following year his father threw himself into his cricket as a distraction. He became the only man ever to score 3,000 runs and take 100 wickets in a season. Only fifteen men have completed the double of 2,000 runs and 100 wickets, Hirst, Rhodes and J.W. Hearne doing so twice, and Woolley three times. Only seventeen other men have made 3,000 runs in a season, Sutcliffe, Hammond and Hendren doing so three times, and Hayward, Mead, Ranji and Tyldesley twice.

Sussex began the 1937 season in excellent form, winning five of their first six matches, one of them against Cambridge University. They went to the head of the championship table, which made them the talk of the cricketing public. Parks was to the fore, making 104 and 40 not out in the eight-wicket defeat of Worcestershire and 144 not out against Cambridge in the 246 run victory. Sussex drew with Nottinghamshire at Trent Bridge, Parks recording 12 and 31, then he made 18 and 78 as they beat Glamorgan at Cardiff by 181 runs, and they were victorious at Lord's by 210 runs with Parks making 97 and 33. Their next game, against Northamptonshire, was their first home game of the season and Sussex won by an innings and 128 runs, Parks scoring 122.

Their next game was in Yorkshire, and, in a high-scoring draw, Parks made 29. At the same time, as part of the MCC's 150th celebration week, the North were playing the South, in what was billed as a test trial. The other game in this week was between an MCC Australian XI – selected from those who had toured Australia the previous winter – and the Rest of England. Parks was chosen as opener for the Rest and scored 2 and 64. He bowled little, only bowling in the first innings, returning figures of 7-1-13-0.

On the previous Australian tour, England's batting had failed to maintain England's advantage. Having won the first two tests, England became the first country to lose a rubber after winning the opening two games of the series. Only three batsmen had returned with an average of more than 30 in the tests and England had struggled to get their innings underway successfully. Worthington and Barnett opened in the first, third and fifth tests, putting on 0, 17, 0, 29, 33 and 9 for the first wicket. Fagg moved up the order from first wicket down, to partner Barnett in the second test and they put on 27. Hedley Verity was pressed into service as an opener in the fourth test, proving to be Barnett's most successful partner, helping him put on 53 and 43 for the wicket. Barnett averaged 44 in the tests, Fagg 14, Worthington 12 and Verity 10.

For the first test against weaker opposition, the selectors tried out two uncapped openers. Barnett was selected but went in down the order, and *Wisden* reported that "the procedure naturally invited criticism." Verity also played, but batted at number ten. The all-rounder Worthington,

despite making 156 not out for the MCC Australian XI, was not selected
and never played test cricket again. He had only been selected for the
MCC Australian team when Voce dropped out, injured.

Parks had been selected as an all-rounder. His bowling that season
had been steady and consistent rather than devastating. He had bowled
in 25 innings, yet had not taken five wickets in an innings, but had only
gone wicketless in six of them, and in these innings he had hardly bowled
– 5, 1, 7, 8, 4 and 14 overs respectively. His bowling was economical: over
a quarter of his overs were maidens and he conceded an average of 2.2
runs per over. His bowling average was 21.33 but his strike rate was
a comparatively modest wicket every 58 balls. Moreover, though
continuing to be successful, his rate of success was declining.

Prior to the MCC game, he had made three centuries and three half-
centuries in twelve innings to average 79. Between the MCC match and
the test he had made one century – 146 versus Hampshire – and one
half-century in twelve innings at an average of 39. Prior to the MCC
game he took a wicket every 50 balls at an average of 16.79; between the
MCC game and the test he took a wicket every 63 deliveries for 25.57
runs. After the test his strike rate declined further and his wickets cost
almost 30 runs each.

In the test Parks made 22 and 7, faring much better than his fellow
debutant opener who made 0 and 1, as England's opening partnership
again failed. England's bowling was criticized as being 'negative'. *Wisden*
joined in the criticism: "Much of England's bowling was of a negative
description, and watching the play one dreaded to think what would
have occurred had Australian batsmen faced such limited resources."

Considering the type of bowler he was, it can be said that Parks
performed creditably. As England were taking 111.2 overs to bowl New
Zealand out in their first innings of the three-day match, Parks was given
only 11 overs. Yet he took two wickets, with a strike rate better than the
innings as a whole and twice that of the next best bowler. In the second
innings he took one wicket in ten overs; all the other bowlers bowled
more, and the only one to take more than one wicket was Voce with 3-
41 in 18.5 overs, as New Zealand batted out for a draw, with two wickets
left standing. The umpires reported that Parks had been England's best
bowler. Parks was never likely to blast through an opponent's batting,
but he would chip away at it, whilst not letting the batsmen get on top
of him. This is exactly what he did in the test. Indeed, had the other
bowlers matched Parks' strike rate of a wicket every seven overs, England
would have won comfortably. Therefore perhaps it was the others'
failings which led to him being dropped. That said, as *Wisden* wrote in
his obituary, "He can never have been a strong candidate for a place
against Australia."

Faced with the failure to bowl New Zealand out twice, the selectors
swept through the bowling, replacing all bar the captain, Robins, who

did not actually bowl in the next test, and Walter Hammond, who had taken his place in the side as one of the world's best batsmen. England won by 130 runs, as Parks' fellow opener from the previous test made a century. Next summer this player, Len Hutton, in only his 6th test, was to make the highest test score by an Englishman.

When the Second World War broke out, Parks was posted to Accrington on police service. Here he played league cricket and, after the war, Sussex not having re-engaged him, he moved north and played for eight years for Accrington and Stanley in the leagues. After this he went to Trent Bridge as coach, then spent three years as a first-class umpire before returning to Sussex as coach.

First-Class:

| Matches | Inns | NO | Runs | HS | Aver | 100 |
|---|---|---|---|---|---|---|
| 468 | 758 | 63 | 21369 | 197 | 30.74 | 41 |

| Wkts | Average | SR | Best | 10wm | 5wi | ct |
|---|---|---|---|---|---|---|
| 852 | 26.74 | 71 | 7-17 | 1 | 24 | 325 |

Players: 2 appearances

| Inns | NO | Runs | HS | Aver | O | M | R | W | Aver | BB |
|---|---|---|---|---|---|---|---|---|---|---|
| 3 | 1 | 83 | 76no | 41.50 | 7 | 1 | 15 | 2 | 7.50 | 2-15 |

# 28  A.D.G. Matthews (Glamorgan)

Born: 3 May 1904, Penarth, Glamorgan. Died: 29 July 1977
3rd Test, 1937 v. New Zealand
Batting:  1st Inns: (No.9)  2 no
Bowling: 1st Inns: 22-6-52-1        2nd Inns: 8-2-13-1

At the beginning of the 1937 season Austin Matthews would not have been considered by anyone as a possible test player. For one thing he had given up first-class cricket, for another he had never been anything other than a moderate county player in a very moderate county side. However, he had already received representative honours – he was a Welsh international at table tennis. There had been a chance of him becoming a double international for he had a final trial for the Welsh rugby union team in 1928.

He was a tall man who had bowled at brisk medium pace for Northamptonshire between 1927 and 1936. He bowled a consistent length, and pitched on line with the stumps with the ability to move the ball away. Northamptonshire were not a strong side – in the ten seasons he played for them they finished bottom of the championship five times

– and Matthews was not more than a solid county player of whom *Wisden* wrote that he "was merely a useful member of one of the weakest county sides, who could not on his performances have kept a place for a leading county."

At the end of the 1936 season he fell out with the Northamptonshire committee when they refused to grant him a testimonial. As a result he left the county and went to Stowe school to coach cricket and rugby.

He had taken 567 wickets for Northamptonshire at an average of 26.45, and, a useful late-order batsman, he had scored two centuries. One of the rare times when he had announced himself to a wider cricketing public was in 1934 when he played for Northamptonshire against the Australians and dismissed Bradman twice in returning figures of 23-0-71-4 and 26.5-3-87-5.

He had showed promise as a young all-rounder with Cardiff in the 1920s, bringing him to the attention of the Glamorgan county club. But, despite an offer from them, he opted against a county cricket career and went to college at Lampeter. He was also a useful rugby union forward, and, after moving from Wales, he captained Northampton as well as playing for the East Midlands. He had also by this time decided to give county cricket a whirl and he joined Northamptonshire in 1927 becoming their regular opening bowler. In 1934 he became coach at Cambridge University, where he coached Wilfred Wooller.

In 1937 New Zealand toured England, and in many respects the rubber against a weak New Zealand side was seen as a preparation for the following year's Ashes series. At this stage England did not have a settled opening attack. Indeed, in her previous eight home tests England had fielded a different opening attack in each game. For the first test the selectors picked an opening attack of Voce and Farnes, which was a new pairing for a home test, although they had shared the new ball in the previous test in Australia. However, Farnes dropped out and Gover was recalled, he and Voce forming the ninth different new ball attack in nine home tests instead. England failed to bowl New Zealand out twice, resulting in the ninth draw in eleven tests between the teams. Voce and Gover were dropped and a recalled Jim Smith and debutant Wellard formed the next opening partnership; F.R. Brown and Goddard were recalled also.

Maurice Turnbull, Glamorgan's captain, knew of Matthews' position in 1937 and knew that, having been born in Penarth, he was qualified for Glamorgan. He had played for Northamptonshire through a residential qualification. Glamorgan's opening bowler Mercer was carrying an injury and Turnbull contacted Matthews and arranged that he would turn out for Glamorgan after the end of the school term. Northamptonshire's committee issued a statement commenting that Matthews could play for Glamorgan "without comment from this committee but without our approval."

Matthews joined the team at the end of July, and by the middle of August had been selected for England after a return of 14-132 on a good batting pitch at Hastings suggested to the selectors that he might be the bowler they were looking for. Farnes was selected to be his opening partner but had to withdraw with an injury, and Gover was recalled to take his place in a bowling line-up of whom only Hammond and Goddard – who had taken 6-29 on the last day to give England victory – remained from the previous test. Having mentioned his 'splendid' bowling since joining Glamorgan, *The Cricketer* heralded his selection: "He may be the type of bowler that England has been looking for. Let us hope so."

The test wicket was easy-paced and on the first day there was only half an hour's play, during which New Zealand made 20 without loss. With the first ball Matthews had a confident lbw appeal against Hadlee turned down. Later he bowled him for 18 at 36, which was to be his sole wicket of the first innings. In the second innings Matthews again dismissed Hadlee for nought with the score on 4, when he fell to a catch by fellow debutant Denis Compton. In both innings he had bowled well, finding pace off the pitch and keeping a good length.

Reviewing the summer's selections, *The Cricketer* wrote on 28 August: "Gover got another chance owing to Farnes being unfit and again did not appear to be an England bowler. Matthews appeared little better than Wellard. [...] All of which means that we have some very good county bowlers but that we have not any England bowlers and that before the middle of June next three county bowlers have got to be found to play against Australia. We have got Farnes of course, but he is so liable to be unavailable or unfit. It is a pity that we have been unable to get a settled attack this summer. The selectors have done their best, but the cards are not on the table and they will have to make the best of what may be admittedly a bad job in the early days of next season."

For the first test of next season the selectors opted for only one specialist opening bowler, Farnes, promoting Hammond to take the new ball with him. Hammond went wicketless throughout 31 overs and Wellard was recalled for the next test, before being replaced by Bowes, who had not been judged fit earlier in the season, and who played in the last two tests as Farnes' partner.

Matthews appeared for Glamorgan in 1938 and 1939 and in 1946 he joined the staff full-time and acted as Assistant Secretary. In this season, aged 42, he took 88 wickets at 14. When younger bowlers appeared he eased into retirement. He had played 71 matches for Glamorgan, taking 227 wickets at 15.88. In 1948 he returned to Stowe as coach. He became a noted rugby referee and toured Argentina with a combined Oxbridge team.

128 England's One Test Wonders

First-Class:

| Matches | Inns | NO | Runs | HS | Aver | 100 |
|---------|------|----|------|----|----|-----|
| 281 | 447 | 70 | 5919 | 116 | 15.70 | 2 |

| Wkts | Average | SR | Best | 10wm | 5wi | ct |
|------|---------|----|----|------|-----|-----|
| 816 | 23.40 | 59 | 7-57 | 6 | 45 | 124 |

Players/Gents: dnp

# 29  R.A. Sinfield (Gloucestershire)

Born: 24 December 1900, Stevenage, Hertfordshire. Died: 17 March 1988
1st Test, 1938 v. Australia
Batting:  1st Inns: (No.9)  6  2nd Inns: (No 5)  5
Bowling: 1st Inns: 28-8-51-1  2nd Inns: 35-8-72-1

Test selection is a matter of being in the right place at the right time. For some, such as Harry Lee, it is a result of geographical coincidence; for others it is a question of consistently being in the right place, and hoping that there *is* a right time to complete the equation.

Test cricketers are almost invariably selected from those playing county championship cricket; this is especially so in the period covered by this book – if you can establish a place in a county side and keep it, there is a fair chance that test recognition may follow.

In 1938, the year that Reg Sinfield earned his test recognition, 358 men took part in county championship matches. By the time of their retirement, 70 of them (almost a fifth) had played for England. Picking at random a more contemporary example I alighted upon 1982. Taking a personal definition of 'English' to disallow those technically qualified but who would not be considered by the English selectors, for example the West Indian test cricketer John Shepherd, there were 302 English cricketers involved in the county championship that year. Of these, 92 – thirty per cent – have played test cricket for England, and one for New Zealand. When one considers that some of those 302 were only briefly flitting across the scene, the percentage increases for those able to establish any sort of a county career. Include only those who played at least twenty-two championship games in their career – a seasonal fixtures-list worth – and the number rises to more than a third.

This is not to belittle the achievement of playing for one's country. Clearly it is still the minority of county cricketers who reach the higher level, but someone good enough to play county cricket over a period of time is in with a very reasonable chance of test honours.

No test side is comprised of eleven test stars. It is normally a mixture of world class players, a few short of this ultimate pinnacle but definitely test class and what now, in the age of the cricketer, rather than professional and amateur, can be termed solid county pros.

The boundaries between these three categories are not hard and fast, but trying to fit players to the already defined categories might validate it. Taking one of the most interesting and stirring of modern English series, the 1981 Ashes, we find England selecting 20 players during the series. The world class Botham, Boycott and Willis played in all six tests and David Gower in the first five. The wicket-keepers, Taylor, three tests and Knott, two, merit the category also. Graham Gooch, who through his efforts in his final test years moved himself up from a test-class bat to world class, was, like Gower, ever-present until dropped for the final test.

The test class Hendrick and Old, played two tests each. John Emburey played four tests and Graham Dilley three, and they merit this category too.

Mike Gatting was the fourth ever-present. At that stage he was a promising youngster, yet to find his feet in test level. This he did for a brief period, when he held the England vice-captaincy and captaincy. As to where he is to be categorised is uncertain. Perhaps he averages out as being test class.

Seven other players earned twelve caps between them in the series, and all would fit neatly into the definition of a good county pro: Tavare, Woolmer, Willey, Parker, Larkins and Allott. Mike Brearley would probably have to go under a separate heading of 'captaincy specialist'.

Some of the definitions are perhaps fine. But any system of categorisation requires them. A 40% mark gives you an exam pass and a qualification, 39% doesn't; and, just like the marking of an exam paper, is also open to different interpretations.

The length of a test career does not necessarily equate with the player's category. Bill Athey played 23 matches, and no one would classify him as anything other than a solid county pro. He averaged 23. David Capel played fifteen tests as an all-rounder, averaging 16 with the bat and 51 with the ball. Nor does a short career necessarily suggest that a player was not test class. Charlie Parker's successes – in that form of cricket for which he could get selected – suggest he could have made a very respectable test-class performer.

'Solid county pro' is an apt description for Reg Sinfield. Although a cricketer who rarely made headlines, or drew people from the refreshment tents, only six people have taken more championship wickets for Gloucestershire and only twelve have scored more runs.

Reg Sinfield learnt some of his cricket on the *Mercury* training ship, run by C.B. Fry and his wife. Perhaps we can deduce that Fry liked the look of Sinfield's mother. As Fry explained in an article in *The Sunday Graphic* in 1947: "The main trouble was that parents applied from all over the United Kingdom, many of them from far away. Distance and expense more often than not precluded interview. And one had to know. What did I do? I simply insisted that with the application papers should be sent the mother's photograph. And if I liked the look of the mother I decided in favour of the son. And it worked."

At the *Mercury*, Fry would use Sinfield for net practice. Fry would ask him hard questions on purpose and when he got them wrong, as a punishment, would make Sinfield bowl to him in the nets. The net sessions seem to have a two-way benefit as Wally Hammond explained in *Cricketer's School*: "Reg Sinfield of Gloucestershire, one of the most staunch and sturdy batsmen we ever had, distinctly showed peculiarities of style that our oldest supporters recognized from the great days of W.G. Grace. But this was only a logical sequence, since Sinfield was a pupil from C.B. Fry's training ship; Fry taught him to bat, and Fry learned some of his shots from W.G. himself."

From the *Mercury* Sinfield moved onto the battleship *King George V*, where he was one of the signals staff, and from there onto the ground-staff at Lord's, and Hertfordshire County Cricket Club. When he joined Gloucestershire he had to serve a two-year qualification period. He played his first game for Gloucestershire in 1924 against South Africa, scoring only three runs. He made his championship debut the following season and bagged a pair, as did his captain. Previously he had played for the MCC, starting his first-class career there.

He bowled right-arm medium-slow deliveries, relying at first mainly on off-cutters and inswing. He often came on as first change, before the genuine spinners, to do a containing job. He was very accurate, able to bowl on off-stump all day, and gradually began to bowl more for the county. As Parker neared the end of his career, Sinfield became more central to the attack, by then bowling mainly off-spin.

At times, Parker, Goddard and Sinfield were the Gloucester attack. In 1930, when *The Cricketer* pronounced that Sinfield "holds out promise of becoming the most useful all-round member of the side," he played in all 28 county championship matches, bowling over 850 overs, taking 88 wickets. Parker bowled twenty more overs for 162 wickets and Goddard bowled 1,225 overs for 131 wickets. These three bowled over eighty per cent of Gloucestershire's overs. The next highest wicket-takers were Hammond and Barnett with 22 wickets each. That season Gloucestershire, with fifteen victories and four losses, came second by three points to Lancashire, with ten victories and no losses. It was the nearest Gloucestershire have ever come to the official county champion-ship, and the first of six occasions when they were runners-up, a position they also held the following season.

Having originally started down the order, Sinfield, a solid batsman, with good footwork and a liking for the leg side, moved up the order, becoming an opener, at first in partnership with Dipper, later with Barnett. As he was required to bowl more he dropped down the order.

In 1926 he scored his maiden first-class century, 101, against Somerset at Taunton. When he asked politely whether this merited his county cap, the captain, Lt. Col. Robinson replied that it did not, but if he could score a century in the forthcoming match against Nottinghamshire and Larwood and Voce it would. He did, and it did.

In 1927 he passed a thousand runs in the season for the first time. The runs came from 48 innings, without the benefit of a century. He scored 1,041 runs at an average of 29.74. The next season he again reached a thousand runs, with 1,047 runs at an average of 24. But that season he took eighty wickets at an average of 26 and bowled three hundred more overs than in the previous year, when he averaged 28.

In the next seven seasons he again passed a thousand runs. In the first six of these he averaged between 25 and 31 but in 1935 he scored five centuries, including a career best of 209 not out, to register 1,740 runs at 35.51 to move into 32nd place in the national averages. That season he played against South Africa at the Fry's ground, a reprise of his Gloucester debut. In Gloucestershire's first innings he made 102 out of 279. In the second innings Hammond scored a century and the South Africans were set 290 to win. At 150-3 they looked like getting it. "With Parker and Goddard doing their stuff I didn't think I had much chance of a bowl. Then I spotted a ladybird on my shirt and told the skipper I thought it might be my lucky day," Sinfield recalled. In 15.3 overs he took 5-51 to bowl Gloucestershire to victory.

In 1934 he had become the first Gloucestershire player to perform the double since C.L. Townsend in 1898, and the first professional to do so for the county. That year he came 79th in the national averages with 1,228 runs at 31.48, with a highest score of 83, and 31st in the bowling averages with 122 wickets from 1271.2 overs at an average of 23. He performed the double again in 1937 with 129 wickets at 23 and 1,001 runs at 24 with a highest score of 74 not out.

This achievement brought him close to selection for that winter's touring party. However he was not selected in either of the teams for the next season's test trial, held on June 1-3. So he played instead on these dates for Gloucestershire against a Bradmanless Australian side – that summer Bradman was to score thirteen centuries and average 116 – and took 8-68 in 30 overs. Meanwhile the test trial was being hampered by bad weather.

When the thirteen for the first test were announced J.C. Clay – who had also not played in the trial match – was in it, but on 6 June he dropped out. His place went to Sinfield.

Sinfield was picked in a final eleven light on pace bowling but strong on spin. Hammond – ten wickets that season so far at 53 – took the new ball with Farnes, the pace bowler Pope being left out, along with Yardley. Yardley spent the day answering Hammond's letters for him, copying his signature from an autograph. The other spinners were Verity who had taken 53 wickets at 16 so far that season, and fellow debutant Wright, who had impressed in the trial and had taken 30 wickets at 24. Sinfield had taken 52 at 23.

England batted first and at close were 422-4. On the second day Compton became the youngest English centurion against Australia, one of many records set in the test. England declared at 658, with Paynter 216 not out. Sinfield had made six out of a twenty minute partnership of thirty-three with Paynter.

Sinfield came on to bowl with the score at 29-0, and at 111-1, Bradman, on 51, pushed forward to an off break which ripped through to Ames who whipped off the bails. Ames appealed to the square leg umpire, who gave a not out decision. Ames then appealed to the umpire at the bowler's end, Frank Chester, who gave Bradman out caught. Sinfield had not appealed. Bradman later confirmed he had got an edge and congratulated the umpire on his decision.

In Australia's total of 411 Verity bowled only 7.3 overs. In their follow on of 427-6 he bowled 62. At the close of the third day, the penultimate, Australia had made 102-1, Sinfield having bowled 15 overs for 23. He was unable to extract much turn on the final day as Australia batted out to safety. *The Cricketer* reported that "Sinfield kept a fine length ... steady without appearing particularly difficult." *The Cricketer* also wrote of Wright, 5-238 in the match, "We have found a bowler. [...] we believe that Wright has come to stay."

It was a match for batsmen; it was the first time that four batsmen had scored centuries in the same test innings, and it remains the only time this has happened in Ashes matches. It was the first time two partnerships of over 200 runs had been made in the same innings, and that seven centuries had been scored in a test match, and that double-centuries had been made from batsmen on either side in a test. Les Ames became the first wicket-keeper to score 2,000 test runs during the match. It was not the ideal match for a bowler to make his debut.

Yardley and Pope were dropped from the party for the next test, which was the first to be televised in this country, albeit to only a few homes in London. The camera was positioned on a fire escape at the eastern corner of the ground, fine-leg when the bowling was from the pavilion end. Hardstaff and Wellard, very much on form – 67 wickets at 19 – came into the party. The only change from the first test was Wellard's replacement of Sinfield as England fielded a more balanced attack. Hammond, who by this stage had pushed his season's bowling average up to 63, did not bowl in the test.

That season Sinfield took 131 wickets at 24.80, but his batting fell away markedly. He scored only 486 runs, top scoring with a 39 not out. In 1939 his batting perked up greatly to the extent that he made 181 not out in one innings, and 1,324 runs at 30 in total. He took 78 wickets at 24 in what he had always intended to be his final season.

Sinfield was liked by team-mates and opponents alike. But his team-mates liked him particularly for being a team man at heart, and for his understanding attitude. Andy Wilson, on debut, missed both a catch and a stumping chance. Sinfield brushed aside the intended apology and assured him that a fifty per cent success rate was certainly acceptable to him. Opponents liked him for he was kind-hearted, softly-spoken and had a friendly word or a leg-pull for everyone.

When he retired he became coach at Clifton College, teaching Denis Compton's son, Chris Broad and John Cleese. Cleese described Sinfield as "quite my favourite person at Clifton, funny, wise and kind."

First-Class:

| Matches | Inns | NO | Runs | HS | Aver | 100 |
|---|---|---|---|---|---|---|
| 430 | 696 | 86 | 15674 | 209no | 25.69 | 16 |

| Wkts | Average | SR | Best | 10wm | 5wi | ct |
|---|---|---|---|---|---|---|
| 1,173 | 24.49 | 64 | 9-111 | 9 | 66 | 178 |

Players: 1 appearance

| Inns | NO | Runs | HS | Aver | O | M | R | W | Aver | BB |
|---|---|---|---|---|---|---|---|---|---|---|
| 2 | 1 | 12 | 12no | 12.00 | 29 | 10 | 54 | 3 | 19.00 | 3-39 |

# 30   W.F.F. Price (Middlesex)

Born: 25 April 1902, Westminster, London. Died: 13 January 1969
4th Test, 1938 v. Australia
Batting:   1st Inns: (No.7)   0   2nd Inns: (No.7)   6
Fielding:  1st Inns: 2ct      2nd Inns: –

Fred Price first kept wicket for Middlesex in 1926 and played his last game for them twenty-one years later. Throughout this time he was an accomplished performer behind the stumps, and a steady bat, good enough in 1934 to score a thousand runs – he missed this total by 23 runs the following year – and reliable enough for Middlesex to entrust him on occasion with opening the innings.

He finally earned test recognition when he was thirty-nine years old, but it could have come sooner. In 1929–30 he was called up to join the MCC touring team in West Indies, as Major Stanyforth was injured.

Stanyforth had one of the more interesting careers of someone who played test cricket. Unable to get into the Eton first eleven, he was also unable to gain a blue at Oxford. His wicket-keeping developed whilst in the army and in 1926 Plum Warner took him on his MCC tour to South America. He was selected to tour South Africa the next winter, and when the original captain, Derbyshire's Guy Jackson, had to withdraw through injury (never, in fact, to play test cricket), he took over as captain, playing in the first four tests, before injury ruled him out of the final match. So he had captained England in four tests without yet playing in the county championship. He made his championship debut the following season, playing thrice for Yorkshire, despite his Chelsea birthplace. That was his whole county career.

Price played in two matches against Jamaica on the West Indian tour, *The Cricketer* declared that "he acquitted himself well." Price's 'keeping was neat and without flourish, and particularly strong on the leg side. At Lord's his abilities were frequently given the most exacting of tests, the pitches there giving the ball a tendency to shoot along the ground.

In 1936 he was thought to be close to selection for that winter's tour and *The Cricketer* reported that "had he appeared to better advantage in batting, might well have found inclusion in the team that went to Australia."

However, Price had his moments with the bat as well. In 1930 he and Harry Enthovan had put on 107 together for Middlesex's last wicket against Sussex at Lord's, of which Enthovan made 102. In 1933, he put on 332 with Patsy Hendren for the fifth wicket for Middlesex against Worcestershire at Dudley. Hendren went on to make 301 not out, Price made his maiden century, scoring 111. The following year he narrowly missed scoring centuries in both innings against Kent at Lord's, making 92 and 107.

In 1937 he created a new world record when he took seven catches in Yorkshire's innings at Lord's. After the match a lady approached him with her congratulations, saying that she had been so excited she'd nearly fallen over the balcony. "If you had madam," assured Price, "I would have caught you as well." The next year he was prevented from having the chance of equalling this record when he took six catches against Warwickshire, but only nine wickets could be taken as the final man was absent.

At the beginning of 1938 Les Ames was ensconced as England's wicket-keeper, but during the second test match he fractured a finger. England needed someone to take over behind the stumps. Hammond would have been an obvious choice, but he was injured too, having had his left leg strapped which necessitated batting with a runner. Eddie Paynter took over, lacking any better alternative, as he had kept wicket as a boy. Having taken over behind the stumps, he had a hand in the first two catches taken. The first catch rebounded from his gloves to first slip, the second ricocheted from his gloves to second slip.

Paul Gibb was chosen as England's wicket-keeper for the third test. His was a surprise selection as he had only played for Cambridge University, and had made a bad impression with the gloves on the Saturday of the Varsity match. On the Sunday he was named in the test side and on the Monday he scored 122 in four hours. Gibb was rare amongst wicket-keepers in that he wore glasses. In his first year at Cambridge he had played as batsman, relying upon very strong back play, fierce concentration and inexhaustible patience. In his obituary *Wisden* wrote, "It would have needed a shrewd critic to discern, when watching him play a long innings, that he was more than a determined and solid university and county batsman. Never once did one catch a glimpse of that spark of genius which normally marks the test player. The figures tell a very different story." The obituary also states that "with his wicket-keeping it was different, not even his best friends would have claimed that he was anywhere near the best of his day."

In his second year at university Gibb took over from S.C. Griffiths when he became injured, and for his third year he replaced him behind the stumps for the whole season. *Wisden* said, "This aroused considerable criticism." Gibb played for Yorkshire from 1935 to 1946. That winter he toured Australia, 'keeping in the first test match, the last of his eight caps, (three of them as wicket-keeper). In his eight tests he averaged 44. He dropped out of county cricket after this. When he returned in 1951 it was for Essex, and as a professional, becoming the first cricket blue to turn professional. He played for Essex for six years, before becoming a first-class umpire. He finished his days as a bus driver.

The third test was abandoned without a ball being bowled, due to rain. Price played for the Players against the Gentlemen, for whom Gibb kept wicket. Price let by only two byes as the Gents made 411 and 172-8. The Gents' innings ended at 6.15pm, and Farnes took the new ball, angered at being left out of the Old Trafford party. His first ball to Edrich reared head-high from just short of a length; his second flicked the batsman's glove before cannoning into his forehead. The next thing Edrich was aware of was someone saying, "have some water, no hurry." In the Players' dressing-room they needed a night watchman. Frank Woolley's gaze alighted upon Price. "Would you like to oblige?" "No I bloody well wouldn't." But he did. He survived one fierce delivery before nicking the second to first slip. Farnes was back in the side for the next test.

On July 16–18, Yorkshire took on Middlesex at Lord's, where, earlier in the season, Ames had his finger broken. On a soft-surfaced wicket with a rock-hard underlay Hutton broke a finger, Leyland a thumb and Gibb was concussed.

The selectors now needed to add an extra wicket-keeper to the fourth test squad in case Gibb had not recovered in time. The selectors' first choice was Arthur Wood, the Yorkshire wicket-keeper. But, in Warner's words, they were warned by 'Yorkshire opinion' that he was not 'keeping well. This was probably the opinion of Brian Sellers, the captain. It has been suggested that he was influenced by the problems he would have had putting out a team which was already heavily depleted through the Lord's injuries and test calls, without having to do without both his wicket-keepers as well. The selectors instead went for Price, who, in Warner's words was "not at all the sort of batsman one would fancy to come off against the bowling of Australia." Warner admitted to having a sleepless night at the thought of England's tail. England were bowled out for 223 and 123 in the test, the last five wickets second time around falling for seven runs. England lost by five wickets and the selection was criticized.

There was a four-week gap between the fourth and final tests which allowed injuries to heal, and Ames was able to take his place in the party for the final test. On the eve of the match the selectors learnt that Ames had broken another finger.

Stories as to how the selection of Wood was made differ. One has Warner, apparently stung by criticism of the last test side, going to ground inside his club with orders that he was not to be disturbed. In the chairman's absence, the other selectors decided to send for Wood. Another has Warner summoning a journalist from the press box at Lord's, telling him that Ames had pulled out and could he recommend a wicket-keeper batsman? Whatever the truth, after the collapse at Headingley the selectors seem to have determined upon a wicket-keeping batsman, consistent with the replacement of another wicket-keeper batsman – Ames – and the original choice of Gibb as Ames' replacement.

But by the time Wood reached the wicket in the timeless test it had ceased to be particularly relevant whether he had the batting ability of Donald Bradman or Donald Duck, as England had already reached 770-6. Dropped on 47, he made 53 in 92 minutes. On his return to the pavilion he was congratulated upon his innings. "Just like me to get out in a crisis," he remarked wryly.

After retiring, Fred Price became a first-class umpire, standing from 1950 to 1967. He became the first umpire to no-ball Tony Lock for throwing, when three times he called him in a match at the Oval against the touring Indians. In another match on the same ground, when Yorkshire were battling to avoid defeat and being baracked by the crowd, he lay down on the ground at square leg and refused to get up until the noise subsided. He explained that he did so "because three times there were catcalls just as the batsman was about to play the ball. That is not my idea of British sportsmanship and under the Laws of 'fair and unfair play' I will not tolerate such things on any ground where I am umpiring." He officiated in eight tests.

First-Class:

| Matches | Inns | NO | Runs | HS | Aver | 100 |
|---------|------|-----|------|-----|-------|-----|
| 402 | 590 | 97 | 9035 | 111 | 18.32 | 3 |

| Wkts | Average | SR | Best | 10wm | 5wi | ct | st |
|------|---------|-----|------|------|-----|-----|-----|
| never bowled in f-c cricket | | | | | | 666 | 321 |

Players: 2 appearances

| Inns | NO | Runs | HS | Aver | ct | st |
|------|-----|------|-----|-------|-----|-----|
| 3 | 0 | 43 | 38 | 14.33 | 8 | – |

# 31  N. Oldfield (Lancashire)

Born: 5 May 1911, Dunkinfield, Cheshire
3rd Test, 1939 v. West Indies
Batting: 1st Inns: (No.3)   80   2nd Inns: (No.3)   19

'Buddy' Oldfield was taken onto the Lancashire staff in 1929, yet had to wait six years before making his debut. In his debut season he made an immediate impression, scoring a thousand runs. That year Cardus wrote, "None so rich in natural gifts has been found by Lancashire since the days which saw the Tyldesleys. If this young man does not go to the top of his calling there will be a scandalous interference with destiny."

A small, quick-footed batsman who was eager to get to the ball, Oldfield was also a fearless hooker and puller, described by Frank Tyson as "one of the finest back-foot players I have ever seen."

He was also a good fielder and, like his county colleagues Washbrook and Paynter, very quick between the wickets. Nervous before going in to bat, he would sit by a window watching the cricket, chain-smoking. He never took breakfast on cricketing days for fear of vomiting through nerves.

*The Cricketer* spoke of the 'sensational success' of his debut season, and wrote, "He has every stroke of the great Johnny Tyldesley except the straight drive, and flashes them with a temerity calculated to delight appreciative critics but alarming to a certain type of selector, who seems to dislike those who take risks – though W.G., Ranji, Hobbs, Trumper and Macartney always did."

In 1935 he scored 1,066 runs at 32 and in each of the seasons from his debut until the Second World War he scored a thousand runs.

Against Sussex in 1937, after the Lancashire side had travelled down overnight from Manchester, in five hours Lancashire made 640-8 declared, Paynter scoring 322. Paynter put on 268 with Washbrook for first wicket and 271 in two and a quarter hours with Oldfield for the third. In the next season Oldfield and Paynter again combined prodigiously for the third wicket, adding 308 against Hampshire. This survived as Lancashire's third wicket record until the batting excesses of the Lancashire Surrey match at the Oval in 1990, when Atherton and Fairbrother added 364. In 1939, A.E. Nutter and Oldfield compiled an undefeated 235 for the fifth wicket, then a Lancashire fifth-wicket record. It was bettered, by fourteen, by Wood and Kennedy in 1975.

In 1938, when Oldfield came twenty-second in the national averages with 1,812 runs at 42, including four centuries, *The Cricketer* commented, "Many supporters of Lancashire were surprised that Washbrook and Oldfield, two stylish young batsmen with plenty of strokes, were not given a chance outside county games. Each fully maintained his form, but failed to gain recognition even in the Festival games."

Oldfield was never to represent the Players, but test recognition came the following season, when he was selected in the place of his team-mate Paynter. In his first innings he began with a risky stroke through the slips, but followed this with a fine cut, off Martindale, and was soon into his stride. A square cut to the boundary in the last over before lunch brought him to his fifty. He continued with what *The Cricketer* described as 'his graceful and enterprising cricket' until, twenty short of a century, he was caught at the wicket on the leg side by Sealy, standing up to Constantine. He had hit eight fours.

Oldfield's innings is the highest by an English one test wonder. Indeed, only three English one test wonders have made a half-century. The others are John King and Charles Absolom.

Absolom was a right-arm slow medium bowler who was an attacking tail-end batsman and all-round athlete who could long-jump 22 feet and 2 inches, put a shot 32 feet and throw a cricket ball a hundred yards. He toured Australia in 1878–79, playing in the sole test on that tour. Coming in at number nine, with England 26-7, he set about the bowling, a contemporary report says that "balls bowled to him to the off he hit to long-on – in fact anywhere but where the bowler intended and hoped they would be hit." He made 53, the next highest scorer, the captain Lord Harris, made 33 and the next highest score after that was 7 by the wicket-keeper and number ten bat Leyland Hone. Absolom made 6 in the second innings and did not bowl in England's ten-wicket defeat. Absolom's first innings performance was one of the rare times that his aggressive batting came off; in 178 first-class innings he made only four half-centuries, and his top score was 70. Later that year he played the last of his 57 appearances for Kent and 99 first-class games. Broken-hearted after a marriage proposal was turned down, he gave up cricket and travelled to North America, where he is said to have lived with the Spokabe tribe of American Indians before moving onto Trinidad. He became purser of the SS *Muriel* and died at Port of Spain, crushed to death whilst super-vising a crane loading bags of sugar.

Oldfield played in the last test to be played for six years and 219 days. When England resumed test-match cricket, two months shy of a seven-year interval, he was no longer playing first-class cricket.

Lancashire offered him the same terms after the war as they had before the war. By now Oldfield had a pub and a family and felt the need for more security. So, having played 151 matches for Lancashire, scoring 7,002 runs at 35.72, with 12 centuries, he declined. Lancashire for their part banned him from Old Trafford; when he took his son to the Old Trafford test he had to hand him over to George Duckworth at the turn-stile. Oldfield, meanwhile, earned money from cricket by playing in the leagues.

In 1948 the registration rules were relaxed, enabling cricketers to change counties without a year spent idling away from first-class cricket. Oldfield thereupon joined Northamptonshire, along with two other ex-Lancashire players, including Nutter who, with a good job as a welfare officer for a cotton firm after the war, had also refused Lancashire's terms.

Oldfield played 159 matches for Northamptonshire. He was more successful for them than he had been for Lancashire, scoring 9,321 runs at 38.51. Of his twenty centuries for them, one was scored at Old Trafford. He made his highest first-class score for them when he scored 168 against Worcestershire at Worcester in 1949. The 361 he put on with Broderick for the first wicket against Scotland in 1953 at Peterborough remains a county record for the opening wicket in first-class cricket.

But Oldfield regretted his move: "Really Lancashire was the only team I wanted to play for and I missed Old Trafford. The money at Old Trafford soon caught up and if I had stayed with Lancashire I think I would have been chosen for England again. Northamptonshire were too unfashionable. I deemed it an honour to play at Old Trafford and for Lancashire. At Northamptonshire it was a job of work."

When he left Northamptonshire he became a first-class umpire and subsequently returned to Old Trafford as assistant coach under Charlie Hallows, from whom he later took over.

First-Class:

| Matches | Inns | NO | Runs | HS | Aver | 100 |
|---------|------|-----|-------|-----|-------|-----|
| 332 | 521 | 51 | 17811 | 168 | 37.89 | 38 |

| Wkts | Average | SR | Best | 10wm | 5wi | ct |
|------|---------|-----|------|------|-----|-----|
| 2 | 60.50 | 95 | 1-0 | – | – | 96 |

# 32  *Predictable?*

There are roughly as many batsmen as bowlers who are one test wonders. There are also a large proportion who are all-rounders. At the beginning of the 1999 season there were 85 one test wonders. Of these, nine can be confidently described as all-rounders; others such as G.F. and E.M. Grace and Alec Hearne might be, although they did not bowl in their single test appearance. There are eight wicket-keepers who 'kept, and another who did not.

The high percentage of wicket-keepers who are one test wonders is unsurprising. More surprising initially is the high number of all-rounders since all-rounders can be, in theory, twice as useful to a side, and have twice as many opportunities for success. As such one might expect them to be more loved by selectors, and more able to produce a debut performance to encourage re-selection. However most all-rounder one test wonders are from the nineteenth century, when cricketers tended to be less specialized in their roles. There are only three one test wonders from the twentieth century who could reasonably be considered all-rounders, and only one post-war one test wonder who was an all-rounder: Charles Palmer, capped in 1953. Palmer was a batting all-rounder; he bowled only six of England's 201 overs in the test, and took only an average of 1.09 wickets per match in his first-class career.

That almost as many bowlers as batsmen are one test wonders, suggests that a bowler is more likely to become a one test wonder than a batter, because a side normally contains more batsmen than bowlers. Bowlers, in theory, have a better chance of creating a balanced impression of their ability than batsmen. Two mistakes – errors, misfortune or bad luck – and a batsman's involvement is over. But a bowler has six opportunities an over. Because poor deliveries can be retrieved by good ones, a bowler has more chances to create a balanced impression of his play.

Yet this seems to work against bowlers. Perhaps batsmen are given the benefit of the doubt more after a poor performance. Denis Compton, whilst undergoing a run of poor scores in South Africa, was asked whether he was in form. "I don't know, I've never been in long enough to find out," he replied. A batsman who is dismissed first ball can give little indication as to his style, strengths and weaknesses or temperament. A batsman, however, who makes twenty may be in long enough to leave his signature. This could work for or against the batsman – even if he scores twenty, he might create a more unfavourable impression than another who makes a duck and has little chance to hint at his abilities. *Wisden* wrote of Bill Edrich's efforts in the Lord's test of 1950: "His scores were 8 and 8: it would have been better for his reputation if he had taken two first balls. Each time he stayed long enough to make it clear he was completely out of his depth with Ramadhin and Valentine." Mark Benson was selected to make his test debut in 1986 against India. He made 21 and 30. However, press reaction to his innings was not favourable, with at least one of the radio commentators opining during his broadcast that Benson had clearly shown that he did not have the technique for test cricket and that he would not play in the next test. Benson, indeed, never played again at test level.

Bowlers are more vulnerable to solitary selection. This may be due to three reasons. They have a better chance to make a firm impression. Bowling attacks tend to get changed more often than batting line-ups in response to pitch conditions. Bowlers, especially fast ones, tend to get injured more often than batsmen, as they put their bodies under more strain; the risk of having a bone broken while batting is shared by tail-enders as well as specialist batsmen.

Logically a cricketer, whether a debutant or not, who makes a century or takes five wickets in an innings is more likely to be re-selected than one who makes low scores or takes few wickets. So performance must come into it to a certain degree. But, as the examples from the opening chapter demonstrate, they are not the defining criteria. Between 1900 and 1939, 82 men made their test debut either as a batsman or an all-rounder. Of those, twelve failed to make a reappearance. The 70 who went on to play test cricket again played 113 innings between them, (five of them undefeated), made four centuries and eighteen half-centuries and scored 2,819 runs at 26.10. The twelve one test wonders made no centuries, two half-centuries and averaged 20.30. Of the fourteen ducks by thirteen debutants – Jim Smith made a pair – only one was made by a one test wonder.

But this is retrospective analysis, and only partial at that. Can one identify the type of cricketer who is likely to be a one test wonder after he has been selected, but before he has played his test? Though every cricketer's circumstances and story is some way unique there are inter-pretations of these stories which can draw similarities between them. What follows is one such interpretation. There are obviously others, depending upon how the pieces of the jigsaw, referred to in chapter one, are put together.

## INJURY AND ILLNESS

Mitchell-Innes withdrew from what would have been his second test due to illness, and this illness kept him out of test cricket for good. Two post-war one test wonders were injured in their tests, making them unavailable for selection in the next. Arnie Sidebottom in the third test of 1985 filled the third seamer role which was an unsettled position for England at the time. Botham played all six tests of the series, and Paul Allott played in the first four before he was dropped and failed to make the winter tour. In all, eight fast-medium bowlers were tried by the selectors during the series. While taking the second new ball, Sidebottom damaged his toe and retired from the match. Injury-prone during his career, he managed only two more first-class matches that season. Andy Lloyd did not play again in the 1984 season after his test debut. Thirty-three minutes into the match, opening the innings for England he was hit on the helmet by Malcolm Marshall and hospitalised for several days with blurred vision.

## CONFUSED SELECTION

Parks, King, and Price all seem to have suffered from selectorial confusion as to the role they were expected to perform. Price was picked as a replacement for a batsman-keeper, when he was not a batsman-keeper, but a competent tail-ender instead. This selection was 'corrected' for the following test with the selection of a batsman/wicket-keeper.

The all-rounder Parks performed his duties admirably in his test. He bowled well, fully in keeping with his style, that of containment with regular wicket-taking. Parks performed the role for England which he had done so well for Sussex that season. Yet the selectors seem to have been wanting something else from Parks, which led to his dismissal from the side.

The only other all-rounder and one test wonder between 1900 and 1939, King, was a fine batsman who scored well for England but was unlucky when he bowled and out of place as an opening bowler. He was caught up in a general purge of the England team, perhaps instigated by a man who had not actually witnessed the test match. King had much to offer to an England side, and, in his brief test appearance, had shown signs of what he could achieve. It appears that King's performance with the ball overshadowed his performance with the bat. As such, his career has similarities to Kinneir and Dipper, where the minor of their two main roles dominated any judgement of them as cricketers.

## POOR FIELDING
Both Kinneir and Dipper seem to have been dropped for lacking fielding ability. In both cases the test side in which they played was below-average in fielding, which may have influenced the decision. Because it was not uncommon during the period of these players' careers to 'hide' certain men in the field, they might also be said to have fallen foul of others' failings in this area too.

## SOCIAL REASONS
Rockley Wilson, and later Charles Palmer in 1953, were chosen for their sole overseas tours, on which they gained their test cap, for what might loosely be termed 'leadership qualities'. Wilson was a late replacement on his tour, chosen as an amateur who could fill the role of vice-captain. Palmer was picked to be the player-manager of the 1952–53 tour to West Indies. Although it seems they were not expected to challenge strongly for a test place, with a limited pool of players to pick from, it is not unrealistic to expect them to play in at least one of the test matches.

Charlie Parker was overlooked for selection it seems because of an opinion that he was an 'undesirable character'. Arnold Warren suffered from something similar, though in his case it was more to do with his unreliability.

## SHORT-TERM SELECTIONS
This is a contentious category, as it is susceptible to post-event rationalization. However, even at the time of selection it is clear that some selections were unlikely to be for many matches. These cricketers can be said to have faced a harder job than most to gain selection for the next match. An obvious example is Lee, who was brought in essentially to

make up numbers in an injury-ridden side, as were Piggott and Ken Palmer.

George Emmett was selected in 1948 when Len Hutton was surprisingly dropped from the side for failing to attempt to dominate the bowling. It was always likely that Hutton's 'punishment' would be brief and he was duly recalled for the next match, in Emmett's place. As the other opener was the established and successful Cyril Washbrook, there was not really a vacancy for an opener which Emmett could have filled, regardless of his performance. Similarly with MacBryan, where again an established batsman, in this case Hobbs, had been dropped for reasons other than form or ability and would swiftly return. There was not a vacancy in the batting order that MacBryan could fill.

More controversially, Sinfield's selection could be considered as a short-term fix, rather than a long-term statement of policy. England went into the match in which Sinfield played with three spinners but only one recognized new ball bowler. This was always likely to be rectified for the next test, with a more balanced attack being selected. Similarly Matthews was given a run out more, it seems, as a way of exploring various possibilities for the opening bowler position for the following season's Ashes series, rather than as a statement of long-term policy or faith in the individual concerned.

There is a danger that this analysis is guilty of being wise after the event. After all, what if the individual concerned had scored a brilliant century or hustled out seven batsmen for little cost? Then a vacancy might have been made for the players, certainly in Matthews' case it would definitely have been. But rarely does a debutant perform so. Indeed, rarely is this done by most players.

## LAST TEST OF SEASON
Anyone selected for the final test of a summer is obviously vulnerable to becoming a one test wonder. This was especially so in the days when not every winter and summer heralded a test series, and the next test opportunity could have been some time away. Marriott, Oldfield, Read and Carr all fit this category, although in varying ways. Marriott went on the following winter's tour, but Oldfield, Carr and Read were not playing first-class cricket when the next test came around. A large proportion of modern one test wonders fit into this category too: Alan Butcher (1979), Paul Parker (1981), Stephenson (1989), Williams (1990), Benjamin (1994) and Alan Wells (1995). Only Benjamin from this list went on the following winter tour.

## BUSINESS COMMITMENTS
Clay and Read turned their back on test cricket for business commitments. In Clay's case the business was as often as not Glamorgan County Cricket Club-based as much as his business interest outside cricket.

Obviously all of these categories are, at least to a certain extent, arbitrary. Also, some players could be placed in more than one category: MacBryan under 'social reasons', Wilson under 'business commitments', in his case school-teaching, etc. This summation does not pretend to be a conclusion, more an extension of the analysis.


# 33   *Failures?*


Cricket, unlike most team sports, isolates its competitors. It takes the form of a series of clearly defined one-on-one confrontations, bowler against batsman. As such, at times, it is a most unforgiving game. Unlike other team sports, the scorecard of the game clearly identifies each participant's individual contribution. As such it provides ready successes and failures, heroes and scapegoats. It is possible, almost a hundred years later, to assess Tate's impact on 'his' test match from the match scorecard, in a way which is not possible to do for all the participants in other international sporting contests of that era.

Cricket can impose very harsh judgements on its participants. Had Fred Tate scored the extra four runs needed for victory, or had Armstrong stopped the ball going to the boundary, resulting in Rhodes facing and leaving him in the position of either getting the runs or getting out, or had Saunders bowled a worse delivery and Tate despatched it for four, or had many of the other possible scenarios played out, then it would have been: "Capital player Tate, dropped a catch but didn't let it bother him did he? No sirree, not a player as good as he. Went in with eight needed after the batsman had failed and smote the runs without a care in the world, cool as a cucumber. Bowled well too, you know. Damn fine chap. Inspirational selection by MacLaren – what a fine captain."

Instead it was: "What was that useless twit Tate doing in a test?"

I have seen it written that "Tate could not bat sufficiently reliably to score the small number of runs needed for victory." But this ignores the reality of cricket. Who could be said to bat reliably enough to guarantee eight runs were scored? Don Bradman perhaps, the greatest run-scorer the game has known, and probably ever will do? The man who, needing only four runs in his final test innings to average a hundred in test cricket was dismissed second ball for nought. Had he batted as successfully in his final test innings as Tate had in his then he would have averaged a hundred.

The reality is that on some days Tate would have not got the runs, and on another he would. And did – shortly after the test when he made an undefeated 22 against the Australians. It is the same with Bradman, though the probabilities of success are different. One of his innings was the then record first-class score, and another was the then record test score – and on six other occasions he was dismissed first ball for nought.

That, in one game, individuals did not score many runs, or take many wickets does not make them failures per se. People who fail on occasion are not necessarily failures.

Perhaps one test wonders can be criticized for failing to seize the opportunity to establish a place in the team. However, this presupposes that the opportunity was always there. In some cases it clearly was not. Read had retired from first-class cricket by the time of the next test. So had Oldfield, who clearly cannot be considered to have failed in his performance at test level – 109 runs in his two innings, and 80 in the second of them, clearly is a successful debut. That he did not add to his test caps was hardly his fault. That Clay did not take up the opportunity of furthering his test career was largely a matter of his own choice as to where his duties lay. Mitchell-Innes' failure to build upon his test debut could also be considered partly his own decision as he volunteered his injury, fearing a potential medical inability to compete successfully at the highest level, but it was mainly a matter beyond his own control.

Other one test wonders started with the odds stacked against them before they even played their test. Lee clearly could not be hopeful of a second cap – probably not something that would have bothered him considering the circumstances of his call-up. Sinfield and Matthews were always going to have to be very successful in their first test appearance in order to get more caps. MacBryan also seemed to have nowhere to go when he made his test appearance, as all the test batting places were already filled. There was, however, a place available on the forthcoming tour which he could have taken; that he did not might have been due to selectorial thinking concerning the desirability of his character; as such, rubbing up his county captain and England selector the wrong way may have counted against him. MacBryan felt so.

This prompts the thought that perhaps it is not just the cricketers who should be examined on the question of failure, but selectors too. Charlie Parker, far more so than MacBryan, suffered from selectorial disapproval of his personality rather than from doubts about his cricket. His cricketing ability was great. So was his ability to antagonize people. But there were often tensions between some of the professionals and amateurs in his day. Parker was not alone in his views, even if he was more vociferous in expressing them. But this need not have counted against him. Throughout many sports there are questions of whether certain players should be selected in view of their temperament, and cricket is no exception. Simon Barnes in *Phil Edmonds: A Singular Man*, quotes a conversation he had with Mike Brearley, and of the latter's reaction when he spoke of Edmonds' lack of caps perhaps being due to a failure to be diplomatic. "When people talk of being diplomatic, I often think they believe they should be insincere in order to get by. Willis was not insincere, nor was he a great diplomat. No more was Botham or Gooch or Hendrick or Lever or Boycott. You are bound to have strong characters in an England dressing-room. There have always been lively discussions and quarrels: teams are not always idyllically happy. A good team is full of conflict."

The half-dozen players Brearley mentions include three of the five men to have played for England over a hundred times as well as England's most capped specialist bowler. These four – Botham, Gooch, Boycott and Willis – also all captained England.

That people do not conform to the norm in one aspect of their life often means that there are other aspects of their life for which this is also true. Ian Botham's almost reckless confidence in his own capabilities, was the foundation of many of his outrageously brilliant performances. It was also the cause of some of his problems. Geoff Boycott owed a great deal of his success to his occasional bloody-mindedness and his single-minded dedication and intense search for perfection. Character-istics that brought him problems off the field, often brought him and his team great success on it. Alone among England's leading century-makers, Boycott's centuries never preceded an English defeat. Graham Gooch was criticized as captain for his single-minded dedication to practice and fitness, but it was this that made him the batsman he was. Botham and Boycott were also criticized as captains. Botham could be said to be the least successful test captain of all as no one has captained in as many tests as he – twelve – without winning. But Botham was given a very hard task when captain through his comparative inexperience and the quality of the opposition. That Boycott led a very average Yorkshire team to second place in the championship suggests more all-round captaincy ability than he is generally given credit for.

That the best use was not made of Charlie Parker's cricketing abilities suggests a failure by various selectors. That he could be an awkward customer is not disputed, but sometimes it is the awkward people who get the best results. Parker was clearly worthy of extended test selection. The case for MacBryan is less clear-cut, both in terms of his ability to compete at test level and of how much his character obscured appreci-ation of his abilities.

Arnold Warren could be lumped together with Parker and MacBryan, but his is a very different case. His character led directly to an on-field failure to perform well and as such the decision not to risk his selection again can be seen as a cricketing judgement. He did not bowl well in the second innings, and the reason for this was his intemperate lifestyle. It can be said of Warren that his unreliability as a bowler caused his downfall. That this unreliability was caused by his personal indiscipline is, essentially, irrelevant to this analysis, although a slight revulsion as to his behaviour may have coloured the decision.

If any one of the cricketers is to be considered a failure from this selection of players then it surely has to be Warren. As a genuinely quick bowler he was always likely to be attractive to selectors, and he did the hard part: he came in cold to test cricket and was a success at his first attempt. He then fluffed what appears to have been a considerably easier challenge: turning up sober the next morning. Maybe this is a harsh judgement. After all, Warren had drunk and bowled before with success. Larwood would relax in the intervals in the bodyline tests with a beer and a cigarette. Gordon Greenidge made his highest score, 273 not out for D.H. Robins' XI against the Pakistanis at Eastbourne in 1974, while hungover. Even the arch-perfectionist Geoff Boycott once batted while hungover – and made a century. But in their cases – and in many, many others – drinking was either in moderation, or they got away with it. Neither of these applied to Warren.

A clear case of failure by the selectors is when their thinking is flawed. They cannot be blamed for players not performing as expected, but when they do perform as expected, yet get dropped, there are clearly doubts as to the selectors' judgement. Why did the England selectors pick Price to replace the batsman-keeper Gibb if the selection caused the Chairman of Selectors a sleepness night because Price was "not at all the sort of batsman one would fancy to come off against the bowling of Australia"?

Parks, too, performed much as would have been expected. He bowled tidily and took wickets regularly, albeit never threatening to run through the batting line-up. This is exactly how he performed at county level. Yet, despite being England's best bowler, and performing 'up to scratch' he was jettisoned, even though he had a useful batting string to his bow. If Parks perfomed well up to his usual standard in the test yet was still not good enough, then what was he doing there in the first place?

Bowlers are also more involved in the team effort than batsmen. Most test wickets are caught, and so bowlers rely on their team-mates to get the majority of their wickets. Batsmen, on the other hand, have far more control over their performance; they rely on their team-mates only to the extent of not running them out. King suffered from his team-mates' failure to take catches off his bowling. His bowling was reported to be better than the figures suggested, but the Chairman of Selectors had not seen the bowling, only the figures. King was caught up in a selection muddle, for which the selectors emerged with little credit.

It is easy to criticize selectors. They defend themselves with the valid point that their selections have to play and so their judgements are tested, unlike the critics, whose teams exist only on paper, and whose judgements go frequently untested. When selectors make an honest assessment between two cricketers' ability in as objective a manner as possible, then their behaviour cannot be criticized, even allowing for the fact that any decision is likely to bear traces of subjectivity. Cricket performance is unpredictable, so when a selector makes an honest 'guesstimate' of whether batsman Bloggs is likely to score more in the next test than batsman Smith, however knowledgeable or dedicated the selector is, there will be a strong element of chance involved. It is too easy, and often unfair, in these circumstances to criticize them for picking Bloggs after he has scored a duck by asserting that Smith would only have been an improvement. Criticism based purely on being wise after the event has little validity.

But when the underlying logic behind a selection is flawed, or when a selection is made from predominately subjective grounds, then selectors' behaviour can be justly questioned. Even when such behaviour is motivated by positive reasons, such as unwillingness to jettison a former stalwart even though it is becoming clear that his best form is permanently behind him. Occasionally, to become better selectors, selectors need to be more cruel to those they select. Well-meant kindnesses, such as giving caps to players in recognition of devoted service, often as faithful fringe members of touring parties, might in fact be unfair, both to the person who might be considered to have a better claim to that place, and also to the national side and its supporters. When Bob Taylor was given his test debut in place of Alan Knott 'for being a good tourist' both Knott and Taylor were upset. When someone like Charlie Parker is not selected because a selector does not think much of the cricketer as a person then they can be seen to be failing in their duty to provide for the best possible national side.

Cricket, unlike most sports, has an unusual aspect to its international contests, in that there are two widely played forms of the same game and its world cup takes place in what is seen as the lesser form – a limited-over competition rather than a test match. An equivalent might be if the rugby world cup were a sevens competition – a challenging and exciting version of the game, but not a format which examines the full range of skills, techniques and possibilities.

In the final of the 1999 World Cup the Australian Adam Gilchrist extended to 68 his dubious record of having made the most appearances in one-day internationals without earning a test cap. In October 1998 Shahid Afridi, the previous record holder, had made his test debut for Pakistan, having played 66 times in one-day internationals. A fellow Pakistani debutant in this match, R.R. Singh, had played in 60 one-day internationals.

There are successful international cricketers who are not test cricketers, but one-day internationals solely. Adam Gilchrist is a world-cup winner but not a test player.

Ian Gould played in a world cup semi-final for England and eighteen international matches, yet never played test cricket. Six other players who have since retired from first-class cricket played for England only in limited-over cricket: Trevor Jesty, who played ten times, Middle-sex's Mike Smith, who played five times, Geoff Humpage, Jim Love and

Monte Lynch who all played three times and Colin Wells, twice an international. Ten other current county players, at the end of the 1999 season, have only played for England in one-day cricket: Adams, Alleyne, Austin, Ally Brown, Dougie Brown, Fleming, Graham Lloyd, Neil Smith, Udal and Vince Wells.

These one-day internationals might be considered the best case of 'so near but so far' international recognition, but for the circumstance of Alan Jones' 'test' career. Picked for the England team for the first test against the Rest of the World in 1970, he never played again for England. But he had become an English test cricketer for, at the time, these matches were deemed to be tests. Later, this decision was reversed by the ICC, and Alan Jones lost his cap, no longer a test cricketer, even though the opposition England faced in this series was considerably better than in the majority of tests she has played. The ICC hold control of the title 'Test Match'.

One test wonders are not exceptional in their lack of test exposure. The average test match career is short. The most common number of caps held by an England test cricketer is one, the second most common is two, and the third is three. Over a quarter of England's cricketers have failed to play more than two tests. Over a third have played in less than four tests and half of England's test cricketers have played in fewer than six tests.

England averages about fourteen caps per player. That the average number of caps per English player is so much higher than the mean – five – is due to the great length of some players' careers. Exclude the five Englishmen who have played over a hundred times, and the average of caps per player for the rest is then only ten. Although test careers are becoming greater as a result of the increased number of tests played, this manifests itself more in giving some players many caps for remaining in or around the test team for a few seasons, rather than in reducing the number of one-cap wonders. At the end of the 1999 season, of the last hundred players to be capped by England, fourteen had only one cap: Giddens, Maddy, Giles, Gloucestershire's Mike Smith, Silverwood, Simon Brown, Alan Wells, Benjamin, Williams, Stephenson, Whitaker, Benson, Sidebottom and Andy Lloyd.

There have always been, and there will always be, one test wonders. It is very hard to view them as failures. In Nathaniel Hawthorne's phrase they 'did not quite make it the most', but at least they made it.

# Index